MW01170385

PEARLS
OF
WISDOM®

1971
VOLUME FOURTEEN

TEACHINGS OF THE ASCENDED MASTERS
DICTATED TO THE MESSENGERS
MARK AND ELIZABETH PROPHET

Summit University S Press®

PUBLISHED BY THE SUMMIT LIGHTHOUSE
FOR CHURCH UNIVERSAL AND TRIUMPHANT

Pearls of Wisdom 1971
Published by
THE SUMMIT LIGHTHOUSE®
for Church Universal and Triumphant®
Box A
Malibu, California 90265

Copyright © 1964, 1965, 1966, 1969, 1970, 1971, 1972, 1974,
1978 by Church Universal and Triumphant, Inc.

All rights reserved.

No part of this book may be reproduced in any form or
by any means without prior written permission from
Church Universal and Triumphant, Inc., Box A, Malibu,
CA 90265, excepting brief quotes used in connection with
reviews written specifically for inclusion in a magazine or
newspaper.

LIBRARY OF CONGRESS CATALOG CARD NUMBER: 78-60619

INTERNATIONAL STANDARD BOOK NUMBER: 0-916766-31-4

Printed in the United States of America

Summit University Press®
Second Printing

CONTENTS

Volume Fourteen - 1971

STUDIES OF THE HUMAN AURA
by Kuthumi

THE RADIANT WORD

Excerpts from Dictations of the Ascended Masters
Included with *Pearls of Wisdom*

The Ascended Master El Morya, Chief of the Darjeeling Council of the Great White Brotherhood, founded The Summit Lighthouse in August 1958 through the Messenger Mark L. Prophet for the purpose of publishing the teachings of the ascended masters. Since that time, personal instruction from the ascended masters to their chelas in every nation has been published in weekly letters called *Pearls of Wisdom*. The anointed Messengers Mark and Elizabeth Prophet were trained by their guru El Morya to receive the Word of the Lord in the form of both spoken and written dictations. Those included in this volume were dictated to the messengers in 1971. Mark L. Prophet ascended on February 26, 1973. Today, Elizabeth Clare Prophet continues to set forth these mystery teachings of the Holy Spirit sponsored by the Brotherhood for the age of Aquarius. For information on other volumes of *Pearls of Wisdom* published since 1958 and additional publications and cassette recordings of The Summit Lighthouse, write for a free catalog.

The Ascended Master El Morya
Chief of the Darjeeling Council of the Great White Brotherhood

Happy is the man that findeth Wisdom and the man that getteth Understanding. She is more precious than rubies: and all the things thou canst desire are not to be compared unto Her. Length of days is in Her right hand; and in Her left hand riches and honour.

—Solomon

Pearls of Wisdom

| Vol. XIV No. 1 | Gautama Buddha | January 3, 1971 |

The Strong Wind of Cosmic Purpose

May the Renewal of Peace Abide in All,

In the stillness of Purpose each new day is born. The responses of humanity either solve or create problems. Lingering struggles remain, but a new cast to the mind provides a strengthening to man that is both refreshing and determined. The marking of dates is lost in the ocean of Eternity, but those who sail upon the ship of time require coordinates that will prevent them from bobbing as a cork upon the sea. And so Destiny is born as an expanded vision.

The transcendent nature of Being has great meaning to the soul that is advancing in those giant strides that require an understanding of the Law of Transcendence. Lesser goals are also important. One's objective should always be to see to it that the Divinity that shapes the ends of man be given voice in his decision. The free will of man ought not to be the voice of permissiveness, but the voice that tethers the soul to those spiritually scientific patterns that have generated a flow of freedom to the souls of millions yet unborn.

Our concerns may delight the Godhead, but greater delight ensues with humanity's performance of God's Will. If men ponder the existence of God, they must open their eyes to see how the methods of the Cosmic Lords have infiltrated the planetary cycles of scientific progress, how the handwriting of Divine Fingers has inculcated in the souls of men bereft of their native purity a desire for true culture, for a code of honor in their dealings with one another, and for crystalline values that are never shattered by the boisterous activity in the marketplace.

In the olden days the few held within the folds of their consciousness the focus of man's infinite Identity and Purpose, while the masses played at competitive games involving an almost animalistic struggle for social and economic survival. The vultures of struggle amplified struggle, and Peace seemed far away. Yet Peace, O Hearts of Light, is a many splendored thing. It is a gesture of Infinity loving the finite into the Greatness of Itself. Peace is the Spirit of the Lord that ponders the little struggles of men—a grain of sand or a speck of dust that becomes a mountain of adversity to their weary souls. In Peace there is always the perspective of focused Reason imploring Destiny to hide behind the screen of the moment until man recaptures the vision of the total Plan.

At a time when Hierarchy faces many tests in its outreach to serve humanity, a more valiant response than that which has been invoked in any previous year must be elected by the true devotees, else there may well perish from the Earth those cultural values and virtues which pave the way for great souls to express great ideas in defense of the divinity of every man.

The balance of the genuine heart should remain undisturbed by the rumblings in the world order while possessing the flexibility of being moved by the gentle winds of the Spirit that bear fresh ideas from God's own Hand, from the realm of Cosmic Purpose. How else shall there be evoked in man a response that will produce the fulfillment of His Purposes in society? How else shall he hold for his fellows true perspective and brotherly love that are not swayed by the invectives of the multitudes?

I plead for the virtues of stability and determination, and for universal effort among the student body as they allow the Spiritual Lords—those who have risen in the hierarchical order because they have given their all in the service of humanity—the opportunity to express the valor of their ideas and to assist the race in the development of that soul consciousness which will cast aside the trivial and concentrate upon the best and highest gifts. If the comparatively few will today, as of yore, keep the Flame on behalf of the many—who would do better if they knew better—we will raise the cultural levels of the world; and in short order you will see those conditions overthrown that literally make merchandise of men in the marketplaces of life.

Everywhere the moneychangers would enter the temple; yet His words, "I AM come that ye might have life," should echo in East and West the glimmer of a great Light. "Life is more than meat," He once said; and we who have studied the many aspects of the spirit of man see in the dawn, as well as in the full-orbed day of his solar (soul) manifestation, a complexity which eclipses the simplicity of his true nature. Oversimplification likewise blurs the focus of Reality. And so we extend to man the proffered gift of perfect balance in the Threefold Flame which stills the soul in the midst of turmoil and shows him clearly that as the Father works he must also work.[1]

The many sons of God upon the planet must rally this year as never before to lift the burden of the world both spiritually and materially. They should understand that the burden of life's responsibility is given to each expression of God. Each person must share in the world responsibility as well as in his individual responsibility. When this is done by all, the Door to Spiritual Octaves can be opened wider, and we can step forth to instruct men in a Righteousness for which their souls have longed. Yet the dharma of the Law is salutary. It is its own cleansing agent; self-purifying and pruning the whole tree of Life, it advocates that Destiny, as the Purpose of God, be espoused.

There are so many unfinished tasks. There are so many that must be begun. But, above all, a new educational system for the youth of the world is essential; for tyrants and dictators who would rule the world, as well as those who profess to be worldly wise, spreading abroad their darkness and false ideologies, have always sought to bend the minds of the very young and to lead them into the realm of hatred and moral decay.

Ours is to train up the child in the way he should go. Ours is to reach out as never before to counteract those conditions in both the ideological and the physical marts that are the destroyers of Life. Ours is to bind up the wounds of the world, to comfort the brokenhearted, and to let the Truth, as fact, literally flood the earth, carving the pathway of the hidden Dream that shall no longer be hidden. For that which is done in secret will be shouted from the housetops, and the Truth shall make men free.[2]

From the East, with the strong wind of Cosmic Purpose, has our voice begun to speak; and the year shall see many fruits of our striving. Will ye unite with us, with the Bands of the Cosmic Heavens that are telling mankind that God lives within them, and that because He lives, they, too, shall live?

Radiantly, I remain

Gautama Buddha

A New Year's Poem
from Kwan Yin

Sunder unreality
   O Mercy's Flame of Thee,
Revere our pure Reality
   And set each soul now Free.

The Flame begins to change the form
   From captive to released,
And drops of Life's Great Mercy Flame
   Infuse the soul with Peace.

The Love of God inflames the heart
   The soul does mold the form,
As Wisdom beams the Spirit-Sparks
   That make each one reborn.

I AM the Servant of the poor
   The Guardian of the pure,
My name is Mercy by the Lord
   Whose Grace let all adore.

Pearls of Wisdom®

Vol. XIV No. 2   *The Goddess of Liberty*   **January 10, 1971**

Ours Is the Eternal Conquest

Children of the Ages:

Stretching the bounds of your imagination, you can reach forward into new dimensions. The individual, determined no longer to succumb to the unfortunate pull of human sense thralldom, seeks new contact with his own Higher Self. As has been said, one speaks of angels and hears the rush of their wings; for even when the consciousness is engrossed with outer darkness, the inner Flame continues to burn, silently opposing the entire weight of man's human creation by its own forcefield of cosmic clarity.

Some men seem to forget that when they have given their all to the moloch of human greed and hatred, they cannot by wishful thinking instantly reap the greatest cosmic experiences. Many times throughout the millenniums Heaven has issued her own mandates with scarcely a response from human levels; but the moment individuals begin to turn toward God, they expect the heavens to literally fall upon them and to shower them with such love as will wipe out all activities of negation in which they have engaged.

Let them understand that while Heaven has love for the prodigal son of creation, that love is tethered to the Reality of Cosmic Law. Although Life peeps through the lattice work of man's consciousness, affording him glimpses of his Higher Self and the promise of those experiences that are to come if he continues faithfully upon the pathway, Life does not immediately expand the fullness of a new sense of direction simply because man wills it so. Let humanity, then, learn the ritual of patient service as they turn toward the Light.

Let the devotees awaken to the realization that there are many levels of human expression, just as there are many levels of divine expression. Many people say, "We have our ups and downs." Practically speaking, you cannot expect that the elevator of your consciousness will remain stationed at one floor simply because you would like it to. One could say that the elevator of the Divine Consciousness is capable of descending to those sub-basement levels where many souls are reaping the ashes of human experience. And, certainly, the elevator of the Divine Consciousness is also able to rise to the highest levels of divine experience. This means that you can rise to the greatest heights as well as descend to the depths of human expression and still remain within the protective forcefield of the Divine Consciousness. But, wherever you go, the practicality of all good that is in store for you is to be found right within the domain of the human spirit, as though it were freshly fallen from the spheres of Heaven in full-blown God-magnificence.

When man begins to bring out this glory from within, it is like the cutting and polishing of a gem. The lodestone of perfection, like the gem in its rough state, does not reveal its great beauty, its lustre, its splendor, until the cutting and the polishing are completed. Then at last it magnifies the wonder of the highest spheres in which a new Heaven and a new Earth appear. The influence of these spheres is real, not only in the outer stream of events but also, and most especially so, in the inner stream of man's own consciousness. Here Cosmic Law registers the very moment that man allows it to by surrendering conditions of hindering darkness and by careful obedience to its precepts, thereby creating within himself the matrices of personal victory.

Out of ignorance, many among humanity refuse to surrender their consciousness to the higher powers of Light; nor will they hold their tapers to the torches of Heaven for divine illumination. Instead, they love to contemplate what they call their own free will—as though the Heavenly Will were distinct and separate from the human will. In reality, the patterns of the human will are changing, and the satisfactions of one moment may become the dissatisfactions of another. This is why mankind should be interested in finding out what the Will of God for them really is.

Men say that they prefer the sovereignty of their own free will. How true it is that they are making the choices. How true it is that while making the wrong choices that appear to them to be right the wonders of God are passing them by. And the fleeting pleasures of life that turn to ashes are a temporary palliative, a chimera shimmering in the ethers of the moment.

Ours is the eternal conquest; however, the infinite cycles are not unrelated to the conquest in the world of form. Man was not created to be a puppet to his own or another's negativity. He was intended to bear the torch of higher wisdom on Earth as a part of the eternal quest. By overcoming outer conditions, man loses nothing, but becomes the recipient of the vastness of the Universal Mind of God.

Down through the historical stream men have often sought to make their conquests in the world—by climbing mountains, by sending rockets to the moon, by biological experiment, by psycho-political control of the masses, and even by evolving new standards of technology and social action—as a substitute for the glorious inner realization of Christ-Reality, which is the only basis for positive change. "Inasmuch as ye have done it unto the least of these my brethren, ye have done it unto me."

Man should not overlook the invisible yet wondrous domain of the soul that to many is a realm of the unknown. Simply because the soul is not a visible manifestation, many believe that the soul does not have a real existence. Yet, what is it that dwells in the body which is called life? Is it not that level of divine awareness that humanity borrows and claims as its own?

When mankind denies the existence of the soul, what shall we do, we who dwell in the higher levels of awareness where Reality is crystal clear? Shall we say to them, "You are right," when we know they are not, when we perceive all around us the glow of His eternal wonder, and the grace of the eternal comfort reaches out to us from the center of Life? I think not. But how shall we convince humanity, who cannot see in the good fruit of human endeavor the reality of the soul and its potential for even greater things?

Beloved hearts of Light, many souls who pass through the veil find those answers in the realms of death that they never found while they were living; for there new perceptions are at last unveiled. Others find themselves trapped in astral pockets of which they had no conception while they were in physical embodiment. When this occurs, regret ensues; and before long they are yearning for a physical body, for a new life opportunity upon the planet Earth. But the portals of birth may not open immediately in response to their plea.

The schoolrooms of Earth are many. The experiences to be had are myriad. The graduates who qualify for the highest octaves are few. We have never remained content to allow the Earth to drift as a hapless experiment in the solar system. Already we have marked vast allotments of cosmic energy for the planet Earth in 1971. We have magnificent teams of conquerors who on other systems of worlds have shown their efficiency in dealing with mortal stubbornness and who, in answer to your prayers, will function as a body of Light reinforcements to the planet throughout the coming year. These Great Cosmic Beings have even volunteered to remain beyond that period as long as they are welcomed by humanity. Thus, on behalf of all mankind, you can literally put out the welcome mat through prayer and invocation to the Invisible Cosmic Servers who have pledged to make every effort to develop in the classrooms of Earth the greatest response of all ages.

Karmic events may seem clouded; some unanticipated troubles

may occur; but we are certain that every benign opportunity that can be directed to humanity will be forthcoming in 1971. We ask the faithful, then, to hold high in their consciousness the concept of cosmic regeneration for the Earth and to recognize that on a planetary as well as a personal level they are truly their brothers' keepers.

We have been summoned by the Solar Lords to assist you in the high adventure of instructing the humanity of Earth in the correct ways of fulfilling their own God-design; therefore, I say, let it be done! Let the deterrent forces be cast aside by a giant whirlwind of the Holy Spirit! Let new vistas unfold out of the cosmic diorama locked within the souls of men, until at last the hopes of the world are filled and the powers of Light are secure in their own domain.

I speak to those who look and to those who listen to the voice within; I speak to those who stop the destructive spirals of life and stand ready at the portal of the year to become as little children and to learn the mysteries of God.

Long have many waited for greater Light to all humanity. Now in the midst of darkness, let the torch of Eternal Life shine upon mankind's face.

For progress and expanding grace unto humanity, I remain

 *The Goddess of Liberty*

Spokesman for The Karmic Board

1. Matt. 25:40.

Pearls of Wisdom®

Vol. XIV No. 3   *Hilarion*   *January 17, 1971*

The Vestments of Reality

Hearts of Infinite Fire:

There are many mysteries in the universe that in this cycle must remain mysteries to unascended man. Yet, man has often sought to decipher the hieroglyphs of cosmos, reaping partial returns from his endeavor, but seldom understanding in the fullest sense the vestments of Reality that are all around him.

May I ask for a moment of introspection wherein you carefully observe the power of Nature within yourself? Examine your physical body in all of its latent wonder. Consider the miracle of a tiny cell. How fearfully and wonderfully it was made! Recall the purity of the patterns Nature impressed upon your form as these were outpictured first in a tiny babe and then in the full-grown stature of a man or a woman. Now turn your attention to the consciousness that has occupied your form, at times passively, and then in a more active way as, with a new sense of participation in your own evolution, you have become tutored by the soul within. Verily, it is time to discover the depths of the wisdom and love that Life has sealed within your temple, that even now are shaping your cosmic destiny.

I come as a teacher of Truth to unlock the treasures that lie buried within your consciousness. Man has many teachers, yet none can compare to the One who extends that divine comfort whereby man becomes self-taught through the tutoring of his soul. The Eternal Spirit teaches His creation in many ways how to become engrossed in a higher form of reverie; among these, soul-tutoring is a unique experience.

Man learns thereby how to exercise his mind in a spiritual outreach of the imagination; and when he has mastered the art of penetrating cosmos, the universe is rolled open as a scroll in order that he might decipher the intricacies of Life. Mysteries he has not even contemplated are unraveled before his very eyes! By the same exercise he probes the unknown within himself, his behavior patterns as well as memories from the distant past that have often puzzled his mind. He learns how subconscious desires, like little coiled springs, do precipitate those acts, sometimes of distress and sometimes of joy, that produce a writing upon the pages of akasha.

Many of our students are overly concerned about their spiritual development, not knowing that their concern is the chief hindrance to their progress. The gentle faith that manifests in the performance of good works and in the belief that God will see to one's spiritual growth does indeed bear the fruit of progress in every area of one's life. For, in reality, God as the Eternal Spirit possesses the potential of man's evolution within Himself. How, then, can those who are striving daily to be His hands and feet be hindered by the suggestion that they are not making the proper spiritual strides? For to serve one's fellowman is to be one with Him, and to be one with Him is to progress.

Dear hearts, it is by leaving all progress to God and by simply drinking in the very atmosphere of Illumination's Flame that you will naturally increase the dominion of your consciousness. It is by using the faculties of the mind and soul to penetrate the intricacy and beauty, first of the physical universe and then of the spiritual universe within, that you will move forward in the fulfillment of your divine plan.

Man is more than a speck of dust. The Earth is more than a ball of mud, as some have said. It is a natural home adapted to the needs of its evolutions, even as the physical body is adapted to the necessities of the soul. Man need not grasp at straws, but he can grasp the poles of the universe to literally vault the heavens in an exercise in cosmic imagination.

What was true during my ministry is still true today: "Eye hath not seen, nor ear heard, neither have entered into the heart of man, the things which God hath prepared for them that love him." These "things which God hath prepared" must be sought and won by the man who—in contrast to those modern disciples whose spiritual muscles have become flabby—does not fear to exercise the faculties of the mind and spirit.[1]

This year we would impart new lustre through our words and designs to every lifestream who comes in contact with our consciousness, together with the blessed assurance that our strength is ever at the door. Some have felt limited by the outreach of their spirits, by their desires and imaginations which do not carry them beyond the confines of their physical consciousness.

Let me hasten to assure you that a call to your own God Self, to the indwelling I AM Presence, or unto me, Hilarion, will be answered by a quickening of your imagination and an outpouring of Light from the well-springs on high. Yes, my friend, there are, by God's grace, many in the higher octaves who are beckoning you to come up the ladder of Life so that you might begin to understand the potential of the soul that God has nourished within you.

You are aware of the many pulls upon the soul of man, in fact upon his whole psyche, pulls that originate in the chaotic conditions of the world as well as in his own subconscious mind. Mankind is looking to the world, with a promise that is mighty, for a fulfillment that is often so lacking that it seems to tarnish the Reality within him. Let him now turn to the grace of God and to those who are above him in a spiritual way. Let him become aware of them, that he may truly gain in stature and advance in the order of hierarchy.

Individuals have unwittingly stunted their own progress by aborting the creative imagination that God has placed within the soul. Many have imprisoned the splendor of God's grace that, if they would only allow it, would shine like a beacon from within. To cover that beacon, to hide it in a shroud of mourning, is to accept limitation in your outreach. Let man then realize that he has unlimited potential, let him call to heaven for an expansion of that potential in his consciousness. For in a very real sense every man is the keeper of his own lighthouse: either he hides the beacon within the self-centeredness of his being, or he opens wide the shutters of his life so that the inner Light can guide all men.

Mortals struggle to grasp the Light they know not of, flashing out their hidden strengths in puny outer-world activities. Their existence is almost a figment of someone's imagination, having a dreamlike quality of unreality. They feel boxed in, and well might they; for their souls are packaged in a synthetic society, and there is no way for them to express the great Reality that God is. But one day they shall burst the bounds of their confinement; and, with the stretching of the cosmic sinews, their entire consciousness will suddenly blossom into glory. Their minds will flex those hidden strengths and springs of heavenly joy that are within the spiritual body of every man, waiting to leap into expansion and progress in the Light.

Yet there remain in the world those concerns and involvements that, like sticky paper, are there to trap man in a round of worldly activities: the ownership of land and property, the maintenance of social status, the acquisition of power, and the manipulation of wealth. But all of these distractions are meaningless once man is able to perceive the boundlessness of God as "the day-spring from on high" that visits his outer self when he taps the inner strength of which we speak. But, unless man receives the messages telegraphed by the soul, how can he entertain other than mundane thoughts and ambitions, seeing that the soul is the screen upon which are imprinted those cosmic engrams of Light which lead the self into higher Truth?[2]

Even the imaginations of man's heart have often gotten him into a hornet's nest of destructivity; but once he is able to let go of himself and to surrender the ego that imprisons his soul, he can understand the Divine Intent with a greater measure of fiery inspiration. He can perceive a rail of heavenly potential, reaching from Earth to Heaven, guiding his soul through the trackless air to the beauties of higher spheres. Then, in the sense of a new beginning, he will start with the alchemy of self-examination.[3]

I long ago said, "Forgetting those things which are behind, and reaching forth unto those things which are before, I press toward the mark for the prize of the high calling of God in Christ Jesus." In

Heaven's Name, you, in reality, are not imprisoned! God Himself wills you free. Every Master, every Angel, every Cosmic Being works ceaselessly for the unfoldment of the divine plan for the Earth. But you yourself must develop the discipline, the steeling of your very mind and soul—the twenty-four-hour-a-day attitude of "pressing toward the mark." And if you do not, another will claim the prize that should have been your own.[4]

There is a vast need for creative men of vision and of science who will engage their minds in new thought and new action. It is well to remember the unborn in prayer and in planning; but, above all, do not overlook your contemporaries who, while enmeshed in worldly activities—the earning of a living, the reviewing of current books and plays, the seeking of new forms of sensual gratification—are very much bound in their finite consciousness to the stream of time, apprehending that one of these days in the not too distant future they will come to the end of their road. These, too, can be the sheep that must be fed, the flocks that whiten the hillsides, waiting to be called to a higher purpose.

You who look to the higher way of Life will understand that Life is destiny. This destiny you will desire to fulfill according to the traditions of the Masters, using the world for the mastery of self, not abusing it in the selfish domination of others. And you will let no outer condition become the bane of your spiritual existence that, like quicksand, will swallow up your constructive ideas.

Remember, beloved hearts of Light, in past ages humanity have dwelled in darkness, forgetting the glories of the Light from whence they came. To the one who does not know the way of the Light, let me say that the only means of finding it is to begin today to invoke it and to keep on invoking it until the road of Eternal Life rises before you, unfolding ever-new vistas of progress and challenges of discovery and attainment.

The Light liveth, the Lord liveth; and this year He is looking for the transformation of many new souls come from the darkness of worldly thought into the Light and freedom of His Mind. He waits with the dawn of a new age. He lives as your Eternal Creator and Friend. One day you will know Him as your Self; and thus in the imitation of the living God, through the Eternal Christ, you will become that which you already are.

As you evolve, remember always, I remain your friend,

Hilarion[5]

---

1. 1 Cor. 2:9. 2. Luke 1:78. 3. Gen. 6:5. 4. Phil. 3:13, 14. 5. Hilarion was embodied as the apostle Paul.

Pearls of Wisdom®

Vol. XIV No. 4   *Meta*   *January 24, 1971*

"Man, Know Thyself!"

To All Lovers of Humanity:

As I gaze upon the faces of men, perceiving their dilemmas, knowing the hungers of their hearts for the overcoming of each condition of body, mind, or even spirit which may be troubling them, I have vowed within myself to give even greater attention to the needs of mankind this year by helping them to know themselves better.

The meaning of the ancient saying, "Man, know thyself," like that of so many other sayings that have become stultified in the consciousness of men, is not readily apparent in the inscription on the temple walls. Why should man know himself? and "What is man," as the Psalmist long ago asked, "that thou art mindful of him?" Obviously, the wonderful Love of the Great Creator of all signifies His divine intent for humanity; for His hidden science, implanted in the very soul of man, is the magnificent formula taught by The Sacred Brotherhood of old. To know His purpose, then, man must first understand himself, and to that end I come as the servant of the Light in all.[1]

Many people today are a bundle of nerves, and their desires are far removed from the fundamental aims of their souls. The soul is very tender within, and from it arises the consciousness that can either introvert to perceive itself or extrovert to perceive the world. Life whispers and Life thunders, but the conditions of the world are often fanciful. They rise from the old and familiar habit patterns handed down from generation to generation, becoming what we have termed "crusty tradition." Man's environment is also invaded with strange manifestations bordering on the psychic world of human emotions, swirling about individuals as a wraith and creating a bounty of confusion.

Now, when I begin to speak of fashioning the bounds of Reality, you should understand that it means that the individual must become aware of that measure of himself which is real and that which is the mere accumulation of centuries of dusty ideas. As man begins to divide the Light and the darkness in himself, he is able to gauge the worth of the accumulation; and, albeit a great deal, suitable only for burning, will have to be cast into the Flame, he will in the process gather little jewels of consciousness. These he will eventually sort out and refurbish with those higher standards that he acquires with the passing of the years.

Thus, little by little, the standards of his life become tethered to the great boundaries of a new reality that is expansive. He is no longer satisfied with the toys and pacifiers of his former existence. He yearns and reaches out for a new healing—a veritable regeneration—of the mind and spirit.

I have often heard many calls made unto me and others of the Ascended Masters, or unto the Great God of Gods; and I have seen the sincerity of these calls which stem from man's desire to be well, to be whole. But when the question is posed as to how it shall be done, people are often caught in the jaws of ancient theological traps. For instance, they accept the idea of God as being a god of wrath—whose sternness in the Law I do not deny—but they overlook in toto the power of the God of Love. Then, too, the meaning and use of Love has degenerated into forms of sexual depravity, denying mankind the correct application of the Life Principle.

To exalt the purpose of creation: this is a creative act. To heal not only the body but also the soul and the fabric of the mind, creating a new garment that cannot be rent in the very consciousness of man—that cannot be destroyed in the very soul of man: this is the fiat of the hour. It is the call of a new age that garners strength because men understand themselves as an aspect of Deity, because they are no longer fearful to advance into the Light. These often ponder the words of Jesus, "If therefore the light that is in thee be darkness, how great is that darkness!" They watch and wait carefully for a manifestation of God, knowing that some manifestations may only seem to be good while actually creating a sense of darkening awareness.[2]

In the healing of the mind and soul we need the air in its natural purity, we need the light in its glowing reality, and we need to understand the meaning of Love as a transforming contribution to all to whom we give it. To so many Love has become a mere feeling of possessiveness, a grasping at life without the desire to convey the enormity of God's grace as a tangible, living gift. When the words, "My grace is sufficient for thee," were understood by Paul, they became a light that substantiated his very being, that lent credence to his existence; for the Love of Christ was a powerful ray pouring healing into the chalice of his consciousness that his cup might run over with joy.[3]

Oh, how often humanity have trapped themselves and allowed themselves to be literally fenced in with barbaric ideas when the infinite Love of God is so real and so practical. In restructuring the soul, then, do not be afraid to discard ancient concepts or dogmatic interpretations, but be careful to preserve the meaning of the altar of God as a hallowed place where communion is not the mere orifice of desire.

Let men understand the Love of God as going far beyond the mere possession of authority, although He has freely given it even to the soul. Men must perceive the grace of Heaven as a gift of worth. They must yearn for newness of life—life not as mere existence which they have already experienced, but life as that infinite bond of freedom which they are beginning to understand. For that bond will one day exalt them into the perfect healing of body, mind and soul, establishing the fountainhead of reality in their beings.

Then they will be able to convey to others the selfsame grace. Then man's ego will no longer be a caged lion, for he will have seen that the strength of the lamb that lieth down with the lion is greater in its purity than the thundering of human authority. For it is purity of motive and intent that structures the soul to newness of life. Then the sun shining in his strength can be retained in the soul as the glow of eternal Light welcomed home by the reflector of man's consciousness.

When the Light received by man becomes an object for misqualification that man consumes upon his lusts, upon his desires, then his degeneration becomes his own self-condemnation. But when at last man understands that God is Love and that he must prepare himself to receive the host of that eternal Love within himself, he experiences the communion that evokes the consciousness of the Holy Grail. He finds that he is able to govern outer circumstances; for the Lord who said, "Take dominion over the Earth!" reinforces His decree by producing self-mastery in the soul. And that self-mastery will never be satisfied with less than total victory over all conditions less than the perfection of the eternal plan.

By conquering the mortal self as well as mortal conditions, man finds the way of true humility which is the way of overcoming victory. And until he does, man lies in chains—chained by his own thought. When he is healed by his own sense of perfection, he may not immediately grasp the fullness it portends; but he stands willing to enter the portals of a new hope in the restructuring of the whole man into the perfection of the universal plan.

Thus does Light overcome darkness. Thus does true beauty appear. Out of the balm of healing Love, I have come; and I remain with the planet Earth this year to assist those who will call unto God and unto me.

As your servant in the Light, I AM devotedly

Meta

Patroness of the Healing Arts

1. Pss. 8:4. 2. Matt. 6:23. 3. II Cor. 12:9.

THE RADIANT WORD
Release of the Thoughtform for 1971: To Forge a Cosmic Union
by Gautama Buddha
Taken from the transcripts of the New Year's Message
of the Lord of the World given at the Royal Tetons on New Year's Eve

"...I, Gautama, in the name of Peace, speak to you tonight; and I say that we must forge such a union amongst all humanity and with Cosmic Beings, as shall unite hearts and prevent those iniquitous inroads in man which divide brother from brother, nation from nation, and people from people, until humanity becomes an armed camp of hostility and destruction.

"Love is the key. Love is the master key by which the world will recognize the potential within themselves, not to destruct the world, but to create in the world those agencies of Cosmic Service and Love which are able to mitigate every human condition, to act as a panacea to humanity, to free humanity from the dregs of darkness and destructivity, which for so long have held sway upon this planetary orb.

"Let us now, then, gaze into the Cosmic Ethers as we see the approach of the Great White Cloud. And behind that Cloud, veiled in pure radiant Light, is the Thoughtform for the forthcoming year—a form of great loveliness and beauty which is the reality of the radiance of every man's consciousness.

"We want you, then, to understand that we have chosen as the Universal Thoughtform for this year the symbol of a great Cosmic Golden Ring. In the center of this great Cosmic Golden Ring is held in the background the image of a world or globe. Superimposed over that, you will find the upper figure in the chart of the Presence, or the Causal Body of every man. [The Earth is suspended within the spheres of the Causal Body.]

"This Thoughtform signifies that the salvation of the planetary body shall also be the transcendent glory and beauty of the I AM Presence in all of its radiant power, as it is acknowledged more and more by humanity. And as they come to understand that through the power of the I AM Presence they can invoke from God those majestic outpourings referred to as 'the latter reign of living loveliness and love,' the world will be literally transformed into the newness of the Golden Age.

"The newness of this Cosmic Fire, the newness of this great Golden Ring, signifies that the Eternal Values have been placed in time and space by the Hand of God, just as a tender seed is lowered into the heart of the Earth for the manifestation of a beautiful tree or a flowering plant. Some have thought this manifestation of His Love to be redundant, but actually the Divine Monad, the Causal Body, like the divine seed, emanates the transcendent manifestation of Eternal Principles which will cause the world to be literally dusted with destiny.

"The Thoughtform is intended to create in the consciousness of mankind the understanding that all of Heaven has conspired to pour out upon the world the waters of the Living Word from the fountain of God's Love, the Strength of His Heart, the Will and Wisdom and Wit to do those things which are necessary, not to make a shambles of it or of the conditions manifesting in the world, but to transform the world by new plans, to educate the young people in a manner in which they have not formerly been educated, bringing them at last into the understanding that their actions toward one another ought to be the actions of the Prince of Peace who long ago spoke to the world and said, 'Love one another, for Love is the fulfilling of the Law'...."

Pearls of Wisdom®

Vol. XIV No. 5   *Cha Ara*   *January 31, 1971*

Sons of Belial: The Problem of Embodied Evil

To Every Lover of Truth:

As there is darkness in the world, so there is Light. As there is Truth, so there is error. As physical light banishes physical darkness, so spiritual Light banishes the ignorance of spiritual error.

There are many who have said that man was made in the image of God. Let it be known, then, that as man was made in the image of God, so he was also made in the image of creative opportunity—he was given the great opportunity to create himself in the image of God. But it is not enough to be created in the divine image; man must also direct his life patterns toward the outpicturing of that image. To assist him in that goal the Great Mediator, the Living Christ, was given to man as the spiritual Light that would banish darkness and ignorance from his consciousness. [1]

Now, the Indian Council has asked me to apprise the students that there are upon the planet sons of Belial[2] just as there are sons of God. These sons of darkness have reappeared throughout the ages desiring the slaughter of the innocents. In the time of Moses they were there, making it necessary to hide him in the bulrushes; in the time of Christ Jesus they were also there, making it necessary for him to be taken in the arms of his mother across the desert in the flight into Egypt.

Many are these sons of Belial scattered among humanity who would corrupt the perfection of the soul of man, who would obscure the divine image. These are the harbingers of destruction that you read about in your papers. Although their goals have remained the same, their methods of executing them have changed with the times.

One day, by reason of the false patterns they have adopted in their lives, by reason of the darkness they allow to lodge within them, they will be no more. Yet, while the sun shines upon the just and the unjust, they continue their machinations as though there were no standard of decency in the universe. They lament their lot as well as the plight of humanity. Seeking solution in the hand of flesh, they deny the pervading order of Spirit.

Some have not considered the parable of the tares and the wheat in terms of the children of darkness and the children of Light, as Jesus explained it to his disciples privately.³ Some have not even thought upon the problem of embodied evil. It is not our intention that any should become unduly upset upon discovering those evil elements in society which have been present for generations. All should recognize the operation of the law of cycles, the inevitability of the harvest when the tares will be gathered in bundles and burned. At the same time they should be vigilant in defense of the Christ Light, seeking to curb the nefarious influences of the sons of Belial upon their children, upon their governments, and upon the educational systems of the world.

Unfortunately, the sons of perdition do not recognize the law of transference of authority given to the sons and daughters of God as filial dominion. Being of the 'bad seed,' they do not recognize the God-given responsibilities of the Christed offspring to hold dominion over nature. Nor do they see that the beautiful rose appears thorn-crowned, not as a divine act, not even as a manifestation of protection, but as the result of man's wrong thoughts, his sharp feelings, his bitterness and hatred toward his brothers.

Nature is a champion mimic, always desiring to design as man thinks, as man feels. Being a reflection of the world of man, the world of nature is at the present time dangerously divided and unbalanced. Bowed down with the pollutions of mankind's consciousness, elemental life can no longer provide the vehicle for the pristine power of the Comfort Flame as was intended by God.

The feelings of the masses, side by side with reasoning minds, vie for control of men's lives. In most cases, neither the feelings nor the thoughts of men are imbued with perfection; yet it is possible for man to so endow them, if he will. Let men understand that even the emotions in all their turbulence can come under the command of the inner power of the Christ Light, the Light of spiritual dominion.

Peace, be still! The waves of mass emotion, choppy, engulfing and humanly erratic, are quieted by the command of the Christ, becoming thereby a calm reflector of the splendor of the Light. The mind can also be stilled, becoming the bearer of good tidings and holy wisdom as the mind of Christ or of God. Unfortunately, even the justice of human knowledge does not always appear to win in the battle between fact, opinion and feelings; for man is more often moved by his feelings of happiness, fleeting though they be, by his emotions and his opinions of himself or others than he is by logic and fact.

Now, let us call upon the Powers of Light, and let us divest the whole self, as each man is able to surrender, of these undesirable fluctuations that prevent him from realizing God as Spirit, enfolding all and teaching all to mimic the divine plan and to avoid contact with the arm of flesh and those worldly spirits that wraithlike, demonlike, bring man into a sea of emotional turmoil.

The day side of beauty and illumination lives. It is abundance and compassion. The night side wallows in alternating harsh and tender dreams, from time to time crushing the aspiration of the young student. May I then urge all who would run with the strong to make provision for spiritual fortitude in their lives. Do not allow yourselves to be thrust from side to side, and then upwards and downwards, making your experiences to be yourself—or yourself to be your experiences. After all, is not your life of greater value, of a more enduring nature than either your perilous or your ecstatic moments? Is not your life able to become a vehicle of expression of such infinite Love, of such infinite Wisdom, as to be eventually enveloped with the infinite Power you seek?

So many would put on the pole of Power before they are given the gift of Wisdom and the gift of beautiful Love. Yet, spiritual man must be unafraid to burn his own darkness, to burn his bridges behind him, and to continue with the utmost determination on the spiritual path, come any wind of hatred from any source, come any destructive emotion or thought into his mind. His life is an opportunity so vast and so utterly filled with divine compassion that nothing shall choke the tender young seed, although it be surrounded by a sea of monstrous emotion or suppressed by the boulders of intellectual pride.

Let the specters of fear and avarice go back into the dark whence they came! Let these fade as phantoms of the night. But let each dawn bring the angels' songs of forgiveness and love into your heart. For there where God lives, in the garden of inner delight, man can become invulnerable like a diamond or lustrous like a pearl of great price, shining either within the heart of the earth or within the heart of the oyster. His soul consciousness is sometimes uncut or unpolished, but it is ever expanding through those experiences which will one day make possible the tender and skillful art of the Master Jeweler who will cut, refine and polish it even as He is wont to do this hour.

Those who yield their lives to Him, who are content to follow His plan as a magnificent reaching-out of spiritual opportunity, will always receive a just recompense for their efforts and devotion. Naught can stay the onward hand of Life when cosmic progress impels the stream of rippling happiness to cast down every idol in its course, to break down every barrier, to pursue every worthy goal, and to see the hand of God, not as an illusive, vanishing dream, but as an invisible but real guardian of man's life.

Unless spiritual opportunity be recognized, you may find only in part that which you seek. But when the hand of spiritual opportunity is seen behind all events as a conspiracy of Light calculated to adorn the soul with garments of greatness—in order that each man might be clothed upon with the proper spiritual thoughts and feelings—then you shall draw near to your own eternal design, then Christ shall come to live in you. On the other hand, your rejection of your own potential can temporarily destroy your spiritual opportunities for attunement with those great Cosmic Friends of Light who would bring your life into perfect balance.

You are creations of vastness, but unless the cup of your consciousness be rightly enlarged, you remain as unborn sons. When you accept as your very own the authority of the Divine Master of Life, the Eternal Spirit in whose image you were made, then true inner progress can occur; for in His hands are wrought such marvelous wonders as man seldom dreams of in his earthly state. But when he embarks upon the higher goal as the fires of imagination intensify, he sees with holy reason that the real purpose of life is to bring each man through the veil to the place where his spiritual merger makes him the author of his own destiny.

Thus, one by one, do all transcend the dust and day by day rise triumphant into the all-enfolding progress of a higher realm, right while their feet pursue the pilgrim path on Earth below.

Heaven waits.

Radiantly, I AM

Cha Ara

Son of Meta

---

1. Gen. 1:26. 2. The "sons of Belial" are mentioned a number of times in the Old Testament. (Deut. 13:13; Judg. 19:22; 20:13; I Sam. 2:12; 10:27; 25:17; II Sam. 23:6; I Kings 21:10, 13; II Chron. 13:7) "Belial," taken from the Hebrew bĕliya 'al, meaning worthlessness, is a term used interchangeably with Satan. Actually, it is the name of another fallen angel whose sons took embodiment after the fall of Lucifer. 3. Matt. 13:24-30, 36-40.

Pearls of Wisdom®

Vol. XIV No. 6   *Saint Germain*   *February 7, 1971*

The Summoning of Freedom
through the Initiatic System

To All Who Would Invoke Freedom:

As recent *Pearls of Wisdom* have directed man toward the study of certain tenets of his own freedom, so does the inward nature of man yearn to know even more of the true meaning of freedom. As man yearns for freedom, Heaven responds with a greater release of freedom's holy Light and wisdom.

What a glorious opportunity the Living Spirit has provided for each vestment of His own consciousness in man! Each investiture of individuality is a transfer of cosmic authority from the realm of Spirit to the realm of form. It is an opportunity for man to see, to know and to be that which he is in truth—a cosmic principle, a spiritual fire, blazing upon the Earth with the shining of ever-new opportunity.

Long ago Jesus said, "If therefore the light that is in thee be darkness, how great is that darkness!" As man measures his own rate of progress by human standards, he often finds himself the victim of pernicious habits of darkness. Sometimes he believes that these habits cannot be changed. In the name of freedom, beloved ones, what hope is there for the world if man cannot till the garden of his own heart, his own opportunity, his own environment![1]

Spiritual fruit is the natural manifestation of that cosmic authority which was bestowed upon man in the beginning. Man was given the fiat to take dominion over his own world, yet he has allowed his authority to lapse. He has failed again and again to uphold the banner of his personal freedom. And because he has permitted the banner to be dragged in the dust, or because someone else has lowered the standards of life, he has often taken excuse and allowed his own standards to fall to the ground.

Now in this year of high adventure, when so many are asking themselves how they may resolve the riddle of life's meaning and their own fruitless experiences, let me hasten to assure the devotees of freedom that once you have embarked upon a spiritual course, the very fiat of movement is itself the bearer of your freedom. By contrast, the inertia of noncommitment and the sense of hopelessness will draw you down into negative spirals of worldly magnetism.

The Cosmic Light investiture, the giving by God of His creative authority to each man, provides him with a very wonderful opportunity when it is properly used. The recognition of the fiat to create will bring to every man a new surge of freedom, a sense of well-being and that practical outreach to his fellowman which is so necessary to the survival of the soul. Through obedience to the divine mandate Masters are born; through disobedience men pale into the insignificance of worldly habits to their own regret and shame, and their "damnation is just." [2]

It is not necessary for man to probe all mysteries, for although he may be aware of them, he may also realize that a partial knowing is the fulfillment of the understanding that there is much about life that he has yet to learn. He need not despair this ignorance—for Cosmos is waiting for the conquest of valiant souls. Some, however, in the name of freedom, seek to conquer worlds in space while ignoring the minerals of seemingly inert vitality right in their own backyards.

Man should not fear the past or the future—that which is near at hand or at a great distance, the known or the unknown—for there is nothing in the universe that does not lie within the bounds of his exploration. In a relative sense he can come to know and to conquer, yet the consciousness of the boundlessness of true freedom is a very essential ingredient in the rightful conquering of each facet of himself.

I once said that man could conquer all of creation by entering into the very Heart of God. Those who know only of the Earth (of Matter) do not consider the higher realms of Heaven (of Spirit); but those who know only of their own hearts can still find God within themselves; and when they do, they will know that the hearts of others also belong to God.

Thus the freedom to know, to do and to dare is a vital opportunity that makes the whole business of living a continuous summoning of new vistas of freedom. Has another discovered a new world, has another planted his flag upon a neighboring orb? Then there is hope for those who follow after. From the standpoint of the individual pursuit of Cosmos, no worlds are conquered until the individual himself conquers. All worlds remain a challenge to every son of God. Has man been there before? Then another can be. Has his spirit been lifted? Then another's may take flight.

Some have said that man is his own worst enemy, and rightly so; for by misusing his creative opportunity he aborts his own creative fulfillment. Some have dwelled in the negative aspects of freedom, taking license to chase the phantoms of their own imaginations. But if the imagination is to be tethered to cosmic freedom, man must first understand the nature of freedom.

Long ago it was said, "Now the Lord is that Spirit: and where the Spirit of the Lord is, there is liberty." The spirit of individual man may feel cramped by his self-created image of an anthropomorphic God; but once God is understood as the all-pervading, all-expansive essence of Spirit, as the divine influx of creative opportunity, man will understand that God will not, cannot, and does not cramp or corrupt His style. Therefore, whenever man finds "that Spirit," he finds true liberty. [3]

How can it be that a Heaven that takes such delight in assisting mankind to climb the pinnacles of achievement would desire to impose upon him any unnecessary restraint? All restraint, then, when it is legal from the standpoint of cosmic law—or, as we have called it, cosmically legitimate—is imposed only upon those who are yet inept in the application of the Law, who are wanderers without knowledge. These Heaven seeks to restrain from committing those acts (such as the contamination of virgin planets with war and pestilence, human hatred and degradation) that in the name of freedom would become the binding cords of their own future karma.

The initiatic system affords mankind the opportunity of receiving the communications of his own Christed Intelligence, who will release to man in his finest moments the knowledge of the Law, enabling him to carry the banner of his own freedom. Men have not dreamed of the vast wisdom that can be theirs through following this system; yet they have applied unto mortal men, unto mortal tomes, the strength of knowing. Let them now in their own minds, and for their own good, accord equal respect to those of us who have sought to guide the race. Let them recognize that we of the Ascended Hosts have, by the grace of God, the necessary cosmic intelligence and cosmic love, and even the cosmic power, that when invoked by 'unascended hosts,' will establish in the world a cosmic forcefield of such magnitude as will restore to mankind en masse that sense of the Divine Reality that shall bring in the Golden Age!

Men cry for the coming Age; they wait for it, they long for it. But if their hearts are ever to be assuaged, they must first begin to experience it in themselves. And this is possible. Men need not eat the whole carcass of their freedom in order to realize certain elements of that freedom. Sometimes a tiny bite will suffice to show man the meaning of true freedom, and thus to stimulate his pursuit of it.

In next week's *Pearl of Wisdom* I should like to deal with an experiment in spiritual initiation. I should like to show each student, according to his own capacity to receive, that tangible freedom is real, that so-called intangible freedom is the spur of attainment which produces tangible manifestation. When one has seen, the need for the appearance of reality is lessened; but while one is still pursuing as an act of faith, he frequently tells himself that once he sees, he will have attained. Let him understand that faith has value, that seeing has value, but that neither can assure man his freedom.

Man makes vows, he seeks greatness; but he is often deterrred by small obstacles. Let all understand that the summoning of freedom is a valid expression of faith, that great help is given to the man who is beginning to realize that he can invoke freedom on his own behalf and thereby come to know that it exists in the higher dimensions of his own being.

Some think they are limited by their past attainments. Not so, for the potential of the mind and spirit is so great that the moment the desire for freedom gives them a higher reign, man breaks the bonds of his mortal limitations. Now his desire is chained to the goal of winning freedom through spiritual experience and attainment. He realizes that he can know, he can see, and he can be a higher expression of his own immortal being. It is freedom just to realize cosmic potential, but it is even greater freedom to attain it.

As I extend these hopeful banners of thought to the world, I cannot help but desire for man a greater moving with the tide of his own reality. Only by the complete repudiation of his past experiences with darkness, as well as the darkness of outer controls, can he free his soul to move with the great stream of Life. The imposition of social, economic or even political controls as a substitute for the freedom of the precious soul is a cheap and pasty design. In their place let us draw the mandala of the future and thereby make way for the cosmic progress of real freedom in man and society.

Devoted to your greater Light, I remain

Saint Germain

1. Matt. 6:23. 2. Rom. 3:8. 3. II Cor. 3:17.

Pearls of Wisdom®

| Vol. XIV No. 7 | Saint Germain | February 14, 1971 |

The Rigors of Initiation Can Be Invoked from the Hand of the Great Initiator

To All Who Would Climb the Ladder of Progress:

The development of an internal sense of fairness, justice and honor is essential if the chela is to progress upon the Path. So long as individuals allow themselves license to do what they will, without first determining by internal deliberation the consequences of their actions upon the lives of others, so long will distortion occur in the mirror of transforming Truth.

What chicanery it is that individuals raise the double standard! How can freedom be won and cherished unless man knows that he has first given justice unto others, that he has espoused the golden rule, and that his intentions themselves have been vigorous in their denial of unfairness wherever confronted? If the standard of Truth is not upheld within, how can it be upheld without?

Once the conceptions of the mind are aligned with the patterns of Truth, the next step is the forgiveness of sins—the breaking of old grudges held against other parts of Life. So long as men harbor these grudges, a certain measure of their daily allotment of energy is taken up in sustaining matrices of condemnation and resentment and thereby diverted from constructive channels. This energy then becomes trapped in the subconscious recesses of his being like a coiled spring that can go neither forward nor backward. Before long, mounting pressure from within these coils causes mental anxiety, frustration, sleepless nights and various forms of psychosis until man becomes a caged lion, pacing back and forth, awaiting the moment to strike against those whom he blames for all his ills.

I speak to all who love freedom. Put your internal house in order and keep it there. Do not allow yourself to become engrossed in the business of vengeance. Why do you suppose the Scriptures warned of old, saying, "Vengeance is mine; I will repay, saith the Lord"? Let all, then, be content to allow the Cosmic Law the freedom to act. As long as people interfere with the karmic patterns of others, so long do they leave themselves wide open as targets for the interferences of others; whereas, by the ritual of forgiveness extended to all—and especially to themselves—for all past wrong, they clear the way for the activation of the Spirit of Truth and their own cosmic initiation. [1]

Yet, it is not enough to clear away the negatives from your world. If you would truly experience the renewal of right action toward your fellowman that will enable you to reach your Divine Presence, you must also understand something about the divine nature in both God and man. The divine nature is real and permanent as the Scriptures record—"Jesus Christ the same yesterday, and today, and forever"— intimating that the Christ Consciousness does not undergo change. Even so, if you would progress, you must be constant in upholding the immaculate concept of the Christ on behalf of all mankind.[2]

One of the great mysteries involving the concept of the changeless nature of being is that whereas the aspects of Deity do not undergo change in the sense of deterioration, they do undergo transforming change "from glory to glory even as by the Spirit of the Lord." This sometimes moot point must be understood: From the human stand-point, the laws of God remain inviolate and cannot be changed as they apply to human conditions. At the same time, the very nature of the Infinite is to transcend itself, to rise ever higher in consciousness into that realm of God bliss, whose vibrations are pulsating in transforming spirals of divine awareness. As the curve of the Infinite appears to be a straight line to mortal eye, so the transcendent nature of God appears changeless to unascended souls.[3]

There are many in the world today who, in the name of God, in the name of Truth, or even in the name of the Ascended Masters, take license in proclaiming erroneous doctrine, not knowing that their concepts represent the astral viewpoint. To keep themselves above the choppy waters of vain rumor and free from mortal strife, it is impor-tant that men shall understand the value of decrees, prayers and affir-mations. That which some men have classed as 'vain repetition' is, in reality, the victorious manifestation of freedom in action in man, accomplished by the ancient power of the Spoken Word.

It is written, "Thou shalt also decree a thing, and it shall be established unto thee: and the light shall shine upon thy ways." The vanity of repetition comes about as men merely utter the words of God without allowing the intense feelings of the Holy Spirit to generate in them that response whereby the very doors of the universe open wide and the windows of heaven shower upon man the answers that clearly are recorded: "...before they call, I will answer; and while they are yet speaking, I will hear." Because some have made vain use of the Sacred Word should all forsake its blessings? I think not. I, for one, shall not![4]

Let it be understood, then, that we do not approve of the astral manifestations of spirits that "mutter and peep" and masquerade in the similitude of God, if for no other reason than the fact that these entities are altogether limited in the realm of response. They may flatter, prate aphorisms and pronounce grandiose schemes, but they cannot act in life; in fact they are utterly helpless to work change in the land of the living—and this is the great requirement of the hour as well as the proof of the spiritual pudding.[5]

The responses of the astral denizens to the pleas of men are doled out as false promise of name and fame; these ultimately dethrone themselves and all who follow them. No pie in the sky is the Ascended Masters' teaching, but a veritable cornucopia of constructive energies invoked for constructive change.

What better action can a man take than to pray, decree and meditate upon the very law of his own life? For born out of his prayers, his meditations and decrees is the power of valiant action; and without them the very stimulus for action cannot be provided. The entire universe was created by the Word of God, and so man himself, by the same power, creates his own world, for good or for ill. Jesus pointed out to his disciples the immediate effect of their words upon their lives when he said,"...by thy words thou shalt be justified and by thy words thou shalt be condemned."[6]

Let men understand the importance, then, of the words they speak and the thoughts they think; for the old conflict, "...shew me thy faith without thy works, and I will shew thee my faith by my works," often becomes a confusing point for those who do not understand the Law in all of its various aspects. But when the Law is understood, it becomes a means of deliverance; and the relationship between faith and works is readily apparent. Those who have no specific inward faith, yet who perform the works of righteousness on behalf of their fellowmen, often find that their faith comes into manifestation following their works.[7]

We are advocates, then, of good works among men; for thus is the Cosmic Law invoked on man's behalf. Furthermore, the whole process of initiation, of testing the soul that it might rise, depends upon the inner action of man's thoughts and feelings as these are implemented through word and deed. But the carnal mind is often the worst enemy of man. Even when the soul of love produces right motive and right action, the carnal mind will place in question the actions of another. Standing guard, self-appointed, upon the activities of men, it waits to plunge its sword into the offenders of its name.

Man should not always be on the qui vive outwardly. Let his protection be from within. In the words of Sir Galahad, "My strength is as the strength of ten because my heart is pure."[8] Unless one's protection issues from the purity of the Christ Consciousness, one is helpless against the inroads of the night visitors; thus do vile men badly motivate those who are inherently good.

By the cleansing process of the Sacred Fire, man invokes for himself a suitable climate for the initiatic experience that necessarily entails the proving of his soul's worth under the most adverse circumstances. Thus is he readied for the appearance of that cosmic virtue which, when multiplied by the efforts of many hearts kindled with love, will relieve the world of its darkness and produce the miracle of Light within all.

One of the simplest methods whereby the rigors of initiation can be invoked from the hand of the Great Initiator is through sustained feelings of joy, of buoyancy, of happiness, of expectancy, of wonder, of trust and of awareness that God is, that He employs in His service myriad hosts of Light, and that these hosts of Light conspire together for the victory of the Light in all who would produce constructive change in themselves and in the world.

In the name of common sense, I implore the citizens of Earth: do not trust the outer hand of worldly circumstances to produce all of the constructive change required for the golden age civilization. Allow heaven the opportunity of expressing within you. Let buoyancy of thought, healthiness of spirit, and compassion for the whole world make life's journey happier. Without this trust, man is bereft even of the opportunity of initiation; with this trust, this faith and this right action, which begins in the inner world of thought and feeling, man can stabilize his entire existence; and through the radiant power drawn from his God Presence, he can pass every test aright and rise swiftly in the cosmic peerage.

First as the servant of all and then as the ruler of many, he will be called upon to strengthen those whose spirits are without hope until the purposes of many lives are at last fulfilled. Bearing the fresh winds of freedom and the courage to undergo any initiation that may be required for his victory, he shall lead others into that realm of joy which the true spiritual man is destined to know and whose manifestation the fleshly garb ought not to prevent.

For your delight in a freedom transcendent and in the progress of the new age, and with the hope that the catharsis of man will become a reality at last,

I remain and I AM

Saint Germain

1. Deut. 32:35; Rom. 12:19. 2. Heb. 13:8. 3. II Cor. 3:18. 4. Job 22:28; Isa. 65:24. 5. Isa. 8:19. 6. Matt. 12:37. 7. James 2:18. 8. From the poem "Sir Galahad" (1842) by Alfred Lord Tennyson.

Pearls of Wisdom®

Vol. XIV No. 8   *Mother Mary*   *February 21, 1971*

The Transformation of the Individual Is the Key to the Salvation of a Planet

To Every Pilgrim Heart:

As the advent of Love comes at times to every man who will open himself to the inward persuasions of his own soul, so I am convinced that all things will one day reflect the glory of God.

So many have retained the image of my Son in those agonies of human persecution that are reminiscent of their own conflict in matter. These involvements with the via dolorosa—the sorrowful way—are a trap that prevents man from seeing and experiencing the glories inherent in the constructive life which was lived by our Carpenter of Nazareth. Let it be known, then, that his was a building for eternity in the finite realm of thought and feeling.

What a tragedy it is that men are so easily diverted by outer media from the true course of their appointed thoughts. How much to be desired, then, is the mastery of one's own thoughts and feelings—the mastery of the flow of energy through one's consciousness.

Because there is no other method of controlling the individual, either from within or without, I wish to stress to every son and daughter of heaven the tremendous joy and freedom that can be theirs as they perceive the import of governing their thoughts and feelings, their attitudes and comprehensions of the Divine Wonder.

All around you beauty exists, yet ugliness seems so often to preempt it. I would remove the crown of thorns that man has unwittingly placed upon his own head, but first I would ask that true reason be utilized in making those constructive changes that are necessary in order that man might secure his cosmic destiny right while in physical embodiment.

Have you thought of what a beautiful gift God has given unto you in your life—even in the manifestation of your physical form which is so often crucified by the harshness of everyday living? Precious ones, the ways of the world are a glaring reflection of man's lack of innocence. When guilelessness and innocence become a part of man's nature once again, he will effectively transform himself in the image of the Christ as was the Will of God for him from the beginning. Then, in emulation of the Masters of Wisdom, man shall not only pursue and be pursued by the Light of The Great White Brotherhood, but he shall also become a true follower of God in all His compassed wonder.

Why, don't you know, beloved ones, The Most High can unerringly guide your thoughts and feelings just as easily as you can weave a simple garment for a child, using the dexterity of your fingers and the flexibility of your mind? With the God-given capacity that you have to direct your physical body and to organize your life, can you not also master the process of controlling your mind and your feelings? And if you do, I assure you that it will contribute much to the alleviation of the problems of the world in its maddened state. It will even counteract the unfortunate manifestations of witchcraft and black magic that are often practiced in the name of religion but are used solely for the psychic domination and control of others.

May I tell you that the one design that Heaven desires to see outpictured on Earth and in the hearts of men is that self-control by which every individual can win his own victory and the strength of his Christlike mind. Therefore do I invoke for all the Christlike mind and the Christlike qualities which will effect the power of self-control that is the requirement of the hour. Whereas from time to time men have misused the minds and feelings that God has given them, those minds and feelings possess the very capacities of the Spirit which Jesus expressed and that he longed to see established in you all.

Through obedience to the law of your inner being, you can effect those self-controls that will make your world brighter each day. And whereas there are some who will despise my message for its simplicity, others will see the need to pinpoint for future action the whole course of their conduct. This need for God-control can be seen in young and old alike—from the little children, in their innocent state, to those wiser ones who, in their maturity, have so often lost those holy threads of innocence which establish the aura of cosmic fortitude in men.

As long as you depend solely upon your human strength, and not upon the power of the Christ, it is easy to see, surrounded as you are by the mosaics of mortal thought, how you can become the victim of those thought-pockets of human degradation. The elimination of the idea that you cannot take command of your lives is the important first step that must be taken before you can begin to weave those spiritual garments of self-mastery we long to see you wear.

Many have thought that in the last days of my earthly sojourn I did not fulfill all my longings. Beloved ones, may I confess to you that even in the ascended state we have not fulfilled all our longings, especially in connection with the Earth and its evolutions. Do you know that out of the teeming millions of mankind, some of the prayers that rise to our level are literally heartrending, and particularly so when viewed in the light of the fact that Heaven has already provided the answer which humanity will not open their hearts to receive. When we stress the importance of the dedication of the individual life to God, it means that we believe that the kingdom of heaven must first manifest within the individual before it can manifest in the world on a larger scale.

So long as men wait upon the world for the fulfillment of their desires, so long will they wait in the recalcitrance and hopelessness of those who do not understand that one is taken and another is left. The justice of God on Earth must become the work of the individual. Those who crave social justice are those who would build worldly fences of unenforceable law and order; they do not realize that the establish-ment of law and order comes about as men claim that holy sense of justice that burns behind the veil of the appearance world. One day they will learn that it is only in the realm within, in the inner thoughts and feelings, that transformation can occur, and that the transfor-mation of the individual is the key to the salvation of a planet.[1]

Whenever undesirable qualities seem to have an inordinate hold upon your consciousness, possessing your whole being, occupying the very fiber of your mind and denying you the peace and happiness of thinking those thoughts that you so long to think, realize that you are momentarily caught in the grips of a terrible force accumulation. In the past we have also been confronted by such forcefields of vicious psychic energies, and even in the ascended state we have been required to meet the challenges of giant floating grids of astral debris. But as we have persevered and prevailed upon God to help us, our minds have immediately become calm and imbued with the power of holy reason and judgment.

Learn not to be rash, to be overly critical, or to unfairly attribute to others those qualities that are in reality no part of the Real Self. Give to all the joy and peace which you yourself expect to receive and watch how the energies of the universe will, in due course of time, like a steadily flowing river, rush into your world to assist you in the whole process of inward purification.

When I think of the long journey of Christendom and of the conflicts into which many have entered in the name of my Son, con-demning as heathen those followers of God in other folds, I am reminded of his words, "...other sheep I have, which are not of this fold: them also I must bring, and they shall hear my voice; and there shall be one fold, and one shepherd." In the name of holy reason, until men come to the place where they are able to see the Body of God upon

Earth as "one fold," even as they behold the "one shepherd," give them their freedom to think as they will, and pray that they may establish in their consciousness that faith in the one God which will make of the whole Earth one family beneath the four winds of heaven.[2]

All conflict must be resolved, all vileness cast away, and the tender beauty of the kingdom of heaven become as flowers beneath man's feet, a high and holy way of joy in the transcendent culture of the Ascended Masters' Consciousness. Then the little children can be trained up in the way they should go, and at long last the travail of the ages that has preceded the birth of the divine manchild will bring forth a golden age of enlightenment, and God will rule in the hearts of men because they love Him and love one another.[3]

Each moment that the individual understands and enters into this consciousness a new beginning occurs. Therefore, be ye followers of my Son and of the invincible Light that presages the eternally progressive Age of the Avatars; for in the beginning was the Light of the Word, and the Light was with God and the Light was God. And out of that Light is born the Flame that pushes back the darkness that never was and never shall be. The illusion of that darkness shall vanish as the coming of the kingdom is heard in a rushing mighty wind and the ground of the heart, like a thirsty ground, laps up the water of eternal Life.[4]

Let men be spiritually filled. Let their goals now be spiritual even as in the past they have been material. Thus shall we bridge the gap of confusion and reveal at last the permanent foundation of the abundant Life.

I remain

Mary

The Mother of Jesus

1. Matt. 24:40; Luke 17:34-36. 2. John 10:16. 3. Prov. 22:6. 4. John 1:1.

Pearls of Wisdom®

Vol. XIV No. 9   *El Morya*   *February 28, 1971*

The Elect Still Pursue the Upward Climb

Savants of the Will of God:

The belt of time has steadily moved from the beginning as the passion of the Light for the expression of itself. The chips of darkness hewn from the Tree of Life by vulgar men have, time and time again, obliterated the radiant view of perfection, but they have not stopped the spiritual evolution of men. While millions move as the restless tide of the masses, the elect still pursue the upward climb.

The Resurrection Flame becomes the fohat of invincibility in the mind and heart of the elect; still, others court vain pleasures. The compensation of the spiritual Path must be understood. The words, "verily, they have their reward," remain the Master's succinct utterance regarding the tone of life when it is linked entirely to the whimsy of the human will.[1]

Men sometimes say they do not choose, but are moved by "powers greater than themselves." Let it be understood that when they are moved by these "powers" to do that which they ought not to do, it is because they have first consented in little things to engage in acts of perfidy against the reality of the eternal Truth. By deviation men are moved, and by devotion men are also moved.

The Path of spiritual devotion may be strewn with thorns, but one does not gather thorns and thistles. The wise man goeth to the cobbler and is properly shod. And so we speak of the gift of preparation for spiritual adventure. Men go into the world well-prepared for high adventure. Let them also gather spiritual treasure and consider the need to make preparation.

Now we come to the problem of communication between the planes. The Scriptures cry out against necromancy, and wise are they who heed their warning. Let men understand the continuity of Life and the value of spiritual attainment. Men ask for the Flame of the Resurrection. They are wise. They ask for spiritual power, and spiritual power is given them. They merit greater spiritual power, and their merit is heard by the Karmic Lords as a request for cosmic action. But the question of communion with higher spheres and the continuity of life after death, so-called, remains a common problem. We shall stress spiritual attainment.[2]

The word of the Lord to the Revelator, "He that is holy, let him be holy still and he that is filthy, let him be filthy still," applies to those who pass through the gateway between worlds. Let it be understood that unless one has first mastered the use of energy in the physical plane, one does not attain in the spiritual planes that progress which can be counted as obedience to the Will of God or the attainment of proficiency in the Divine Nature.[3]

The question has been asked why some of us choose to work with the evolutions of Earth and why some who have attained to the ascended state do not compile those magnificent utterances which glorify the Supreme Spirit.

First of all, let it be understood that there are evolutions upon the planet who are not of this world, but of another; and there are also evolutions on the planet who, while spiritually holding fast to divine ideals, do not have that mental development which would enable them to draw the balance of the Christed Self into manifestation. The problem of the various life waves upon the planet is a factor which determines who from our octave shall come forth to serve and who among us shall remain in the Great Silence or active in other sectors of cosmos.

Although individuals do not draw forth while in embodiment the victorious manifestations of self-mastery that marked the life of Jesus and other avatars, they may still earn their ascension by balancing fifty-one percent of their karma; yet this will not automatically give them those virtues which they have not attained. However, the availability remains; and they have the opportunity after the ascension to increase their momentum of both virtue and attainment. And so every star that is born of God does not necessarily exhibit the same magnitude. Every soul does not manifest the same attainment, "for one star differeth from another star in glory. So also is the resurrection of the dead."[4]

Then there are those of us who hold spiritual office by reason of our spiritual initiation. We have no pride in this but only devotion to the purposes of God; therefore, we were especially chosen, and this is the meaning of the Chohan of the Ray[5]—those who are chosen of the Rays of Divine Will, Wisdom and Love, of Purity, Truth, Devotion and Freedom, to act as guardian spirits to teach mankind the Way, preventing, when possible, their betrayal of those ideals that when espoused will provide the opportunity for the greatest attainment.

I must take my stand for the banner of the rule of attainment. Let those who study to show themselves approved unto God be considered as those who hold the Divine Wisdom to be a thing of worth. When men seek after phenomena or exhibitions of the fires of another, let them realize that the inward attainment is the measure of a man.[6]

When I speak of the power of the Spirit of the Resurrection Flame, I include its power to resurrect the attainment of the soul garnered in all past ages. It is necessary that you call for the resurrection of your own momentums of self-mastery; for the spiritual business of mastership has sometimes gone lagging insofar as the evolutions of Earth are concerned. We wait to see those who will attain proficiency in body, mind and spirit—who will understand the need to serve and to be prepared; for there is a mighty work to be done in the name of the Lord by those who know the meaning of discipline and sacrifice.

We intend that our forthcoming university in the world of form will be a noble beginning for a quickening in the souls of men, a fiery realization that life is more than just an amusement game, that it is a transcendent experience of climbing the stairways of opportunity. Wise is the man or woman who prepares for proficiency in the divine art. And let this also be understood: man can do many things simultaneously; he can cast out unwanted darkness while drawing into himself those treasures of wanted Light that create new dimensions and new resurrections.

Why, I almost feel like exclaiming at the very top of my lungs: What glorious opportunities are given the soul that opens the doorway to the understanding of itself! When we say man can become God, do we desecrate God? The highest form of valor is the imitation of perfection. He who imitates The Most High, bearing the mantle of humility, will rise far in the Cosmic Hierarchy. Remember the Parable of the Talents and the fate of the unprofitable servant who buried his talent in a napkin. Remember the possibility of the correct use of Life's energies and the setting of the sails of cosmic desire.[7]

Attainment in the world of form is attainment in the world of the formless. Spiritual communion with those Arhats (the Ascended Masters), who are never content to ignore any spiritual treasure trove, will make of each *Pearl of Wisdom* a jewel in your crown of spiritual rejoicing. Men have supposed that God would reward them for well-doing by crowning them with His own crown of cosmic honor; they have not understood that He fashions that crown out of the substance of their own victorious achievement, and that their crown can be no bigger and no better than they themselves make it.

In the name of common sense, why will men wear the crown of thorns in an act of self-obliteration, when in reality the ego is intended to be divided in half—the lower ego being stomped upon by the victorious feet of the Higher Ego? Every man must put down his own delusion, sort out his own confusion, create his own lawful 'intrusions' into the divine domain, and understand that he has within himself a Christ-ladder that will lead him to victorious attainment—if he will only use it.

The beauty of communion can be sustained when one is in communion with those bright Spirits made in the similitude of God, but certainly not when one is in communion with the spirits of darkness. Saint John said, "Beloved, believe not every spirit, but try the spirits whether they are of God." The astral realm is unprofitable. It is a realm of twirling emotion, a baton of phenomena bereft of worth or permanence.[8]

Work toward permanence, toward eternal spiritual progression, toward attainment; and Heaven will bless you for it. Consider the boundlessness of the great Divine Identity. Your God Presence created you to share in the bounties of the universe and the Resurrection Flame to quicken your appreciation of the Divine Nature. It should be invoked to inhabit not only the body, but the mind and spirit as well. Then you shall learn to soar victoriously, and you shall be tethered to the practicality of releasing the fruits of reason unto your fellowmen.

In this *Pearl* I desire to sunder the veil that divides man from his God. I wish to show the importance of the True Self in the divine mystery, so that every man will in love preserve his way into the divine domain and will not sell short the victories that are possible through service and attainment. Knowledge is a gift of your Christed Self. When rightly used, it is priceless. Through the perfect balance of the Eternal Spirit—Love, Wisdom and Power—man attains that immortality which he deserves; for God wills it so.

Peace, victorious ones. The dawn cometh.

Your Morya

1. Matt. 6:2. 2. Deut. 18:10-12. 3. Rev. 22:11. 4. I Cor. 15:41, 42. 5. The Seven Color Rays are the natural division of the pure White Light emanating from the Heart of God as it descends through the prism of the Christ Consciousness. The Seven Rays and their Chohans (Chohan means "Lord" in Sanskrit) are as follows: 1st Ray of Power and Faith (Blue)—El Morya, embodied as Sir Thomas More; 2nd Ray of Wisdom and Illumination (Yellow)—Lanto, embodied as a sage in ancient China; 3rd Ray of Love and Beauty (Pink)—Paul the Venetian, embodied as Paolo Veronese; 4th Ray of Purity and Ascendancy (White)—Serapis Bey, embodied as Phidias, the famous fifth century B.C. Greek sculptor; 5th Ray of Healing and Supply (Green)—Hilarion, embodied as the apostle Paul; 6th Ray of Ministration and Service (Purple and Gold)—Nada, embodied as a priestess in the Temple of Love on Atlantis; 7th Ray of Freedom, Transmutation and Ritual (Violet)—Saint Germain, embodied as Sir Francis Bacon. The Offices of the Seven Chohans of the Rays are divinely appointed by the Cosmic Hierarchy, who make their selections from among the most qualified Ascended Beings who have arisen from Earth's schools. Those who retain the Office of Chohan hold sovereign responsibility under divine ordination for the administration to mankind of all of the qualitative aspects of their own specific Ray while harmonizing their administration with the other six Rays. The Chohans always obey Cosmic Law; yet they are given certain latitude, in keeping with their manifest individual evolution, capacities and special endowments, to direct mankind in the most adroit manner, giving such loving assistance and spiritual direction as may be the requirement of the hour. They retain in their service legions of angelic hosts and Ascended Brethren who carry out the plan of The Great White Brotherhood for the most complete expression of the Seven Rays that is possible among the mankind of Earth. 6. II Tim. 2:15. 7. Matt. 25:14-30. 8. I John 4:1.

Pearls of Wisdom®

Vol. XIV No. 10   The Maha Chohan   March 7, 1971

He Who Loves Best Serves Best

To Those Who Would Commune with the Flame of Life:

Green are the fields of Ceylon, beautiful in their own right the fields of India. Yet, to the Lord belongeth the harvest of men's hearts. They cry out for guidance when in turmoil and trouble. Then, content with their own small measures of attainment, they remain aloof from divine ideals. Little do some know of the virtues of the Holy Spirit and the mastery of the Ascended Jesus Christ Consciousness.

They speak of the Second Coming, but they do not understand that, above all, the attainment of the Great Master must come into their hearts. His Light, that does not fail in the highest dimension, must not and should not fail upon Earth. Man must not confuse his opportunity for rapport with the Holy Spirit with sense delights. He must see and hear behind the veil of matter the rippling of spiritual expansion. He must commune, if he would expand, with the higher thoughts of God that hover behind the visible form.

What composes the wheat—golden treasury of the bread of Life? Out of human greed men have robbed the golden waving grain of the natural life-giving elements. Because their control of the processing goes unchallenged, they continue to misuse modern methods of refinement, not to promote better health, but to deprive their fellowmen of the vital powers of Christ-wholeness contained within the natural grain. As they have done in the realm of the material creation, so have they done in the realm of the spiritual. The modern day robbery of the Christ potential at every hand is reminiscent of the words spoken long ago by one of the holy women: "They have taken away my Lord, and I know not where they have laid him." [1]

The knowledge of the Holy Spirit as the indwelling Presence is foolishly regarded by many to be a myth. Then, too, there are those whose longing for power and phenomena leads them to commune with the dark spirits that bestow "power without payment"—that is, without exacting that individual self-mastery which the Lord requires of His sons and daughters ere they receive the mantle of the Holy Spirit. Yet, the Cosmic Law clearly states that man must earn the right to do and to be that which he already is; for man is a dual being: he is manifestation and he is potential. And the word, "Whatsoever a man soweth, that shall he also reap," is a spiritual word of great promise; for in the bestowal by God of the right of every man to become the Christ, He has taken nothing from Jesus, whom He sent to exemplify that Christ Grace which is the Light of all. [2]

The Christ is the bestower of each man's own inherent cosmic identity, the power of the divine seed that lives within him. Invoking this power of the indwelling Christ, every man can create a furnace, white-hot, of aspiration that will draw to him the magnitude of the Cosmic Light by which the worlds were framed, by which the Christ was raised from the dead, by which all spiritual attainment, whether it be in Saint Francis or in Lord Gautama, was made.

Men speak of heathens and Christians. They speak of Jews and publicans. Yet they know not of what they speak when they speak of division. They know not of what they speak when they speak of oneness. Oneness is the Divine Nature of the Father-Mother God, it is the oneness of the Holy Spirit; whereas division is the self-created schism of men by which they sunder their bond with reality. Each man should understand his own divine potential as utterly important; for without that potential and the oneness of his Higher Self, he has no vehicle through which to express his devotion to God or to his fellowmen.

In assisting mankind to realize their God-appointed course, we would make plain that with the passing of the cycles and the years, when all is said and done, attainment, God-given, is the purpose of existence. Men are content to praise God when the highest praise of God is attainment. They are satisfied when their tiny needs are met. Little do they know of the great vacuum that exists within themselves which can be filled with the great treasury of the divine potential. Little do they know of the great opportunity that also lies within themselves. All of this is a part of the treasure of the Holy Spirit. It is a treasure of service; for he who loves best, serves best. And he who serves best has the greatest treasure.

As I gaze upon the waving grain and the rich vegetation, the green beauty of the foliage, I am reminded of the soul's inner beauty, nourished by the Holy Spirit. I am reminded of the Fire of the Sun that gleams in every heart. While the insects crawl upon the ground only to be crushed beneath the feet of man, the civilization of man and the marts of commerce march on, crushing beneath their feet the tender aspirations of the souls of men. Man does not fancy himself an ant pressed beneath the boot of world karma; yet in the Armageddonlike conspiracy of world karma that he is weaving from day to day—

through his neglect of the Holy Spirit and his failure to properly train the young—his very life opportunity is being literally snuffed out.

In a recent meeting with me, the Members of the Indian Council spoke of the sending of grain to India by generous hearts in America. They talked of assistance that had come from many parts of the world, and at the same time they acknowledged that only the few in India and the world understand the need for the unification of the soul of man with his Real Self. Only the few understand this unification as a necessary prerequisite in combating inherent superstition, ignorance, and compounded failure that lead first to hopelessness and then to moral degeneration. The world has often sought an end to armed conflict; but who will end human bigotry, religious intolerance, and the scum of immorality that corrode the souls of men?

We are particularly concerned with those fresh lives—the babes and youths—who come into embodiment with the hope of a new opportunity of fulfilling their life plan. Their ancient karma, conspiring to produce unwholesome conditions in the domain of their individual consciousness, could, if mankind were only more wise, be so tenderly mitigated by the loving care of a more appropriate educational system, one that is less geared to the perpetuation of those human qualities men hold dear, which are nothing more than a passing chimera. Yet, again and again they have demonstrated a preference for whimsy while ignoring the need for universal brotherhood. Alas, their preferences, which reflect their improper training and lack of exposure to the culture of the Christ, have determined the course of history!

I have asked the Indian Council and the Karmic Lords to withhold, if possible, until Easter, certain impending cataclysmic developments upon the planetary body. The matter is in consideration before the Council.

Love remains in the universe, everywhere positioned to rush in with that valiant assistance for which man hopes. As in the time of the death of Lazarus, the Christ Spirit of the Resurrection yearns to bestow upon man and society that comfort which is not dependent upon either social or political conditions, but upon the receptive chalice of fiery hearts who genuinely love and move quickly to act without fear or favor.

I cannot foresee the advent of a world resurrection until there is a greater measure of world response. But I must urge those valiant disciples of Christ to continue to bring forth the divine manchild as a cosmic image in their minds, as a glyph of such strength as to make its mark upon the wall. Then the Lords of Karma, in seeing the handwriting on the wall and the weight of man's negativity, will also see that there are those whose every sacrifice and thought hold out against the darkness the magnificent torch of eternal Life.

To preserve the world in a sea of myriad lights is our hope. To preserve it as a platform of graduation for the millions evolving here who must learn to esteem the Love from the Heart of God: to preserve it as the prospect of a new resurrection of hope to mankind—this is our hope.

Charged with the Hope of the Holy Spirit, I remain the advocate of eternal Faith, Hope and Charity.

The Maha Chohan

Representative of the Holy Spirit[3]

1. John 20:13. 2. Gal. 6:7. 3. The one who presently holds this office was embodied as the blind poet Homer. His retreat is in Ceylon where the Flame of Comfort (white tinged with pink, with gold at its base) and the Flame of the Holy Spirit (white) are enshrined.

Pearls of Wisdom

Vol. XIV No. 11   *Jesus the Christ*   *March 14, 1971*

The Union of Heart and Mind

Blessed Are They That Mourn for They Shall Be Comforted with Truth!

As men and women of today gather photographs of loved ones, as they preserve mementos of other days and other times, so do the akashic records marvelously preserve the goings and comings of men.

One of the sweetest thoughts for all who have lost those whom they love through the change called death is the concept that every young atom of each person is immortally preserved in the Consciousness of God. All care lines, all sorrow, all undesirable episodes are forgotten; and only that which is deemed worthwhile in the Mind of God is preserved in His foreverness. But men sometimes fear the realm of akasha, and even the nature of the Father Himself, to be as a vast ocean that swallows up their loved ones and their cherished moments, nevermore to release that which is absorbed. Let me elucidate.

Each day, each cycle, out of the depths of God's Love, from the hand and wheel of the great Master Potter of all, come forth new moldings according to the ancient patterns and ideas of His creative intent. Nothing worthwhile is ever really lost. All is preserved in the miracle of the eternal resurrection as fire sparks of cosmic magic, revealing the infinite care of God for each creature made in His own image.

And how the ritual of preservation bespeaks His Love even in the beings of mere mortals! Even the factors of instinct, reaction and response are preserved for a time; and that which man creates according to his sovereign will is honored in the world of form for the duration of its cycle.

Until man learns to apply the higher laws that govern his being, he will continue his energy output according to old patterns of human habit and tradition. But when he understands at last the great tide of reality that is onward moving, that is progressive, that demands the discarding of unwanted qualities and conditions, and that continually directs and redirects all parts of his being into the patterns of perfection, then he will shine outwardly like the inward radiance that is reflected in the image of God placed within himself by the Almighty.

Why are the soul ties to the Father so relevant to the heart of man, and yet so meaningless to the head? First, because the heart relates to love, and love relates to the universe known of the soul; secondly, because the head relates to the examination of objects and concepts by the fingers of the mind. Standing alone, without the employment of the heart, the head often makes those brittle decisions which shatter on impact the tender and intuitive feelings of the soul.

Stern, then, is a man's own life record and self-judgment when shaped after mortal design; but, when the natural faculties of the soul are allowed to breathe out the radiance of the Light, the whole world of man can be an eternal resurrection of loveliness. Then the strength of his mind, tethered to the radiance of his heart's love, becomes a shining armor for the protection of the emerging Christ Consciousness. Then the middle wall or partition between the Holy of Holies of his heart and the focus of his mind is rent in twain; and man, having access to the corridors of both mind and heart, fashions new wonders of perception and precipitation out of his total being.

Wherever the wall of partition exists between heart and mind, wherever one predominates over the other, there is bound to be an imbalance in the expression of the Christ—whether the corpselike gloom of the carnal mind that goes about classifying and devouring everything and everyone with its cutting criticism, or the unbridled passions of fruitless desire issuing from a heart untutored and impure.

But when the union of heart and mind occurs under the aegis of the one eternal Father and His eternal Son, then the meaning of the resurrection is revealed in the pulsating identity of the Christ, delineating mastery for all and in all. Then the soul looks on as from the Flame within his heart, the Flame of balanced Love, Wisdom and Power: a new age man is born. Leaping over the pages of history in giant strides, he rides upon a white horse, the master of his destiny and of his karma. His image is not cast upon a cross of human torture and debauchery but upon that masterful building which appears on the horizon of the new age; for man has first built the kingdom within, utilizing the rock and the timber, the chemistry and geometry, the very laws and elements of the firmament on high in his mastery of self and of the abundant Life.

When this happens in the inner beings of sufficient numbers of embodied men and women, then I am certain that the kingdom of heaven will become a reality in the world of form. But so long as the sense of struggle pervades the world's thought, so long as life is considered a race of competition for the accumulation of worldly goods, wherein man's life becomes based upon the abundance of the things which he temporarily possesses, his life is not the abundant Life, his life is not based upon the knowledge and victory of the Resurrection Flame, and the kingdom that is not within will not manifest without.[1]

We come in this twentieth century to give new concepts to man that are relevant to today, to relate his mind to the marvelous cosmic outreach of the Mind of God, and to teach him how to tether his being to the rocket of the Spirit that soars the untrammeled heights and discovers a design so vast, a reality so supreme, as to liberate his very soul from the socket of mortality. By a like token we teach the leap of the Ascended Masters' consciousness into the domain of the self, into the microcosmic world of man's thoughts and feelings. Can man realize the mastery others have accomplished? Then let him also realize that he, too, can master himself and his world. Let him be unafraid to advance in the God-design.

The myth of glorifying the outer identity of any man, including that of myself, must be perceived for what it is. Men must understand that "there is none good but one, that is, God." Therefore, why callest thou me, or any man, good, thus attributing to the transitory manifestation that which can only be a part of the permanent reality of God and man?[2]

Men must understand that the greatness of God and the potential of Christ accomplishment lie within themselves. They must see how cleverly the lie was woven by those ancient traditionalists who, in denying to mankind their God-ordained right to manifest their divine inheritance, created and labored the fatal view that I, in the person of Jesus, am the only door to salvation. This pernicious doctrine has replaced the teaching I gave to the disciples that the Christ, the "I AM" of every man, is the open door which no man can shut.

The only begotten of the Father, full of grace and truth, is the Christ Spirit that before Abraham was—I AM. Let men realize that the door of the "I AM" is a universal Presence, that the door of the all-pervading Spirit, whom I revealed as Father, is the Father of every man, that the Light is the Light of every man, revealed in the Gospel of John in written form, but first revealed in the Presence of every man that openeth his eyes.[3]

Some have feared this to be the saying of antichrist. Let not your hearts be troubled, but be comforted in the Truth that I bring. I AM the Living Christ who dwelleth in you all, even as the Father dwelleth in me and I in Him.

Those who confess that I AM come in the flesh must also confess that the Christ is come in them. This is the meaning of the Word made flesh—it is the power of the Light that descendeth into the form of every child of God. Am I the Son of God? Then ye are also sons and daughters of The Most High. Do you testify that the Father sent the Son to be the Saviour of the world? Then look within, for the Christ who overcomes the world lives also in you—one and all.[4]

This teaching I gave to Beloved John, who clearly understood the relationship of the outer self to the divinity of the I AM Presence. He saw and believed my admonishment to the disciples to do even "greater works" than I had done, because he knew the unlimited potential of the only begotten Son—the Christ of every man.[5] Therefore did he write my testimony for the ages:

"Behold, what manner of love the Father hath bestowed upon us, that we should be called the sons of God: therefore the world knoweth us not, because it knew him not. Beloved, now are we the sons of God, and it doth not yet appear what we shall be: but we know that, when he shall appear, we shall be like him; for we shall see him as he is. And every man that hath this hope in him purifieth himself, even as he is pure."[6]

When men understand the nature of true being, they will perceive that God fashioned a new potential for every man in the earliest beginning of the creation and endowed him with the authority of the Christ. Out of His fiery Spirit—all-pervading, all-loving—He directed to all of His sons and daughters the eternal resurrection of body, mind and spirit.

In the light of this understanding there can be no separation from any part of God; for the form, the body terrestrial which comes from the realm of Spirit, is perceived as manifesting for a little while upon the mirror of the appearance world and then vanishing away, to be reborn in more wondrous form, the body celestial, ultimately to become one with God Himself. [7]

And thus God is perceived as the advancing radiance of His creation, the transcendental crest of the wave of a glorious future, safe in the arms of eternal reality made clear. And if the fruit of mystery seem too difficult to perceive, then let the language of the heart and the mind of the universal Christ speak of new resurrections, of greater tomorrows.

Let divine comfort be administered to all who have ever been bereaved. Let all understand that their life is in reality the Life of God, and that the moments of time, ticking away by the rhythmic beat of the clock, are actually sublime moments of opportunity wherein the realization of cardinal truth can at last be imparted to the soul that opens mind and heart to the reality of Christed Being. Then sin and darkness and error shall be no more; for these graveclothes are put off by the universal man who, stretching the limbs of the universal Christ, appears reaching unto the stars and the glorious sun and beyond until he finds the Great Heart of universal passion for the abundant Life.

A God is born in man, and man becomes that God, according to the original intent; and the Spirit of the eternal resurrection is the face of the eternal morning.

> I AM He who loveth every child,
> Every man and every woman,
> Every creature great and small -
> With that transforming Love
> That transformeth all.

> Your Elder Brother on the Path,

> *Jesus*

1. Luke 12:15-21. 2. Mark 10:18. 3. John 8:58; 1:14; 1:9. 4. I John 4:2, 14; John 1:14. 5. John 14:12. 6. I John 3:1-3. 7. I Cor. 15:40.

Pearls of Wisdom®

| Vol. XIV No. 12 | Archangel Michael | March 21, 1971 |

The Leap of the God Flame

Flames of Faith, Kindled by His Love:

In one of your earthly tomes there are written these words: "For of all sad words of tongue or pen, the saddest are these: 'It might have been!'" [1]

What folly it is to pursue a pathway of thought that droppeth to the ground devoid of meaning or fulfillment! Faith was written by the hand of God. By it He framed all manifestation. Let the dregs of past ages, the historical record of man's infamy, and the burden of Egyptian bondage be no more as a darkening plague!

Instead, open the eyes of the spirit that you may see; for mortal eyes, blinded by the mad rush of world events, can scarcely make out the purposes of heaven. But inner eyes, opened in the childlike wonder of a newfound faith, can commence to string upon the great rosary of life's experiences that response to faith which evokes the leap of the God-Flame.

Content with the creature comforts, man at times does not understand the meaning of Life. Caught in the net of negative spirals and his own degenerate karma, he does not rightly put together the story of his own life. How, then, can he be expected to put together the drama of the ages and the lives of others? Yet human attitudes are so blithe, and at the same time so prone to belittlement, molded as they are in the age-old spirit of mockery. Long established in the business of tearing apart, they seldom reckon with the intense need, from both a spiritual and a material standpoint, to put together.

I AM an Archangel, and I deal with the passions and feelings of Gods and men. When I speak of "Gods," I trust you will understand that there is but one Lord—"Hear, O Israel: The Lord our God is one Lord!" remains the fiat of the ages—but there are many sons and daughters who have begun to exhibit that self-mastery and cosmic control which lead to higher initiation and engagement in the eternal track of universal certitude. They have become, as it were, Gods in their own domain. These, too, must be reckoned with—these Cosmic Beings, Ascended Masters, Angels, Archangels and Mighty Elohim;

for they have become co-creators with Him by virtue of the Godlike qualities they have externalized. [2]

Finite man seldom thinks on such as these—servant sons who have risen in the cosmic peerage to adorn the heavens with His expanding Love. And this is the meaning of the statement, "Ye are Gods!" cited by Jesus who had the courage to preach the cosmic truth that every manifestation of God has the opportunity of becoming Godlike, even as the Father is in them and they are in Him. [3]

The faith of mortals is usually centered around this one or that one among their contemporaries, for whom they have changing esteem or contempt. What a pity! For all men are becoming, all men are evolving, even when the forward movement can only be measured in inches. Let men learn, then, to have faith in the potential of their own evolvement, and let them accord the same to others; for the arc of God stretches across the heavens and reaches the life of each individual according to his capacity to receive.

Human turbulence is confined to a finite span by divinely imposed proscription; nevertheless, its unfortunate sphere of influence includes other men evolving within that given span. Thus the vortices of malevolence which have accumulated upon the planet Earth are attested by the fact that the angels of my band, when coming into the realm of Earth, wear crystalline helmets of cosmic light substance that are impervious to dense human vibrations and thoughts of faithlessness.

Would it not be more beneficial to the evolution of the individual, as well as to that of the race, if your thoughts—everyone's thoughts— were more constructive and were not so wedded to the past history of human infamy? The plays and novels that are written, the dramas that are unfolded before the eyes of the very young so frequently contain within them elements of human passion rehearsed over and over again. Yet mankind is seldom bored by his own depredation; and the relatively few choose the outlet, so temporary and so destructive, of human suicide. [4]

Let all understand that Life is meant to be a progressive outreach, an experience in Faith, Hope and Charity, an onward movement for the elusive perfection man seldom finds but often feels impelled to seek. But where are they seeking? Not in the realm of perfection, but in the domain of the familiar, in the transitory world which they have called the stable, which to us is most turbulent and uncertain.

Let them turn to faith in God and in the divine plan. Let them not continue to lament the failure of heaven to appear, when all around them the drama of heaven is appearing, and the only failure is man's failure to recognize that God is, and that God does appear in all of nature and in all of man as the sublime outreach of the immortal Spirit toward perfection and hope.

What a strengthening comes to man when he becomes willing to accept change in his own life. And this change should not be temporal but wedded to a spirit of ongoingness. His must be the realization that the cogs of progress are geared to a cosmic chain capable of raising an entire civilization, if man wills it so.

As surely as the canopy of a blue heaven is overhead, so in moments of faith that refuse to be shaken, man can consciously tether himself to the Holy Will of God. Each time individual man reaffirms his faith in the good and the real, this tethering creates a strengthening of the bond of purpose in every man, and the unshakable conviction that because God is, man is.

The duality of the ages—the Spirit that is, and the spirit that is becoming—showers upon mankind the opportunity of severing the veil between the reality of God and the reality of man. When he accepts the proffered gift through that valiant flow which is the spirit of overcoming victory, man understands his own divinity and the great fact that God wills it so. Then he is no longer a fatalist, wandering the streets of dense desire, forsaking his divine birthright, satisfying his hungers with the husks of life, again and again finding himself bereft of the very means of existence.

Once trapped by astral denizens, now he cries out in the pain of being clothed with unworthy garments, albeit they were made by his own hand. Now he asks to be delivered from the painful exigencies of his karma. He asks for Life; he seeks once again to walk the streets of Earth, to recapture a lost opportunity, to fulfill his newly found destiny. Spirit responds to his plea, and from the orb of opportunity he is launched into wholeness of being.

And so I speak of the Pathway. I speak of the spiritual Path. I speak of faith, and I trust that men will understand why we do not appear to the merely curious. When we have appeared as a man, they have maimed us. When we have appeared as a divine being, they have pointed the finger at themselves saying, "You hallucinate!" And so the only sign given by God to man is the sign of the prophet Jonah: As Jonah was in the whale's belly three days and three nights, so shall the son of man be in the Earth three days and three nights. [5]

Thus the drama of the life of Christ Jesus and of his crucifixion, death, and burial become, as a universal initiation, the story of every man's adventure in form; for that which is earth, earthy, that which is crucified in form, must rise into the realm of Spirit whence it came. Thus the spirit of man must also become willing to be molded and to mold others in the divine image. Rising at last into the realm of immortal Life, man becomes that faith which he seeks, a living faith of fire, tested for all ages and attesting the dignity of the Son of God.

"Made a little lower than the angels," he is crowned with glory and honor.[6]

So do we exhibit the facets of eternal faith to every man, that he may be clothed and in his right mind, one with God, yet the servant of all.

The cosmic arch spanning the heavens reveals universal purpose. The magic of believing is the gateway to immortal Life.

In the name of Eternal Faith, I remain

Archangel Michael

1. "Maud Muller" (1856), by John Greenleaf Whittier. 2. Deut. 6:4. 3. Pss. 82:6; John 10:31-38. 4. By Karmic Decree those who take their lives are required to reembody immediately in circumstances similar to those from which they sought escape. This is done in order that the soul might learn that there is no escape from life's solemn responsibilities and sacred opportunity, and that he must stand, face and conquer right where he is. 5. Jon. 1:17; Matt. 12:39, 40. 6. Pss. 8:5; Heb. 2:7-9.

Pearls of Wisdom®

Vol. XIV No. 13   Lord Maitreya   March 28, 1971

The Way of the Eternal Christ

O Mankind, Awake!

Myriad diversifications, like glittering pieces of glass strewn in random fashion upon a game board, litter the world with confusion. The kaleidoscope of human nonsense, rearing its head from human slime, dares to poke fun at those towering manifestations of Cosmos to whom is accorded the direction of mortal affairs from inner levels.

Strident voices, raised in a cacophony of mockery reminiscent of the last days of Atlantis, echo as a solemn warning to those who are dedicated to producing a spiritual climate upon earth. That which can be brought to pass through many hearts and hands united in holy service will enable all people, from the little children to the aged, to receive the bountiful gift of divine aid, if those who have been called will stand, ready and willing to do whatever is necessary to produce the miracle of the Golden Age.

Men say that social pressures and the trends of the times, like crushing and grinding gears, have eliminated the high standards of living and have trapped them into those degrading actions which throughout the entire historical stream have spelled the doom of civilization. Let me say, then, to those men and women of cosmic vision who can see the beautiful glyphs of spiritual initiation standing as marble stairs, whitened and waiting the feet of the initiate: Now is not the time to raise the white flag or to throw in the sponge!

Those who know how to divide humanity have been quite successful in so doing. The battle has been long, but the war between the Legions of Light and the denizens of darkness is not yet ended, although the victory is unquestioned.

They have sought to divide those whose skins are darker from those whose skins are lighter. They have gloried in the responses they have evoked from the ignorant to promote a din of destruction in the family of nations. They have exulted in racial dichotomies and in their dividing of the generations, turning fathers against their children and children against their fathers. They have gloated in the mockery of one religion by another, hoping all will fall under the hammer of self-destruction.

Without recognition of their Divinity, without compassion for their humanity, civilization cannot mount; the nations of the world will be as nothing—reduced to the chaos of whistling winds shrieking in the dark night of their souls' anguish and desolation.

Ours is the hope that climbs into the Master's chair. The tiny babe born in hope, nurtured with wisdom, and schooled in courtesy and order will bring to fruition a Golden Age society longed for by many hearts, both Above and below—and there the Light shall beam.

Two thousand years ago a wise carpenter born in Bethlehem prophesied the signs that would appear in the last days. Later the Apostle Paul, tutored by this Prince of Peace, commented, "When they shall say, Peace and safety; then sudden destruction cometh upon them." The beloved Master, in his presentation of timeless Truth, always showed the great unity of Life and its divine purpose. He revealed this purpose as the kingdom of God within every man. He taught Paul that this kingdom was not meat or drink, "but righteousness, and peace, and joy in the Holy Ghost," albeit he also stated that all substance is holy—vibrating, dancing electrons, joyously fashioned by the eternal God—saying to Peter, "What God hath cleansed, that call not thou common." Thus the Great Alchemist affirmed for all time the impartial law of the kingdom of the Spirit, the mighty airy voice of a Cosmos directed.[1]

Without cosmic direction so beautifully born within him by divine decree, man could not govern his thoughts, his feelings, his desires. He would fall deeper and deeper into the bottomless pit of the carnal mind. And as the theologians of the world have through the centuries distorted the great Christine truths, so without cosmic direction humanity would continue to distort the interpretation thereof.

But we are concerned to open the eyes of all, to show them cosmic consideration. His eye is over the righteous and His ear is open to their prayer. Men seek in mysticism, in theology, even in the study of the ancient art of necromancy to find some power unto salvation or unto their own design. Let them know that a God of infinite love has long ago completed that design which is the joy of the eternal Spirit, the cup that runneth over.

Let men hasten to do His will. Let men understand that in all their getting they have not gotten understanding. Let them be made to know that their theology is devoid of practical meaning and of the infinite perceptions of the Masters of spiritual Wisdom. Let them understand that there are great treasure houses of knowledge guarded by the Hierarchs of The Brotherhood who stand ready to reveal the Law of Life, waiting hopefully to bestow upon mankind the eternal Truth that will make them free. But when they hear it, they do not recognize it; for they suppose that some strange craft of the wit, some ancient ritual of darkness will lead them to a higher dominion.[2]

There is only one way, and that is the Way of the eternal Christ. It is the way of victory, of vision, of beauty, of transcendence, of eternal love.

Let the little children be taught cosmic Truth. Let them be taught how to live in harmony with the universe. O mankind, awaken to the world of true spirituality, the golden circle of pure Light and Love, vouchsafed to you in the name of the Christ! This is the cup of cold water that you may drink in hope and thereby perceive that in Him your life is at last elevated out of the harshness and cruelty of a mundane existence. "They shall all know me, from the least of them unto the greatest," the Lord has said, "for they shall see Me face to face. And I will be their God and they shall be my people."[3]

Let all men understand that they must garland together those spiritual flowers of cosmic devotion that in united love speak of the promise of one kingdom under God. These are not the harbingers of the schemes of the dark ones who would rally mankind under the satanic banner through a host of traps they employ to hypnotize the brains of the people. Let all understand that the Spirit does not require such underhanded devices to achieve its glorious ends; for the great bond of cosmic Love is a magnet of such force and dimension as to call all homeward through that sweet obedience which is true cosmic joy. Other devices may temporarily titillate the senses, holding mankind's beating heart in a vice grip of passion; but these can never deliver the human race from its misery, nor can they provide the Sacred Eucharist that will change them from darkness into Light.

I am called the Initiator, but how shall I initiate those who do not even understand the meaning of initiation? Men have a long way to go, "because strait is the gate, and narrow is the Way, which leadeth unto Life, and few there be that find it." Wise is the man who understands the tactics of the dark ones who would divide the world and plunder its temporary glitter. Wise is the man who understands that the real satisfactions of the soul emanate from the Spirit of Life and from those cosmic dogmas proven by Angels, Archangels, and Cosmic Beings to be a measure of the eternal Path.[4]

Follow onward, for my Way is Light! Those who walk in darkness as the deceivers of mankind, those haughty spirits who disavow the laws of God and the calling of the saints—they shall fall into their own snares, and when they cry out, no man will answer them.

Long ago he said to the children of the Light, "Come unto me, all ye that labour and are heavy laden, and I will give you rest. For my yoke is easy, and my burden is Light." Let all take on themselves the burden of the Lord and be diligent workers in the Father's vineyard. [5]

While the day is yet with man, I remain devoted to the salvation of humanity from darkness unto Light,

Maitreya

1. I Thess. 5:3; Rom. 14:17; Acts 10:15. 2. Prov. 4:7. 3. Jer. 31:33, 34. 4. Matt. 7:14. 5. Matt. 11:28, 30.

Pearls of Wisdom®

Vol. XIV No. 14   *John the Beloved*   *April 4, 1971*

Love Is the Magnet of the Heart

Brethren in God:

All men were created in the same Image. All differences are the result of man's choosing, in free will, to expand upon the original nature of infinite Love within him.

Love is like a great magnet. It is the magnet of the heart. Those who yield to the nature of the heart without the guidance of reason are often emotionally warped, and they do not understand the perfect balance of Love manifest in the triune nature of God. Naturally, Love is manifest in Love; but Love is also manifest in Wisdom and in Power. Unless it be included in these other aspects of the Trinity, man does not walk in that balanced consciousness of the Christ which enables him to retain his harmony with Life.

Harmony comes about because man is truly imbued with the love-nature of God. But how easy it is to confuse human loves and desires with divine Love! Once divine Love is understood as the great givingness of God that is also mindful of every precept of cosmic law, try as he will, man realizes that he can no longer function from the plane of human desire and human opinion and still be in harmony with the law of infinite Love.

The reason for this is quite simple. Human desires and human opinions are fluctuating, whereas true love is constant and even-flowing. Man, as a child, mimics the life-patterns of his elders; yet because of his soul's lack of development and his karma that is periodically harvested as the fruit of former lives, his instincts are often not in keeping with divine grace.

Whenever a man is persuaded to move against divine grace, against the prompting of the inner voice, to commit those acts that are in violation of cosmic harmony, he is creating an etching upon his soul that will remain not only for his current life but also for the term of his individuality, until one day he finally comes face to face with the law of sin—of inharmony—which he created "within his members" and which he therefore must balance. This is why man in the lower aspects of his nature is admonished to be mindful of God; and, because man in the higher aspects of his nature is made in the Image of God, he must one day face the results of his own sowings ere he can return to that Image.

Tiny seeds of doubt and distrust sprout just as well under the present burden of world thought as seeds of faith and inspiration. There are times that, in all cosmic honesty, because of man's affinities with the world and his carnal desires, it is the opinion of many in heavenly places that it is easier for him to become the victim of his own evil tendencies than it is for him to drink the cup of his own innate goodness. But, beloved ones, just because in the past you have created in darkness, there is no reason to continue sowing seeds of shadow that you will reap in the future!

Let all realize that "Whatsoever a man soweth, that shall he also reap" is a cosmic fiat which was never abrogated either by the words or the works of Christ Jesus. He himself declared, "Think not that I am come to destroy the law, or the prophets: I am not come to destroy, but to fulfill. For verily I say unto you, Till heaven and earth pass, one jot or one tittle shall in no wise pass from the law, till all be fulfilled." Yet so many are eager for an excuse for their actions. If the excuse please their own minds, they somehow forget that which is pleasing to the Mind of God, that which has been made plain in His commandments, in the teachings of the prophets, and in the example of the avatars.[1]

Contrary to the law of divine Love, people throughout the world criticize and condemn those who are not so much guilty of evil deeds as they are the victims of other people's careless remarks and their prattle about things they little understand. Thus Saint Germain has frequently admonished the Keepers of the Flame to refrain from criticism, condemnation, and judgment, which always snare the very ones who are engaged in these dark doings. He counseled instead that they should call forth divine Love daily on behalf of all and especially in the administration of their affairs.

Now, divine Love is not always obvious. Sometimes it is but a feeling in the heart. How foolish are they who judge without knowing what really is in the heart of another, for so often their judgments are unfounded save in the mass creation of darkness that spreads as an infectious plague amongst the people, causing them to eye one another suspiciously and to doubt the integrity of the inner man.

Let us replace distrust in the world order with confidence in the good inherent in man, with faith in the God who has placed it there, and with that unity of God and man exemplified in the mission of beloved Jesus. Let the children of darkness continue in their condemnation of the children of the Light; by divine decree they shall reap that which they have sown! Let the children of the Light continue to build the constructive spirals of the Spirit that tower over all; by divine decree they shall also reap that which they have sown.

To lean upon the compassion of our Lord, to draw close to his humility, and then to trace the great divine strength God has placed in one's own character, magnifying His good in all—this is the way of salvation that clearly directs man to higher spheres of thought and feeling. Unless he pursue the quality of infinite grace, bestowed upon man because he has learned to love, he will find himself the victim of an entirely different quality—one lacking in the graciousness of the Holy Spirit which enables the individual to sense and fill the needs of others.

Pliability of the spirit is the fashion of the Christ. Compassion for men's ignorance goes hand in hand with that sternness of the Law which compelled the Christ to speak fervently to his disciples, "What, could ye not watch with me one hour?" We often marvel at the great fountain of devotion within the hearts of many, but we also admonish that no reed of bitterness should ever be allowed to creep into man's world to separate him from the grace of God and from the sheepfold of the Ascended Masters. How futile it is that the very ones who are harnessed to their own changing personalities will allow the personalities of others to become the objects of their ridicule and scorn. Truly the Master's way has always been "Father, forgive them; for they know not what they do." [2]

Those who know what they do and why they do it are the advanced disciples of our Lord. I gladly call them brother, for they lean as I did upon the bosom of the Master.[3] The idealizing of the Masters requires more than the mental imaging of their physical appearance or making a pilgrimage to the places where they walked. Those who would be close to the Masters should realize that their universal consciousness is wherever you are. We are here and we are there, and we yearn to convey without further delay the marvelous God-feeling that we have for Life! Never sanctioning abortions of Life, we recommend that mankind walk circumspectly with God and understand the meaning of Being itself.

Through the gates of birth and death pass many souls. All were intended to move in pathways of divine Love. Other habitations not of God's creation have come into being only because man has provided thought-fields and force-fields of his own unrealities without understanding or invoking the actualities of divine grace. If men would only create themselves in the Image of God, in the Image of Love, rather than spend their time creating a God made after their own likeness, they would soon discover for themselves how Love can literally sweep into all their activities until darkness would no longer be without

Light, but would disappear in the sunburst of the reality of Cosmic Love.

Devotedly, I AM

John the Beloved

1. Gal. 6:7; Matt. 5:17, 18. 2. Matt. 26:40; Luke 23:34. 3. John 13:23.

Pearls of Wisdom®

Vol. XIV No. 15   God Tabor   April 11, 1971

"The Earth Is the Lord's, and the Fulness Thereof"

To Those Who Would Harvest the Abundance from the Heart of God:

From our retreat in the Rocky Mountains near Colorado Springs flows the love of our heart's eye. Beholding immaculately, we invoke in all Life a greater realization of man's inner power over the field of his own consciousness.

Now, consciousness is a moving, vital essence that possesses the Divine Tao, conducting through the mind's fingers of contact that Spirit by which men cognize the manifestations of themselves and nature. All of man's acts, the great and the small, take on new meaning when he realizes that his consciousness is a gift of the Spirit Most Holy. Wherever consciousness preordains action, there is responsibility to the Holy Spirit; and where there is responsibility, there is also the need for understanding, in order that the responsibility might be fulfilled.

Many have pleaded ignorance while others have ignorantly engaged the teeth of their energies in opposition to the highest plans God has for the earth planet. When we pause to consider that attitudes of just plain meanness—and there is no other word for them—have passed among mankind through the educational systems of the world and the marts of commerce, through the exploitation of the credulous and the proliferation of dark designs of thought and horror, we realize how important it is that all men be reminded once again, before it is too late, of their solemn responsibility to guard the Christ Consciousness in others as well as in themselves. Those who are concerned solely with their own accumulation of wealth seldom realize that unless they possess the abundant Life, they will one day lose all that they have temporarily gained; for "the earth *is* the Lord's, and the fulness thereof." [1]

If any man would shew himself "approved unto God" and to the Powers that Be, spreading abroad the word of Truth from the mountains to the great plains, he should understand that above all is the need to "train up a child in the way he should go, (that) when he is old, he will not depart from it." All have accumulated karma and records of the past, much of these being shaded in darkness; yet through the centuries all who have had any degree of openness of mind and heart have also absorbed some Light. But when we pause to consider the responsibility of man to accurately teach man, we perceive that in order to pass on higher Truth he himself must have a more than ordinary training, and his consciousness cannot be limited to the accumulation of things. [2]

Many of the teachers of the world today are so wrapped up in the little knots of their own personal lives and karma that they are incapable of truly caring for the spiritual-material needs of their pupils. Their outlook is not only worldly-simple but almost vulgar, because they are saturated with egoism. Parents who send their children to be trained by these highly unqualified individuals, who deny God and pridefully strut their designs before the youth, fancying themselves architects of a new age, are already reaping the karma of their neglect.

The saddest part of this misadventure is that humanity seldom realize that into what to them seems a relatively unimportant matter— the education of their youth—goes the entire adventure of their own becoming. For, so long as humanity are kept busy in the toils of their karma, which as a treadmill regurgitates their experiences and spills them forth as a vile suds upon one another, so long shall they be bound to the world of form.

Only when humanity's teachers understand the true meaning of training up a child in the way he should go, only when they understand the cosmic responsibility to cleanse their own spirits so that their teachings may become a vital communication of cosmic ideal wedded to the entire accumulation of man's knowledge, cleansing and purifying all—only then will humanity begin to build once again a Golden Age. Then what some might call Platonistic, but what is actually the divine society of the Ascended Masters, the kingdom of heaven upon earth, will become a reality because the enlightened potential of the Spirit of man will be not latent but apparent in conscious manifestation.

We of the Ascended Masters' realm, overseeing humanity with the radiation of our love and the eye of our attention, pinpoint once again in this unit of cosmic knowledge, this *Pearl of Wisdom*, the need for all to face squarely their cosmic responsibility to employ the energies of consciousness, the faculties of mind and heart, to build a Golden Age civilization solidly based upon the Golden Rule. It is in the hope that loving parents, young people, and even the elder stewards will bestow upon the tapestry of the coming age a restoration of prayer in the schools—not, as it has been for so many years, a mere token offered unto God, but as a vital communication of the heart of the child to his Creator—that we advocate the bolstering of faith, hope, and charity in the hearts of all. How sad it has been, but how true, that where God has been moved out, men with atheistic and damning concepts of dialectical materialism have moved in.

In the asteroid belt of the solar system, located between Mars and Jupiter, revolve magnetic chunks of the ancient planet Maldek, a monument to the perfidy of the laggards and their denial of the power of the creative Spirit of pure Being. Will you then, parents and teachers of this age, allow your children and your children's children to imitate their degenerate ways and then to literally destroy this planet before you lift a hand in defense of Righteousness and Truth! How men can deny God and expect to build a socialistic, utopian society of antichrist in the place of the kingdom of heaven is difficult to understand; but it has happened in nation after nation, while the Scriptures declare, "The wicked shall be turned into hell, and all the nations that forget God." [3]

The youth of the world, who have been hypnotized by the dark doings of the Luciferians rampant in this age, should wake up to the fact that they have been made the puppets of darkness. They should understand clearly that they have been manipulated by those who have used the television and moving picture industry of the United States and other nations to brainwash them with a decadent philosophy and a decadent music—the same old theme that caused the destruction of Maldek. They should see, before it is too late, that the jaws of a vicious trap are closing in upon them—and even if the plot should fail to actually materialize as their perpetrators plan, mankind stand to be the losers, because the youth who have defected from the Spirit of the living God will be the ones who will not only bear the coming generation but also set the example for it. Yet all of this can still be avoided by their parents, teachers, and elected representatives, who thus far have allowed the misapplication of the cardinal principles of Divine Reality in school, church, and society to go unchecked.

In heaven's name, do you think that humanity can escape the penalty of their own deeds exacted upon them by an inexorable Cosmic Law! If they neglect the training of their children, they are neglecting the most vital part of the structuring of the social order. When it is time for them to reembody, who will teach them what they have not taught the very ones who shall bring them forth? Mankind's current concern with the pollution of the elements is a hollow mockery of their pollutions of the human spirit and the human mind through their failure to stop the trafficking of dangerous drugs and pornographic art. The flood of degrading concepts now being released into the world of man at an alarming rate, unless reversed in its course, will destroy this planet as surely as it did Maldek.

O humanity, hearken to thy Cosmic Teachers who are no longer removed into a corner but stand before thee face to face to reveal the Truth of the ages and the Law of thy being! The way of cosmic history is plain. The way of the Great Law is also plain: "Whatsoever a man soweth, that shall he also reap." [4]

The advent of Cosmic Truth can be brought to bear upon human needs if hearts will open and respond. If they will not, and I speak to each little spark of the Divine Spirit, I am certain that we will not be allowed from our level to interfere with human free will. The hope of the world lies in man's acceptance of the grace of God.

Never fear, the grace is there. Never fear, the wisdom is there. Never fear, the mercy is there—just waiting for man to appropriate it.

Today as never before, man must take a good look at himself, at his world, and at his life in its universal context. He must realize that in this vast network of universal Life which he calls Cosmos are framed such mysteries as to delight his eye and to bring wonder to his heart. But if he is ever to know these graces, if he is ever to become an Ascended Being, if he is ever to enter into the fruit of holy reason, it will be because he acknowledges that spark of Life in himself and in Nature as the inviolate creation of a Reality so far beyond his finite self as to be labeled by him "infinite." If he acknowledges the spark, then I say, there is hope.

I AM Tabor. My concern is with the proper utilization of the abundant Life that God has placed in the hills. In reality man is like unto a hill, one that we would till and cultivate; for the cultivation of the spirit of man and of spiritual goals is our desire. "The earth is the Lord's, and the fulness thereof," but no one is more eager to bestow it on man than God. It is man and man alone who, by the schisms he has created between himself and his God through his doubts of his own immortal destiny and his questionings of the divine plan, has frustrated the grace that God has, and is, from manifesting right where it is so badly needed.

"In God We Trust," written on the coins of the United States of America, is a mantram invocative of cosmic protection to the earth that ought never to be removed and that ought also to be written upon the heart. Then the movement of the nation toward the reestablishment of an Ascended Master culture can rightly begin. These words should also be enshrined in the hearts of the people of the whole world, for all nations can benefit from the radiance released through this simple yet powerful fiat. The people of Russia and China, dominated as are the people of Tibet and Eastern Europe by the red dragon of communism, have found their dreams of culture, of beauty, of love, of order, and of the strength of the law of infinite Love suppressed by a godless tyranny that is spreading as a looming shadow across the face of the earth, blighting the world with a plague of darkness, hopelessness, and despair.

The only pathway toward the Light lies not on the altars of Baal or other pagan gods, but upon the altar of the living God where there is wrought a Golden Age civilization through the malleability of man's free will and his acceptance of the chalice of opportunity to follow the Ascended Masters in the regeneration of the spirit of Life, that all may be found not wanting but enjoying and progressively assimilating the abundant Life.[5]

Fruitfully, I remain

Tabor

God of the Mountains

1. Pss. 24:1. 2. II Tim. 2:15; Prov. 22:6. 3. Pss. 9:17. 4. Isa. 30:20; Gal. 6:7. 5. Judg. 6:25.

Pearls of Wisdom®

Vol. XIV No. 16   *Kuthumi*   *April 18, 1971*

Fervent Devotion
to the Unwavering Principle of Love

To Those Brothers and Sisters in Christ Who Find Acceptance of the
Word *Holy:*

Miracles, miracles, miracles! Men are always hearing about
miracles; and when they witness them they seldom realize the
ingredients that are in them, the application of cosmic law, and how
devotion and holy prayer fashion in man the required faith by which
the Reality of God at last takes shape in mortal form.

"Oh, shed Thy Light on me!" This simple statement—invocative to
God because man believes He is, invocative to the Spirit because man
believes the Spirit hears, invocative of results because man believes
that results are forthcoming by His Law—should be uttered from the
depths of the soul and breathed as holy prayer, daily, hourly, and
whenever His grace is required.

The grace and Light of God have not changed their nature through
the long centuries of mankind's submersion in a material consciousness. Religions may change through the misappropriation of the
Law by those who should correspond to Holy Fires but often do not;
but no man need give to the Christ as an excuse for his spiritual neglect
the fact that he has been misled by his teachers.

Each man, if he will, can still find the pathway of communion with
his God. Each man, if he will, can imbue himself with that devotion
which will attract the attention of the highest peers from inner levels of
Light and draw to him the mantle of humility. Thus he can focalize a
greater measure of the devotion of his Real Self, until he is no longer
imbued with the idolatrous image of himself as the ruler over his
divine Presence.

Many there are in the world today who are content if they can
pursue the pathway of whimsy, if they can do what they want to do, if
they can be what they want to be. But once they reach their goal, how
frequently they are bored with the results, for somehow even the most
spiritually unenlightened know when they are not fulfilling their
reason for being.

In the eleventh hour men build cathedrals of human accomplishment when they should be building cathedrals of divine accomplishment. The stones of their labors are as difficult to handle today as were

the stones of the temples built by artisans and priests of God in days of old; but the results are entirely different. Because their labors are centered in the human self, they have builded upon the sand of which our Lord spoke; and one day they shall see that their labors were in vain. [1]

The floods have come as they have been predicted—floods of permissiveness, of inexcusable hatred, of the accentuation of human misery, and of an almost fanatical dedication to the mania of the ego. Yet our Lord stands the same today as he did two thousand years ago. He can pass through the walls, disappear from their midst, walk upon the water and say, "Be not afraid, it is I." But the nations of the world have forgotten the depth of his blazing Reality, which has not diminished through the centuries; and those who have seen his glory know that it has taken on even greater lustre. [2]

I make a plea, then, not only to the Franciscan Brothers but also to all who would take upon themselves the yoke of responsibility of our Lord—wearing the rough garment of obedience, the hairshirt of fervor—to be dauntless in their faith. Let other men shed the skin of their bad example in the world order! The brothers and sisters of our Lord must go onward mindful of Him, realizing that the best fruit of good example to the errant ones is fervent devotion to the unwavering principle of His Love.

The world will always plague the devotee, and the carnal mind will always attempt to beleaguer him with doubt and argumentations on the fruitlessness of his search. But he is not afraid of that. He is not moved, because he knows that as the antipode of Reality, there exist those voices of the night that speak simultaneously with the voices of the day.

Therefore, man must first of all determine with whom he speaks and what force he allows to speak through him. When he speaks on behalf of faith and love, he must understand that God speaks; and when he speaks on behalf of human folly and human vileness, he must recognize that darkness speaks. The voices of the night will attempt to lead him into paths of unrighteousness that always end in unhappiness, and through him they will attempt to lead others down the path of spiritual neglect. [3]

As the cosmic law is ever vital and alive, so the Tree of Life is vibrant with the fruit of new meaning, changing day by day through the hidden miracle of changelessness. Here the fruit of newness of Life is found never shedding the stamping of the Divine Image with the giving away of itself; for when one measure of delight is taken, another replaces it so that the fruit of the vine is always found to be the same yesterday, today, and forever.

The cup of cold water given in the name of Christ is the elixir of hope to a world maddened by blackness and despair. As in the parable of Lazarus and the rich man, until man has seen them for himself, he may be unable to realize his own injustices; and when he does, it is often too late. The motivation of the soul to higher expansions of faith and service is a noble undertaking. Blessed, then, are the men and

women who do not fear to make public their service to the needs of our
Lord. Let them not be afraid to renounce the things of the world;
instead let them be afraid to renounce Him.[4]

Out of the depths of our Brotherhood, out of the fountainhead of
cosmic experience, arise new steps of opportunity, new dimensions of
spiritual attainment, the measure of which is beyond the ken of man's
present knowledge. How many activities of The Great White
Brotherhood are hidden from the view of the merely curious! Men
think of themselves as being involved in the decades, when their
existence spans centuries and millennia; yet they decry the failure of
their memory to span the centuries when they cannot even remember
what happened yesterday!

> O Chalice of Holy Wisdom,
> Mind and spirit of man,
> Wear thy garments as you can
> And do the things God hopes for you
> With sacred memory of the few,
> Groping through the darker strands
> Until you find at last the plans
> God has made for thee—
> Truly made for thee,
> Creative still to be,
> Transcendent yet to see.
> Freedom and love are bold;
> Hope far greater than gold
> Gilds the Holy Plan
> Revealed to seeker. Vanguard Teacher
> Of freedom in the soul,
> Mold and make man Whole!
> There is no night so dark
> To drive God out of it,
> No day so bright that embodied man
> Can flout the darkness
> That attempts to steal his peace.

By vigilance and by the drawing forth of cosmic strength, the
renewal of hope to the ages is born and rises as a symbolic metaphor—
sunlike, dawning in consciousness, embellishing all with a greater
measure of themselves. Man lays in the crèche of his own rude making
the vital, immortal image of the Son of God. Cradled within himself are
the leaps of life and the childlike wonder of beholding Good.

> Sharingly, I remain

Kuthumi

(Saint Francis)

Lord,
    make me an instrument of Thy peace.
    Where there is hatred let me sow love;
    Where there is injury, pardon;
    Where there is doubt, faith;
    Where there is despair, hope;
    Where there is darkness, light; and
    Where there is sadness, joy.

O Divine Master,
    grant that I may not so much
    Seek to be consoled as to console;
    To be understood as to understand;
    To be loved as to love;
    For it is in giving that we receive;
    It is in pardoning that we are pardoned; and
    It is in dying that we are born to eternal life.

                                        Saint Francis

1. Matt. 7:26. 2. Rev. 12:15, 16; John 20:19; 8:59; 6:20. 3. I John 4:1. 4. Matt. 10:42; Mark 9:41; Luke 16:19-25.

Pearls of Wisdom®

Vol. XIV No. 17   *Paul the Venetian*   *April 25, 1971*

In Christ "without Blemish and without Spot"

To All Who Love Truth and Beauty:

One of the magnificent feelings that God has ordained for every man is the sense of being in Christ "without blemish and without spot." How marvelous is the soul stamped with the Divine Image, framed in the elements of universal Truth foursquare, perfect in body, mind, and feelings, perfect in memory!

Unfortunately, feelings of personal guilt for wrongs real or imagined, for sins committed or contemplated, interfere with the beautiful and harmonious state of the soul fresh from God's own hand. In this frame of mind man becomes unduly uncomfortable; his emotions become unstable, his thoughts confused, until finally his whole being is guilt-ridden. In the name of the beauty that the Lord has placed in the souls of all men as well as the mercy He has extended to all, let me warn those who aspire to do His will that just as it is dangerous to be without conscience, so it is dangerous to be possessed with an unwieldy one.[1]

The forward movement of a lifestream is best organized and directed by God through the Threefold Flame within the soul and through the Holy Christ Self, who is the Divine Mediator poised just above the physical form, dispensing the energies and graces of the Presence into the human chalice. Thus has God provided the means, the link with Himself, whereby man can receive the correct administration of cosmic justice and mercy in perfect balance—if he will invoke the legal aid of Heaven and accept the Hosts of Light as the advocates of his Real Image.

Ah yes, there was a day when man was free from sin, when he walked in the paradise of perfection, which has been called the Garden of Eden. And all can walk there again when, through the Divine Mediator of the Holy Christ Self, the Lamb "without blemish and without spot," they are able to absorb the cardinal principles of universal beauty and loveliness, to cleanse and free themselves by the electronic shower of the mercy of God of all energies stigmatizing the human soul and creating individual and national guilt.

How the manipulators of the world love to create segmental guilt, the guilt that arises when one segment of society is pitted against another. How they love to do the diabolical work of castigating and then fragmenting the peaceful nature of man, making him into a hunted animal that can no longer hold high his head and exhibit his true Divine Nature.

Our thought for man today is first the thought of God—a thought of blamelessness, sinlessness, and perfect beauty. The despoiling of the pristine state came about as the result of man's violations of the unwritten Law—for the perfect Law of Love between God and man does not require recording without; it was already recorded within the soul of man from the founding moment when his Creator gave him individualized existence.

"The strength of sin," as Saint Paul says, "is the law." Therefore, once man had broken the Law inscribed in the heart and made his sin the law of his world, the Great Law was enforced as the ordinance of God, as a wall of Light that would keep man within the bounds of order and decency. If it can be said that the strength of sin is in the restrictive covenants invoked by a wayward generation, it cannot be said that the strength of sin is in the universal Law of Cosmic Love which first framed the worlds. For it is the letter of the Law which killeth, when man is driven into a state of harassment wherein the Law itself becomes a barrier to his progress, repressing the design of his nature and replacing the Spirit of the inward Law which giveth Life and which was intended to be an expression of his buoyant, God-ordained freedom.[2]

Let men perceive the various methods of stimulating the divine sense of beauty that is within. Through the ritual of forgiveness of sins, through the balancing of man's individual debts to Life, through the desire to do well wherever he finds himself, man is able to rise above his environment into the arms of his universal purpose which, when projected upon the screen of man's vision, becomes almost apocalyptic. It speaks of a New Jerusalem, of a Holy City, of a Holy Brotherhood, of a magnificent domain of consciousness in which man can forever happily dwell—if he elects to follow the high calling of the sons and daughters of God and the Law that is written in their inward parts.[3]

So long as man is content to feed upon the husks of life, to hold vision of lesser dream, so long will he remain in bondage unto himself, a victim of his own desires. When the people of the world illustrate their faith in the divine design through an active sense of commitment to the principles of the Great Law, they will begin to invoke the protection and the direction necessary to find their way out of the maze of problems that beset the race. For faith begets love, and love obedience, which reaches up to a state of consciousness wherein man takes dominion over the earth. Then his concern will be not so much with outer conditions as it will be with inner causes. Then, from the heights of communion with Reality, he will begin to untangle the skeins of the world web of deceit which, originating with the few, has gnarled the lives of billions of earth's evolutions.[4]

But today such freedom is not the common lot of the race. Human greed, lurking in the hearts of the many, blinds them to the deceitful purposes of their overlords and closes the gateway to the realm of spiritual truth and perfection; thus they go their separate ways as neighbor is set against neighbor, race against race, and men demand economic equality in defiance of the law of their own karma.

Long ago the Master Jesus reminded Peter of this law when he sought to take justice into his own hands: "Put up again thy sword into his place: for all they that take the sword shall perish with the sword." Thus man should not seek by intellectual or religious doctrine to cheat Life or experience, which, in returning to him that which he has sent out, would teach him those momentous laws that alone can give him his individual freedom. [5]

If the economic standard of the whole world is to be reduced to a common denominator, as some would have it—mostly those who have nothing to lose—the law of karma could not function. Albeit all men are created equal, they have not always acted as good stewards, allowing their lives to be used as vehicles through which the living Law of Cosmic Love could function. Therefore, the Law of Love decrees that they cannot reap that which they have not sown. [6]

In state-dominated countries, where the central government has become a millstone around the neck of the people, the enforcement of an economic determinism, inconsistent with the divine economy which of necessity is determined by Cosmic Law, is wreaking havoc with the natural distribution of labor, talent, and supply planned by God. Here the course of human life is no longer divinely directed; but instead the strength of sin is in those laws which have not been sanctioned from on high, which bind the people to a system that utterly frustrates the soul's harmony with Nature, until there is nothing left but a form of life devoid of meaning, empty and futile.

Those who understand the meaning of true love understand that this love is the result of God's infinite compassion and concern for the world as well as for the individual. When in the course of human events men inject into the stream of civilization those factors of deviation from natural law that abort their opportunities and prevent the onward movement of their progressive enlightenment or those of the race, they become the victims of their own misuse of free will. Then, when the law of their own sin has removed them from His Presence, they speculate that if there is a Deity, He must be very far away, when in reality God is very much involved with the evolution of the creatures of His own Heart and has placed man above all upon this earth to take dominion over the stream of life in manifestation.

The current trend to demoralize the youth and to pit one segment of society against another through the misuse of those wondrous media and electronic facilities of the age is a sin against the Almighty, reminiscent of the violations of Cosmic Law which preceded the destruction of the planet Maldek. The Hierarchy never threatens, but it does warn humanity. This is not a situation where the Lords of Karma say, "If mankind will not do what is right, they will be punished"; but it is simply the inevitability of the outworking of Cosmic Law.

Because the mandates of individual as well as collective karma prevent the light of true beauty from shining through in its total spectrum, we are concerned that the beautiful evolutionary pattern be sought in its entirety by men and nations. Those dark threads that are appearing on the surface of civilization may be cut away and removed from the garment; and in their place the motif of Divine Love, embroidered by millions of devoted hearts, will one day reveal unto all a more perfect structuring of universal purpose. Until the tapestry of Life is thus completed, men must in patience possess their souls, putting on the whole armor of God, being "strong in the Lord, and in the power of His might."[7]

In closing, may I remind you of the words of the Apostle who admonished the early Christians as The Brotherhood would also admonish you: "Stand therefore, having your loins girt about with truth, and having on the breastplate of righteousness; and your feet shod with the preparation of the gospel of peace; above all, taking the shield of faith, wherewith ye shall be able to quench all the fiery darts of the wicked. And take the helmet of salvation, and the sword of the Spirit, which is the word of God: praying always with all prayer and supplication in the Spirit, and watching thereunto with all perseverance and supplication for all saints."[8]

Let men be about their Father's business, that the kingdom become a harvested Reality.

For the increase of Virtue and Beauty, I AM

Paul the Venetian

1. I Pet. 1:19. 2. I Cor. 15:56; Heb. 10:16; II Cor. 3:6. 3. Rev. 3:12; 21:2; Jer. 31:33. 4. Gen. 1:26. 5. Matt. 26:52. 6. Luke 16:1-12; Gal. 6:7. 7. Luke 21:19; Eph. 6:10. 8. Eph. 6:14-18.

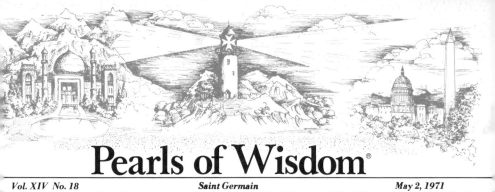

Pearls of Wisdom®

Vol. XIV No. 18   **Saint Germain**   *May 2, 1971*

A Summoning to Cosmic Purpose

Devoted Friends of Freedom:

The grasp of the divine sciences lies within the domain of all, but it requires of man certain significant dedications and consistencies of application. Many have cried, "How long, O Lord, ere freedom be trumpeted over the whole world? How long, O Lord, before the victory of the Light?" They must remember that never in recent history has the world enlisted the aid of the total body of humanity in the defense of freedom. The relatively few have consistently held for the many the balance of spiritual power by which marvelous accomplishments have been made upon earth and by which the quality of man's life has been correspondingly enhanced.

Now we stand at the crossroads of Light and darkness. Man is crucified upon a cross of iron and steel that he himself has erected. The mechanistic diorama which appears everywhere on the horizon has multiplied variegation and destroyed simplicity. People long for a quiet spot in the country, by the sea, or in the mountains. They yearn to "get away from it all," and they are finding the process increasingly difficult. The world seems a giant ant hill and man but a slave of his own crucial endeavor.

This season I wish particularly to call to the attention of all who will lend an ear to The Brotherhood, that those who raise themselves up among men, those who insist upon being "king upon the hill," ruling large blocks of people, have throughout history employed the tactic of dividing the populace, setting one group against another, thereby creating those divisions necessary for controlling the masses.

The alert must become wary of smear attempts, from whatever source, leveled against individuals and organizations. They ought to recognize from their study of history, past and present, that there do exist in the world unscrupulous men and women who do not hesitate to tactically employ the accusing finger, thus diverting the spotlight from themselves and their own nefarious doings. There are many crafty ones embodied upon the planet who take advantage of the tempest in a teapot that is typical of society today. Peering over the affairs of men, they lay their plans according to the ebb and flow of the tide of mass emotion and the cycles of the moon, taking advantage of the susceptibility of human beings to idle chatter and their failure to investigate the source of communications they receive.

In the past, rumors have unseated kingdoms as well as kings; and today the world is being racked by a literal war of nerves calculated to destroy the poise of nations and individuals. Those who are devoted to spiritual truth should take care not to allow themselves to become the victims of these contemporary plots, thinking they are too wise to be fooled; for I assure you that in other ages these same plots have been employed most unscrupulously and most successfully.

Man should realize that the most important quality of individual life—that which will raise the entire world, that which must be placed above all else if a planet is to be righted in its course—is the glorious mastery of the self by the power of the Christ. This self-mastery of which I speak is the true definition of individual freedom; for freedom, as I have said before, is never license. There is an area of interaction between peoples and nations which must be respected. None can practice depredation upon another with impunity; likewise, courtesy, tact, and diplomacy, universally employed, are always a source of blessing to all. This is freedom in social interaction.

If at this hour I could safely say that the gentle folk of the world were in complete control of the governments of the world, the marts of commerce, the religious temples, the moneychanging institutions, the entertainment industry, the news-reporting agencies, and other vital arteries of human life, I should be most content. But such is not the case. Instead, what amounts to a cloak-and-dagger situation is and has been going on during this entire century and many before, and so the various segments of the people have danced as puppets not only in the minds of the puppeteers but also in actuality.

The lamentable state of affairs in the world order has left the man in the street entirely confused, for he knows not where to place his allegiance. Almost numb with unbelief at the changes rapidly taking place in the world, some do not even feel that life is worth living; still, they hesitate to go about ending it all, and wisely so.

What is needed is a summoning to cosmic purpose; but ere they respond to the call from cosmic heights, all who love freedom must recognize that they are being victimized by unseen forces in treacherous ways. Saint Paul said, "We wrestle not against flesh and blood, but against principalities, against powers, against the rulers of the darkness of this world, against spiritual wickedness in high places." Thus men must be willing to face the truth that their favorite organization, church, or party is no longer necessarily finding favor in heaven—if it ever did. People must be loyal to Principle, not to personality—let the chips fall where they may! Above all, men must not allow themselves to be driven by a competitive or a self-righteous spirit into a state of fury where, in defending their so-called rights, they destroy a culture and an age and then go down themselves with the destructive spirals they have initiated.[1]

The people are not "dumb cattle," as the manipulators suppose; they are becoming increasingly aware of the manipulation of the news media and the gross economic deceits practiced against them. The very fact that the entire population of the planet can be in instantaneous contact through vast communications networks such as Teletype and Telstar provides even more reason why those who would manipulate the mankind of earth choose to obtain control of the media as well as the dissemination and interpretation of the news. The motion-picture industry has become a disgrace not only to the people of earth but also to those of us who observe from on high. Meanwhile, the Karmic Lords have almost tottered in their decision betwixt mercy and swift justice. As you say upon earth, "The fat is in the fire."

The Brotherhood, in addition to censuring the entertainment industries of the world, perceives the cosmic justice that must one day fall as a bolt of lightning from the skies upon the moneychangers and their manipulative tactics in the world of finance. In the fields of government, cowardly legislators have continually allowed the disgraceful erosion of the freedom of man to go on before their very eyes. In many nations, government has become a mechanical monster, greedily grinding its gears of inefficiency while world progress literally staggers in its course.

Now, what shall I say of freedom? It is an airy creature of the heart, ever rising, ever moving forward; but if the outer man will not keep pace with the advancements of his own soul, he may find himself "tail ending it" and falling to rise no more. The soul will go on. It is a flaming radiance from the Heart of God. It has beckoned and called; it has patiently sought to glorify in man the Divine Nature and that loving-kindness in all man's doings which is promoted by the spirit of holiness and righteousness.

While justice is frequently our concern, we love mercy and understanding with an equal heart; and we see the need for the millions of mankind to focalize the spotlight of their attention not upon those dribbles of human emotion that splash upon the floor of the human playground, but upon the realities of the human soul that sparkle from within and shed light upon every human problem.

People must not despair of hope for a solution to the world's problems; but they must understand that all of the problems upon the

council tables of the world are possible of solution if the human heart
will submit itself to the freedoms inherent within the soul. Until they
do, and until they are better able to draw forth from God a greater
measure of understanding, in all probability they will stew in their
own juice.[2]

At the same time, the spiritual people of the world ought not to
become disturbed by these outer conditions to the extent that they lose
their own souls or become enmeshed in such a consciousness of doom
as to be almost unfit for spiritual service. What is needed now more
than anything else is the understanding that what God hath wrought
God can work again, that God can do these things through the invocation of His strength by those peers of humanity that stand ready to
cooperate with The Brotherhood.

The day of salvation is at hand—the day of renewal. Freedom is a
part of the Nature of God. Like the May flowers, it blooms upon the
crest of the land; and it is also to be found glowing upon the crest of
the wave. What a bounty is to be found in freedom by those who know
where to look!

> It is freedom to employ the mind and heart
> And consciousness and will
> In the majestic service of being still
> A friend to God and man.
> It is freedom to reject
> All that opposes the divine plan.
> Upholding banner, guiding star,
> Shedding Light rays from afar
> Into nearer newness, holy fragrance,
> Man at last becomes content
> To follow God's Will—the way He bent
> The twig of opportunity.
> Dark has the hour of present time
> In shadow shaped the world.
> Now let the Sun of Love come out,
> Its banner be unfurled.
> The way of strength and brotherhood,
> The way of peace made plain,
> Will bring to all upon the earth
> The Glory of His Flame.
> The Flame of worth and strength and purpose,
> 'Neath the banner of the free,
> Conceals no virtue, utters purpose,
> The way each man can be.
> If you will to be, the pure equality

Of freedom all can see
Appearing in the Flame
To keep the heart still free—
No darkness in its motive,
No failure in its heart—
The Way I AM is Freedom.
Oh, won't you now, then, start
To realize at last
The brave New World to be—
When man all one does understand
His graceful opportunity.

It is to this end that all men were born, conceived in God's likeness; and the living Word remains a lamp unto the feet of those who are willing to consider the way in which they shall walk. Because this is a time of the dividing of the way, a time of separation between segments of humanity, when the children of Light shall espouse the banner of freedom and the children of darkness remain the slaves of that darkness, I cannot fail to invoke freedom this year as never before by making plain to mankind the hierarchical intent and the correct use of the Law of Life and Liberty.[3]

O sons of Liberty, awake! As Saint Paul said: "Ye are all the children of light, and the children of the day: we are not of the night, nor of darkness. Therefore let us not sleep, as do others; but let us watch and be sober." While I do not urge upon you a witch-hunt wherein the fires of fanaticism, enflamed by senseless fury, create even darker deeds amongst men than those which they seek to expose, I do urge that vigilance upon man which in sanity and reason will see the course of human events as they are taking shape as the handwriting on the wall.[4]

The fierce determination of the hordes of darkness to capture the minds of the youth of the world, that they may trap in one Babylonian world-government of chaos the very wave of the future generation, is something to behold from inner levels! If you could see as we do, I am certain that you would not let an hour pass without invoking assistance and protection on behalf of the youth.

There is a renaissance coming all right, and there is a revolution coming; but these need not have as their objective the destruction of the sovereign governments of the free powers of the world. Let change take place first within the heart and soul of man, creating there that determination which will enable him to overcome all negative hereditary and environmental influences; then, having mastered himself, let him introduce a kingdom of spiritual values where Life and Light and Love under brotherhood will at last bring in a Golden

Age of understanding and peace because man wills it so.

Let none fail to realize that to merely cry, "Peace!" does not in itself produce it. Man must work and serve his Creator and his fellowmen; for the fires of freedom are not fanned by indolence, but guarded by eternal vigilance. Therefore, in the words of Paul, we leave with you in this hour of supreme testing the warning of The Brotherhood: "Let no man deceive you with vain words: for because of these things cometh the wrath of God upon the children of disobedience. For ye were sometimes darkness, but now are ye Light in the Lord: walk as children of Light and have no fellowship with the unfruitful works of darkness, but rather reprove them. . . . All things that are reproved are made manifest by the Light: for whatsoever doth make manifest is Light."[5]

In the heart of the struggle, we stand as Captains of the Lord of Hosts and enlist your aid.

Devotedly, in Cosmic Service, I remain

Saint Germain

1. Eph. 6:12. 2. Karma. 3. Pss. 119:105. 4. I Thess. 5:5, 6. 5. Eph. 5:6, 8, 11, 13.

Pearls of Wisdom®

| Vol. XIV No. 19 | El Morya | May 9, 1971 |

The Pillars of Eternity

O Hearts of Fire!

The Banner of Maitreya is the Banner of Christ. Light from Alpha Centauri is Light from the Sun, Light from the heart. He who would delude himself, or be deluded, speaks of the fractioning of the Body of God as though in reality the parts were separate from the Whole. How can man separate from Life and still bear it?

Men speak of the rays and understand not that they emanate from the one Source and combine into the pure White Light. Yet many are the misqualified shadowed ones, the gray ones, the dark ones, and those who, in departing from the way of scintillating Reality into the darkness of egomania, are also breaching the covenant of Life and thus becoming like "wandering stars, to whom is reserved the blackness of darkness forever." [1]

Within yourselves, O men of vision, pursue the one God! What do you care that the prattlers say, "He is not," or that some say, "He is Jehovah"? Others proclaim Him in the holy mountain at Jerusalem. Still others acknowledge the coming of Muhammad, of Buddha, of Confucius, while some say there is only one "begotten of the Father" and understand not the meaning of the Word.

The one who exemplified the only begotten of the Father, full of grace and truth,[2] said, "Before Abraham was, I AM."[3] Clearly, the Way is shown as the emanation of the First Cause, or Logos, doing battle with the subsequent darkness of men, that they that walked in darkness should see a great Light.[4] There is but one Light, one Spirit, and one God in us all.[5]

Hierarchy acts with His permission, in His Name, and as the extension of Himself. He has proclaimed, "Lo, I AM with you alway, even unto the end of the age."[6] Slices of cycles are perceived, and men do not understand the balance of the cycle. They do not understand that as it was a thousand years ago, so a thousand years hence the mercy of God endureth still. Yet episodes of thundering karma are wreaked upon humanity as the spur of chastisement that draws men to His everloving Heart.

Men banally proclaim the wrath of God. In the same manner, they proclaim His Love. They do not understand that both are facets of His domain. In ordinary situations, His Love withers darkness; but the

belt of mortal karma, as the wrath of a Holy Fire, returns to awaken the
dense ones who sleep. Opening their sleepy eyes, they see at first dim
and shadowed shapes; for the transition from darkness unto Light is
not made in a moment. But Reality has always blazed as the noontide;
it has never wedded itself to those who deal in the merchandise of
darkness.

The Light of the risen Christ Consciousness cannot be claimed
exclusively, even by those who proclaim themselves Christians. More
than name is contact and love. Again and again, Hierarchy steps
through the veil to individual hearts. The nearness of the cosmic intent
at this moment in cosmic history is very great; yet the peril of
shadowed monsters without standard or purpose poses an equal threat
to man in the present state of his acceptance.

When humanity are told the whole truth in forthcoming releases
of The Brotherhood, they will perceive at last that in the hands of
Hierarchy—by the infinite grace of the Eternal God—are momentous
truths, childlike in appearance, but full-grown in maturity to those
who can read between the lines.

The burden of perception is upon man. Let the idle and the
careless pass by. The grotto of Reality becomes to them a grave; to
others it becomes the crucible of the resurrection. Light expands
within; and the kingdom of the individual, sharing the open sesame of
cosmic invocation, brings no dishonor to any, but to all the understanding of a vessel of honor, God-made.

Wrong thoughts should be cast off and burned. As useless garments, they clutter the ethers with effluvia. It is time for men to
exercise their prerogative concerning the quality of their thoughts. Let
them choose the creative essence of the New Day. Let them choose to
honor themselves and humanity with thoughts of the abundant Life,
with thoughts of cosmic vitality, with the resurrection flame, with
regret for evil, and with the all-embracing spirit of cosmic harmony
toward all Good.

Have you considered the Reality of Good? Have you considered
the leap of Good toward the arms of man? Have you considered the
need to embrace the Good, to express to the Good your appreciation,
that it might expand and break the bonds of momentary limitation?

Morya speaks. The will of God is Good. It is embraceable, enforce-
able, cumulative, and infusive. Space may indeed be hallowed. The
accumulation of cosmic fires is not the affair of a moment. Lifetimes
unending are not enough to express or to realize it.

Only eternity can suffice for man to grasp one moment of immortality. Yet God has said, "Ye are the abundant Life." Today men snuff
out their realities in temporary magnetizations to the trivial grasping
for control, for worldly power, for hypnotic exhibitions and the
banality of phenomena.

Why should Heaven declare itself the advocate of magic when all
around us God has placed

The Pillars of Eternity

Men have made them stones of stumbling,
But they are monuments to the Reality of God;
And they live, conveying the fruit of the earth,
The flower of the grass and the symbology
That year after year withereth not away
Never to come again,
But continue to appear until that morn
When in the dawning consciousness
Of each individual man is born
The strength of purpose in those words, "I can!"
Perceive again the wonder of it all,
Remove from life the vacant stare—
Boredom, human pall:
Majestic is the purpose of us all.
We yield one glance to God
And look no more upon the pastures of the world,
Human barns to store the fruit of passing moments—
Ours is the banner of everlasting Life.
No strife, delusion, or outer-world concern
Will hold for us allure;
Our hearts do burn with longing
For the passion of Christ Reality, ours to see,
Our life's motive once again to be.
O God, do speak and break with us Thy bread,
Anoint our head with Light and set us free,
For bondage chain and earthly claim
Cannot keep us from Thy Immortality.

Devotedly in His Name, I remain

El Morya

Chief of The Darjeeling Council

1. Jude 13. 2. John 1:14. 3. John 8:58. 4. Isa. 9:2. 5. Eph. 4:4-6. 6. Matt. 28:20.

Sweet Surrender to Our Holy Vow
by the Ascended Master El Morya

Meditation upon the God Flame:
> Our will to Thee we sweetly surrender now,
> Our will to God Flame we ever bow,
> Our will passing into Thine
> We sweetly vow.

Affirmation of the God Flame Merging with the Heart Flame:
> No pain in eternal surrender,
> Thy Will, O God, be done.
> From our hearts the veil now sunder,
> Make our Wills now One.

> Beauty in Thy Purpose,
> Joy within Thy Name,
> Life's surrendered purpose
> Breathes Thy Holy Flame.

> Grace within Thee flowing
> Into mortal knowing,
> On our souls bestowing
> Is immortal sowing.

> Thy Will be done, O God,
> Within us every one.
> Thy Will be done, O God—
> It is a living Sun.

> Bestow Thy Mantle on us,
> Thy Garment living Flame.
> Reveal creative essence,
> Come Thou once again.

> Thy Will is ever holy,
> Thy Will is ever fair.
> This *is* my very Purpose,
> This *is* my living prayer:

> Come, come, come, O Will of God,
> With dominion souls endow.
> Come, come, come, O Will of God,
> Restore abundant living now.

Pearls of Wisdom®

Vol. XIV No. 20   *Nada*   *May 16, 1971*

Love, the Wings of the Soul

To Those Who Know the True Meaning of Love:

The key to happiness is to be found in the correct use of the power of love. Just as the true concept of love becomes a garment to clothe the nakedness of man, so the false concepts about love tear from man the covering he already has, leaving him tattered, an object of pity. Wrongly qualified love is a drain down which the energies of humanity flow. Rightly qualified love becomes the wings of the soul that lift the consciousness of humanity into a state of cosmic bliss that they can seldom envision in the former state.

Blessed ones, the consciousness of man cannot be receptive to good and evil simultaneously. By his preferences and his choices man determines the state of his soul. The ingesting of putrid novels and psychic episodes involving the lives of others or the figments of some author's imagination does not produce the fruit of happiness. Many of the works of modern fiction writers are transient charades based on man's supposed need for lurid entertainment. If the consciousness is creative, vibrant with the joy of the living God, as it rightfully was endowed, does it then require additional stimulus from without and forms of entertainment based upon the escapades of the human consciousness?

Little do individuals understand the laws governing the flow of energy so freely given unto them, for which they are truly accountable. One day, when there dawns upon the consciousness of humanity a greater understanding of the Source of all energy, they will realize the importance of qualifying their thoughts and their feelings according to the patterns that resemble the Source. And they will realize that these patterns are almost universally distorted in the entertainment media of today.

How beautiful are the thoughts of God, but how seldom do humanity, in their strata of consciousness, actually pause to give consideration to God's thoughts. The very idea of being entertained by His thoughts seems startling to them. But when they pause long enough in their busyness to ponder upon the flow of the Divine Love into their consciousness, when they consider the magnitude of the divine intent, they are almost immediately polarized to a Godward movement.

Then no unhappiness can come nigh their door, and they are able
to adjust to all of life's situations in perfect divine order. No longer is it
a question of not liking what the day brings, but of understanding that
whatever happens—even a matter involving karmic return, wherein
they become the recipients of that misqualified energy which they had
formerly sent out—theirs is to joyously balance life's energy, to set it
free and thereby free themselves and all life forever from whatever
condition they at one time sent out into the world.

In Heaven's name, beloved ones, understand that by cosmic law
God Himself is not required to wash the dirty linen of humanity. One
day He gave man the gift of Himself, of His Consciousness. Simply
because humanity have changed that consciousness until it has
become old and familiar, although often undesirable, there is no
reason why humanity should continually repeat the same mistakes.
Now, when the individual becomes determined that he is no longer
going to submit to the depredations of the human consciousness, when
the soul of man is recognized as the vehicle of the living God, he is able
to summon the strength to cast off those undesirable thoughts and
feelings that formerly troubled his mind.

Isn't it marvelous, beloved ones, that freedom can come unto
mankind as naturally as the unfolding of the petals of a pink rose? The
soul is very delicate, yet at the same time it possesses great resiliency,
the hardness of the diamond, right within the cells of its fragrant
petals. By the diamond-shining virtue of heavenly Reality, man clearly
perceives at last that he holds within the chalice of his own being all
the wonder, perfection, and love that is in the universe.

The emergence from chrysalis can take place right where he is. He
does not need to wander hither and thither upon the surface of the
earth seeking Christ, albeit there are important things that he can do to
carry the Light to all humanity. The Christ is within him and requires
development only in the sense that the Christ Consciousness, the
consciousness that was in Christ Jesus, must remold and remake the
human consciousness until at last it no longer resembles its former
self; for old things are truly passed away and all things are become
new.[1]

The spiritual garnering of holy wisdom from the Heart of God
requires the mind of a little child. All of the sophistication of the world
that has unfortunately become a part of the learning process has been a
trick—and a very bad one at that—played upon mankind by the
serpentine mind. God is not devious, beloved hearts; He is as clear as a
bell, pouring forth the notes of the magic flute of spiritual
comprehension.

The Christ Consciousness leads the sheep of God to the still waters
of true knowledge[2] where outer conditions can no longer affect man,

for they find that all things are governed within themselves. Truly, man is a divine alchemist, rightfully compounding the facets of his life into a wondrous whole, as God ordained. Truly, each man must bear his own burden;[3] yet there are so many, in misunderstanding, who would say, "Another bore it for me." Let them understand the real meaning of "savior" as relating first to God and then to the Beloved Son, whose radiance universally enfolds everyone. Then, at last, by consecration and effort, the mantle of be-ness falls upon the heart in contrite majesty, as man finally realizes that he was made in the Divine Image.

> A rose so tall crowns us all,
> God's mercy 'round our feet.
> His Light of Love from Above
> Reveals man's life complete.
>
> No flaw can mar His Reality,
> No blight can harm the soul.
> Before the heart the rose does start
> To make all mankind whole.
>
> Domain of Light and beauty,
> Freedom rules the mind.
> The hand of Christ Reality
> Teaches now, Be kind!
>
> I AM all one, enfolding all.
> My Light Rays from Above
> Renew in heart the divine spark
> For which the Christ does call.

Devotedly, to the need of mankind's perennial renewal of the Christ Consciousness, the Rose of Sharon,

I remain

Nada of the Heart of God

Chohan of the Sixth Ray
Member of The Karmic Board

---

1. II Cor. 5:17. 2. Pss. 23:1-2. 3. Gal. 6:5.

THE RADIANT WORD
Excerpt from a Dictation by Beloved Archangel Raphael
The Gift of an Archangel: A Crystalline Star of Understanding
given at the 1964 Easter Class

It is my God-determination to let the atmosphere quiver with the healing Light of God. The blue radiance, the green radiance, the pure central white fire radiance—these flames combine to form a triad of healing significance. Precious ones, the white fire core is surrounded, for purposes of healing, by a mighty tangible blue sheath of Light. The blue sheath denotes the will of God, which is the manifest perfection for all mankind. The mighty sheath of green, vibrating and quivering around the blue sheath, is the substance of the healing qualification for the earth and for the evolutions thereof.

I call your attention to the fact that the central focus of the green healing ray is the pure white fire core, which is able to touch the responsive chord within every lifestream, even those who may be vibrating on a different ray than the green. Therefore, all lifestreams of every ray are entitled to receive the fullness of the pure healing power from the mighty cosmic fount, which descends into the forcefields of mankind's being in order to bring about the perfection which already is and will remain forever inviolate in the octaves of Light.

While visualizing this thought form, you may give the following prayer to your own Beloved I AM Presence, also by Archangel Raphael:

Beloved God Presence of me, take command of my four lower bodies and of my being and world. Create and sustain in me a perfect picture of the Divine Design so wonderfully and fearfully created. See that this action of Thy divine-eye picture of my being is established in the forcefield of my whole being and that it maketh me whole both now and forever. See that this mighty focus is expanded without limit, establishing forever the patterns of the Divine Design in the temple immaculate which I AM. Conceive in me anew a clean heart and restore in me the fullness of a right mind in action, which shall remove all distortions in my flesh form and mental body, bringing about and establishing in me the wondrous purity of God as it descends, bearing the great power of the bells of freedom which shall ring in my soul, saying:

"With the sounding of the death knell, I spell an end to human creation, which would give power to disease and the wrong use of divine substance and Light's energy. I call forth and I invoke and I AM the fullness of the Infinite Immanuel— God with me and within me; God established here; God in all His purity; God that is the Manchild that taketh dominion here and now in my being and world and is the fullness of my immortal perfection, conferring upon me the eternal vestments of God, which shall be without end, in accordance with the jewel-like perfect design, the holy symmetry of the ageless perfection of my being. All this I AM!

"All this I ever shall be and all this shall manifest in all and be all, for God alone is in His holy temple and all of the world and its discordant voices shall keep silent before the perfection of my being until the dominion of God is given to the whole earth. The earth which I AM is the Lord's and the fullness thereof. The earthen vessel which I AM shall now become the refined gold of the Holy Spirit. The radiant power of that Spirit shall stream forth from my heart's Light and kindle around me the aura of the Infinite One. Circling me now is the angelic power of Light and the magnetization of Light! and the magnification of Light! and the attenuation of Light over the entire planetary body!"

Pearls of Wisdom®

Vol. XIV No. 21   *Kuthumi*   *May 23, 1971*

STUDIES OF THE HUMAN AURA
The Perfecting of the Aura
I

To All Who Would See and Know and Be the Truth:

As we commence these Auric Studies, let it be understood that the combined manifestation of body, soul, and mind creates around the spinal column and the medulla oblongata those emanations called by some the human aura and by others the magnetic forcefield of the body of man. Let it be understood by all who read that each individual in whom is the Flame of Life reveals himself as though he were to shout it from the housetops—all that he really is, all that he has done, and even the portent of that which he shall be—right in the forcefield of his being and in the magnetic emanations surrounding his physical form.

The reading in depth of the human aura is no ordinary science. Those who would undertake to do so should understand that by a simple change in thought the fountain of the human aura, which pours forth from its own orifice, can change its color, its emanation, its magnetic affinity—its complete identity; yet at the same time it may retain beneath the surface the capacities to poison the atmosphere of the individual or the auric emanation within, by virtue of his failure to cleanse himself in heart.

"Blessed are the pure in heart: for they shall see God"[1] is more than a beatitude issuing from the mouth of the living Christ. It is a fiat of strength shining, promised to all who behold it. We have pondered the great need of humanity for purification, and we advocate above all the purification of motive. But when individuals do not see clearly just what their own motives are, it becomes exceedingly difficult, by reason of their own internal blindness, for them to purify themselves.

Therefore, the purification of the faculty of vision has been given top priority by the Masters, because it has been our experience that when men learn to see as God sees, they perceive the need to correct their problems and in most cases do so without further delay. In the matter of our Brotherhood, those unascended devotees who wear the golden robe of cosmic illumination, who in truth are illumined concerning the many subjects ordinarily hidden from the average seeker on the Path, are expected to perform more advantageously in directing their lives according to the instructions issuing from their lips. A good example is the best teacher.

Now, what is the object of humanity's desire to read the human aura? Is it simply to satisfy some quality of human curiosity, or do they find satisfaction in perceiving the wrongs of others without correcting their own?

All who undertake this study of auric emanations and of the human forcefield as it pours forth into space should recognize the creative nature already existing in mankind. By the misuse of the creative nature, men have fabricated in countless lives undesirable and unwholesome conditions which plague their young, disturb their elders, and in no way contribute to the growth of the quality of human life as originally envisioned by Almighty God.

The hope of the world as the Light of the world is to be considered. The world today emanates an aura not at all resembling the Christic aura of the Universal Christ Consciousness; and the bulk of the people remain in ignorance of the simplest cosmic truths because the powers of darkness that are in the world have accomplished the distortions of the Scriptures which they desired long, long ago. Man's interpretation of his relationship to the Divine involves itself in pagan, anthropomorphic concepts. God is seen as being appeased by sacrifice; even so, men fail to understand the true meaning of sacrifice.

In the case of the Master Jesus, because of the perfection in his nature, which he clearly perceived, he did not require any propitiation for sin; yet he is portrayed as one who is able to save to the uttermost those who believe in him. Those who understand the meaning of God, Christ, and Life from a real standpoint see that there is no difference between the divine nature in Jesus and the divine nature in themselves. They understand that there is no partiality in heaven. All can equate with the image of the beloved Son. The ninety and nine must be forsaken,[2] for they already possess the strength within themselves to perceive this truth. And the one who is lost, caught in the brambles of confusion, blinded to his own Reality and the inward radiance of the Divine Image, must now forsake the false doctrine of the blind leaders of his blindness; he must heed the Voice of God and return to it.

Through our Auric Studies which we are releasing herewith, we anticipate that many shall find their way back to the Father's house. There they will perceive that they must present themselves a living sacrifice unto God. It was never the Father's intent to collect penance from humanity, nor to exact a form of sacrifice as appeasement of His wrath; for the only wrath of God that is valid in the cosmic courts of heaven is that karmic recompense, that weight of sin which imputes to humanity the darkness they have created, acceded to, or acknowledged.

In reality man lives in a universe of Light and purpose. To veil that purpose from man was never the intention of God; for He has clearly said, "That which has been hidden shall be revealed."[3] In this sense, then—the higher sense of releasing the divine knowing within man, who in reality is both the knower and the known—do we finally establish the Reality of God within the consciousness of the individual, thus producing right there in man the perfection that he craves.

It is amazing how by ignorance men are thwarted in their attempts to understand Life. Simply because they do not know, they do not find out. Therefore, as our beloved Master once said, "For whosoever hath, to him shall be given and he shall have more abundance: but whosoever hath not, from him shall be taken away even that he hath."[4] He spoke of understanding. This most precious treasure we shall attempt to bequeath to you in our releases on the Studies of the Human Aura. All who read should bear in mind that we cannot increase the knowledge of those who do not first invoke it from the throne of grace.

It is of utmost importance that the student understand that there is a process whereby every observation of his five senses is transmitted automatically to subconscious levels within himself where, by inner hieroglyph, events he has witnessed or matters which he has studied are recorded; thus the entire transmittal of data from the external world to the internal lies in the akashic records[5] of his own being. The process of recall, while quite involved from a technical standpoint, is almost instantaneous. Out of the storehouse of memory, man quite easily calls forth these treasures of being. Unfortunately, not all events are benign; not all recordings are examples of perfection.

The sorting and classification of these records is the responsibility of the body elemental and the recording angel of the individual lifestream. You will find mention of the recording angels in the words of Jesus when he spoke of the little ones, "For I say unto you that their angels do always behold the face of my Father which is in heaven."[6] Each individual has such an angel representing the purity of the infinite God, assigned to his lifestream by divine decree from the very foundation of the world. This angel has not only the ability to read the life record of everyone upon the planet, but also to commune directly with the Heart of God, "to behold the face of my Father which is in heaven." Thus the intent of God to reveal Himself unto the angel of His Presence, attached to each of His children, operates through the Holy Christ Self in perfect harmony with the divine plan.

How unfortunate are those who, while always perceiving the height and depth of man, are never able to become impersonal enough in their approach to endow "the least of these my brethren"[7] with the quality of the living Christ. Men find it not at all difficult to believe that the fullness of the Godhead bodily dwelleth in Jesus,[8] but they do find it difficult to believe that it also dwelleth in themselves. Yet this God has done. He has in the bestowal of the Christ flame placed the fullness of himself in every son and daughter. When the divine nature is properly understood then, how easily humanity can bring forth the antahkarana[9] and thus begin the process of correctly weaving their life manifestation.

Now, as man studies the science of perfecting the aura, he should also understand that through the misqualification of thought and feeling, many undesirable traits are brought into manifestation. Most dangerous of all is misqualification in the emotional body of man, in the feeling world; for thereby the heart is touched and in turn often sways the whole life record of the individual into a miasma of doubt and questioning.

I do not say that the sincere student does not have the right to question or even to doubt; but I do say that once the truth is clearly presented to him, if the door of his heart be open, he will never doubt and never question the truth of the living God. He may not leap over the hurdle; but he will clearly perceive that it can truly be, that he will be able, yea, that he *is* able to realize more of God than that which his present awareness allows. Let us free humanity by right knowledge from all that has bound them and blinded them to their own great inner power, to the treasure house God has locked within their consciousness.

Now I want to make very certain that all understand that misqualification in the feeling world—such as anger, self-righteousness, fear, hatred, jealousy, condemnation, and resentment—gives a certain leverage to the power of amplification. This is similar to the transponder system on your large aircraft. When the transponder button is pushed by the pilot, it triggers a signal from the transponder which causes an enlarged blip to appear upon the electronic board of the airport traffic controller, thereby enabling the plane to be easily identified. Thus do the emotions of mankind often falsely amplify misqualified thoughts and feelings to the point where a dominant position is assumed by these misqualified feelings. Although this takes place without the consent of the real being of man, nevertheless, darkness does, then, cover the earth. Yet Christ has said, "I AM the Light of the World."[10]

I have given you many thoughts in this my first release on Studies of the Human Aura. The Brothers of the Golden Robe will joyously respond to the depth of His wisdom which we shall release in the completed series. From the archives of The Brotherhood our love pours forth.

Devotedly,

Kuthumi

World Teacher

1. Matt. 5:8. 2. Matt. 18:12. 3. Matt. 10:26. 4. Matt. 13:12. 5. Akashic records: The recordings of all that has taken place in an individual's world are 'written' by recording angels upon a substance and dimension known as akasha and can be read by those whose spiritual faculties are developed. 6. Matt. 18:10. 7. Matt. 25:40. 8. Col. 2:9. 9. Antahkarana: The web of perfection within the thread of Light connecting each one with the Heart of God. 10. John 8:12.

Pearls of Wisdom®

Vol. XIV No. 22   *Kuthumi*   *May 30, 1971*

STUDIES OF THE HUMAN AURA
The Susceptibility of the Aura
II

To Every Chela Who Seeks the Light of the World:

Continuing auric studies, we examine the influences of the world upon the human monad. Man is a creature of simple design, yet complex in the externalization of that design. Little do men realize, when first they ponder the nature of themselves, the ramifications of the consciousness of each individual. The influences of the world, the thoughts of the world, the feelings of humanity are easily transmitted consciously or unconsciously from person to person; and in the transmittal of thoughts and feelings, neither sender nor receiver has any guarantee that the patterns of his intent will be preserved intact.

If the Light that is in man that he transmits is undesirable,[1] those who are easily made the victim of his thoughts and feelings or those who are naturally affinitized with him may reproduce the effects of those thoughts and feelings in their own worlds. So many in the world today are victims of the thoughts of others—even thoughts from other eras, which endure because mankind have fed their attention and their energies into them.

In effect, it can be said that man has endowed either his evil or his good deeds with a semipermanent existence, and that the consciousness of good and evil partaken of by Adam and Eve, because it has been perpetuated by his free will, is living in man today. Yet, through a return to the Edenic Consciousness of God, man is able to find the Tree of Life, which is in the midst thereof, and to eat of the fruit and live forever.[2]

There is much that we shall transmit in our studies, but first we must ask that the students approach them with the right attitude in order that we may create a climate of the practical use of right knowledge. Through the ages that have passed from spiritual innocence to worldly contamination, men have seldom observed the recycling process by which there has been regurgitated upon the screen of life a flood of undesirable qualities. Both world and individual problems have been prolonged entirely because of the vibrational patine of blackened and tarry substance with which man has coated his very being and then refused to surrender.

It is time humanity began to examine themselves as individuals having a creative potential which they may use to influence the auras of others and which in turn makes them susceptible to influences from others, both good and bad. Thoughts of love, joy, and peace—divine thoughts created in the hearts of the saints and the angelic hosts—should never be avoided, but should be enhanced by the magnetic forcefield of the aura. Men can learn from one another, and their auric emanations can benefit from contact with those whose auras are filled with virtue.

Because it is just as easy for the aura to absorb vice as it is for it to absorb virtue, the individual must understand how this process of thought and feeling transmittal can help or hinder him in his daily occupation. Because people are so completely unaware of the effects of the mass consciousness, as well as the mental pressures from neighbors and friends, we continue to stress the importance of using the violet transmuting flame and the tube of Light as effective deterrents to the penetration of the aura by undesirable qualities and to their effects upon the mind and being.

Needless to say, I am determined to transmit, in this series, definite information that shall make it easier for the soul within man to hold dominion over his life pattern, thus improving the quality of the human aura. Unless this be done, great pain and suffering will undoubtedly come to humanity, and that unnecessarily. The Brothers of the Golden Robe, in their devotions and study of the holy wisdom of God, have recently considered that a clearer revelation of matters involving the human aura would make it possible for more individuals who are oriented around spiritual knowledge to be assisted and to assist others; hence this series.

Now, without question there are problems manifesting in the world wholly as a result of the individual's contact with the auric field or forcefield of embodied humanity. Therefore, defenses must be clearly shown. They must be understood at the level of the individual. In addition to that, methods of projecting the consciousness or the forcefield out of the physical body and to others in one's immediate family or circle of friends must be understood and then effectively mastered as a means of sending hopeful Light rays of cosmic service to those who, while in need of assistance, have no idea whatsoever that such possibilities exist.

Although people are brought under the benign or harmful power of various auric manifestations and forcefields, they do not understand how this is done; and many times they are unaware that it is being done. It is not a question of scientific marvel to them or one of strange phenomena—they simply do not know that it exists. But we do. Working effectively with this knowledge from a wholly constructive standpoint, the angelic hosts and Brothers of the Golden Robe yearn to see the day manifest when humanity, one and all, will understand how they may use this beneficent force of the human aura in a correct and proper manner. For they will see that the aura is designed to be a reflector of Good to all whom they meet and to the world at large.

Those skilled in mortal hypnotism and seductive practices have a partial knowledge of the use of auric and forcefield projections; and they do achieve limited results that lend credence to their work in the minds of some whose goals are likewise limited. As our beloved Master Jesus once said, "The children of this world are in their generation wiser than the children of Light."[3] In conference with us, beloved Jesus has made very clear that in making that statement it was never his intention to see this condition prevail. Rather it was his promise to all who believed in the Christ, "Greater works shall ye do because I go unto my Father."[4]

Thus it is the will of God that each generation should attempt to improve the quality of the abundant Life upon the planetary body through every available means that is in keeping with the teaching and practice of the Christ.

It has been our intent in these first two releases to give certain vital bits of information on our subject. Later in the series we shall develop that understanding of our instruction which, if correctly applied, can change your life and the lives of countless numbers among mankind because they will be better able to appreciate and to follow the way of truth and the way of hope.

Do you know how many individuals there are in the world today who by reason of their ignorance on these very subjects become the victims of the manipulators? Well, beloved ones, there are many, I assure you. And I do not want the graduates from our class to ever again be among them.

Let me, then, go back to the basic principles of Ascended Master law by citing for all the need to use your tube of Light and the violet transmuting flame as the greatest protection you can ever have against the forces of manipulation. How very dominant, God-endowed, and beautiful are the fragments of divine knowledge that have been received by you thus far.[5] Do you truly meditate upon them? Do you make them a part of your life? Or do you find them to be entertaining flowers that somehow the mind takes a fancy to?

Beloved ones, I want to prepare you for a most tremendous piece of information, which I will transmit to you in a forthcoming lesson. But I want to make certain that when you receive this concept which I will bring to you, you meditate upon it like a flower. I give you a full week from this *Pearl of Wisdom* to the next to prepare yourselves in your meditations for this concept, which I assure you will give you a very concrete idea beyond the mechanical as to just how you can accomplish the purification of your aura. Without this knowledge that I am about to reveal, a great deal more time could very well elapse before you would truly understand the real freedom you have and how to use it for the blessing of all Life.

When you divinely apply the wisdom of The Great White Brotherhood to the correct manifestation of Reality in your world, I am certain that the improvement in your aura and in the quality of your life will be very great indeed. Remember that I want you to be a flower—a rose or a lotus—waiting in the swamplands of life to receive the precious drops of truth that Heaven has prepared for you. If you will do this, I am certain that you will need no further proof of the reality of your being, of the unfolding kingdom that is within you, and of how you can take dominion over that kingdom, as God intended, in a way that is safe, sane, and correct.

When there are so many books being written today, so many words being released into the stream of mankind's consciousness which are almost a complete abortion of the divine intent, I must urge you to appreciate the opportunity we are releasing to you today.

Devoted to your heart's Light,
I remain

Kuthumi

---

1. Overlaid with his imperfect thoughts and feelings.　2. Gen. 3:22; Rev. 22:14.　3. Luke 16:8.　4. John 14:12.
5. The basic precepts of the Ascended Masters' teachings given in their retreats are published in the Keepers of the Flame lessons in the Masters' own words; they provide an excellent foundation for those taking up beloved Kuthumi's Studies of the Human Aura.

Pearls of Wisdom®

Vol. XIV No. 23   *Kuthumi*   June 6, 1971

STUDIES OF THE HUMAN AURA
The Colorations of the Aura
III

To the Keepers of the Light in Every Age:

The Reality of your God-perfection, latent in all Life, is continually releasing the current of its magnificence into your consciousness. Whenever an impediment blocks the flow of this magnificent God-energy, it is as though an object has opaqued the Light of the sun. As the sun has its corona, so there is always a spillover of the delightful radiance of the vital Life forces in man, which are so easily subjected to his negative influences and misuse. This discolors the aura with negative vibrations and leads man to draw the conclusion that he is less than the perfection of God.

Just as men recall on a cloudy day that the radiance of the sun is behind the clouds and can be seen from an aircraft which penetrates the clouds, so man should also begin to develop and maintain the habit of constantly telling himself that the blazing, dazzling Reality of the fullness of God is being released to him moment by moment as the master plan of eternal purpose. Thus he should develop the habit of counteracting all examples of shadow and misqualification by applying the principle of internal Reality.

What is real? What is real is released to man as he practices the ritual of penetration—of penetrating the Light of the Son of God by the very power of the Light that is within him—and thereby more and more of the divine radiance can infuse the aura in its manifest pattern. Therefore, today the delight of the Law of God will be in the mouth of the man or woman who will speak the living Word,[1] invoking from the Heart of God that magnificence which he already is, claiming in the Word, I AM, the fullness of the Godhead bodily in himself[2] as a joint heir with the universal Christ Consciousness.[3]

Now, in the matter of the effects of one's thoughts and feelings upon the human aura, we shall briefly touch upon the subject of coloration. As the intensity of the white and the violet Light is increased in the aura, especially those shades which are pale and ethereal, one notes the enlarging of man's perceptions and an increase in spirituality. As the pale yellow—almost golden—Light floods through the mind, the very fingers of cosmic intelligence manifest as interconnecting Light rays, enabling the mind of man to contact the universal Mind of God.

By amplifying in the aura the beauty of pastel pink—vibrating fire of the cup of universal Love—man is able to spill over into the world the very thoughts of divine Love. As so many know, the color of violet, vibrating at the top of the spectrum, is transmutative and buoyant. Born to the purple, the man who so infuses his aura is cloaked in the invincibility of the King of kings. This royal color is the cosmic fire of the Holy Spirit, which, when blended with the azure blue of the will of God, manifests as divine Love in action in that holy will. The green light, eternally new with abundance, charges the aura of man with the power of universal healing and supply. To seal all in the will of God is to drink from the goblet of that holy will. In the electric blue of the Ascended Masters, it denotes both purity and power.

Now, not all of mankind see the aura, and for some it is perhaps a misstatement to say that they do. What happens in most cases is a sensing, by the inner being of the reader, of the auric emanations of others and the interpolation thereof by the mind through the organ of vision. The impressions of the impinging aura carried over the nerve pathway as a result of the extension of the reader's consciousness into the domain of the magnetic emanation, seem themselves to be seen, when in reality they are only felt. Vibrations of anger often register as crimson flashes, just as black is seen in the aura as the opaquing by negative thoughts and feelings of the otherwise natural release of the Light of the Presence through the being of man.

Remember, beloved ones, that the tone of the divine aura is an extension of God, just as the mode of thinking and feeling is the extension of the human consciousness. The interference with the aura in its natural, pure state by the mortal consciousness and its misqualification of Light create the negative colorations that are both seen and felt by the more sensitive among mankind. The muddying of the pure colors of the aura occurs whenever there is a mingling of the emanations of imperfect thoughts and feelings with the pure colors released through the prism of the Christ. This marked change in color and vibration is obvious to the trained eye.

In this connection, may I say that one can learn to discern the thoughts and feelings of mortal men and to perceive what is acting in their world. The difference between momentary passions, consciously willed, and sustained deep-seated emotional trends must be considered. How easy it is to see through the process of auric discernment that which is not immaculate in someone's feelings, thoughts, or acts without understanding that only a temporary surface disturbance may have taken place. Much later, if that one is not careful to override such disturbances by retraining the mind and feelings and consciously governing the energy flow, an in-depth penetration may occur whereby auric contamination will reach subconscious levels and thus prolong the time span of man's indulgence in negative states.

Great care should be exercised by all who desire to amplify the immaculate God-concept of others to see that they do not, by their incomplete perceptions, actually intensify those negative conditions which those whom they would assist may not be harboring at all, but are only entertaining momentarily. Then, too, there is the matter of the projection of mass forcefields of negatively qualified energy which can become a patine, or layer of substance, overlaid upon the natural vibration of individuals. Although totally foreign to their forcefield, this overlay of darkness, if seen at an inopportune moment, may be diagnosed by the careless or untrained observer as an outcropping of the bedrock of his identity.

Always remember, dear hearts, that those who fall in the swamp may come up covered with mud; for the quicksands of life, by their very nature, always seek to drag man down. But man can and does escape these conditions, overcoming through the same glorious victory that brings forth the lotus in the swamplands of life. I want you to understand, then, that by a simple act of invoking the Light of the Christ Consciousness, man can overcome the ugly chartreuse green of jealousy and resentment, the muddied yellow of selfish intellectualism, the crimson reds of passion, and even the almost violet black of attempts of self-righteous justification.

To see others clearly, beloved hearts, remember that man must first perceive in himself the beautiful crystal of cosmic purity. Then, casting the beam out of his own eye, he can see clearly to take the mote out of his brother's eye.[4] By the purification of your perceptions, you will be able to enjoy the entire process of beholding the Christ in self and others, as one by one the little disturbances of the aura are cleared up through the natural manifestation of the childlike beauty of cosmic innocence.

What is innocence but the inner sense? And the poem of victory that God writes through man is already there in matrix and in creative form, waiting to be delivered upon the pages of Life. Human density may have interfered with the manifestation of the Christ in man; but the Light and Love of the Law will produce for him the greatest purification, making possible the penetration of the aura by the beautiful colors of the Christ Consciousness.

I should like our students throughout the world to join with me this week in a determined effort to let the crystal-clear grace of the Throne which is within you as the Threefold Flame (three-in-one, hence *throne*) ray out into your world such ecstatic, electrical cosmic energy, that you will literally vaporize the darkened elements of your own aura and hence develop that magnificent seeing that will bring the joy of the angels and the Light of God to all whom you meet.

Perhaps we shall become more technical, but I think in no way can we become more practical than we have in that which I have already spoken.

Will you follow the Christ of your being in this regeneration?

Devotedly,

Kuthumi

1. Pss. 1:2; Josh. 1:8. 2. Col. 2:9. 3. Rom. 8:17. 4. Matt. 7:3.

Pearls of Wisdom®

Vol. XIV No. 24 — *Kuthumi* — *June 13, 1971*

STUDIES OF THE HUMAN AURA
The Reading of the Aura
IV

To the Pupil in Search of a Teacher:

The trials of life that come to man are in reality his teachers, that is to say, they substitute for his teachers because he will not hear them; yet it has been clearly recorded in the scriptures and ancient writings that the time would come when man should see his teachers and that they should not be far removed from him.[1]

So many today are concerned with the facial expressions and appearances of the teachers, without ever realizing the lines of character and soul reality that comprise the inner being of a man or woman. Let the true seekers be concerned, then, not so much with the outer beauty of appearances, but with the inner beauty that produces those manifestations in the human aura which bring the admiration of every Ascended Master because they are the fulfillment of the God-design.

If any of you have ever been judges in a contest of beauty, you will understand the difficulty in making a selection from among the manifold aspects of God's beauty. In the case of the Ascended Masters and Karmic Lords, it is sheer delight that motivates them to pronounce their seal of approval on all that is the God-intent in those who aspire to represent The Brotherhood and to glorify God in their body and in their spirit.[2] And what a marvelous forte of possibility exists for every man! I want our students to think of the richness of the natural, radiating, consecrating devotion that God has placed within man. The opportunity to express the perfection of the Holy Spirit, when rightly apprehended, enables man to fashion the wedding garment of his very Christed Being.

Now, I know that through the years many of the students of the occult have stressed the ability of the advanced disciple to read the human aura, to interpret it, and, in effect, to see it. May I say at this time, and quite frankly so, that no psychic ability or even the ability to read the human aura denotes in the person who does so, that mastery by which the true adept overcomes outer conditions.

I do not say that adepts do not have this ability. I simply say that the possessing of this ability, in partial or even in total proficiency, is not necessarily an indication of the advanced spiritual development of the individual. Also, it should be realized that those who profess to read the human aura may do so very poorly, in a confused manner, or in a very limited depth. In order to correctly interpret the reading of the human aura, one must be able to read the karmic record and to have some insight into the total being of a man.

I would far prefer that the students would consider the benefit that can come to them through beholding Good in themselves and in others and through striving for the good, as my beloved cohort El Morya has said. For the fruit of striving may not always be apparent on the surface, even on the surface of the aura; but it stands behind the real life record of man's attainment. This is why God has said, "Judge not, that ye be not judged."[3]

Here at Shigatse we concentrate on the sending forth of holy wisdom; we concentrate on harmony and on true loveliness. There are times, of course, when man must perceive that what is acting in his world is not of the Christ. It is then that he must be able to disentangle himself from his problems and to recognize that neither his problems nor the unwholesome conditions that surround him are the nature of God. Therefore, the Lord does not require him either to prolong his problems or to be weighted down by his environment. Might I add that by nurturing the divine nature, man finds that the aura will quite naturally resemble the Presence in its radiant perfection. This is the pattern that appears in the heavens of God's Consciousness and that can appear in the heaven of every man's consciousness; for it flows out from the seed pattern of perfection within man even as it manifests in the Presence above.

When Jesus said, "I and my Father are one,"[4] he referred to the balancing of the divine radiance of the God Presence and Causal Body within the outer manifestation, which through his reunion with Reality had become one with God. Hence the color rays which had been focused through the "coat of many colors"[5] now became the nimbus, halo, or radiance of the Christ Consciousness around him—the seamless garment that he wore as the Son of God.[6]

We have tried to make apparent in this discourse the fact that ordinary human beings are not endowed with this sense perception of the human aura, and this should always be borne in mind. Pilate heeded the dream of his wife, who warned him to have nothing to do "with that just man,"[7] more than the testimony of virtue manifest in the one who stood before him. He could find no fault with Christ Jesus;[8] but he did not bear witness to his perfection, else he would never have permitted the crucifixion of Christ, nor would he have turned him over to the Sanhedrin.

The commonsense approach to the realities of God is to be found in depth in the being of man. Man is a veritable treasure-house of beauty and perfection when he returns to the Divine Image—and I know of no better way to produce the miracle of the star of divine radiance in the human aura than to become one with God. This seemingly impossible hurdle is the panacea man seeks, and he shall find it if he seeks diligently enough and does not fear to surrender his little self; for all human ills will be cured by virtue of his becoming the Divine in manifestation. More harm has been done in the world by fraudulent readings of the human aura and false predictions based upon these readings than man is aware of. What a marvelous thing it will be when man turns his faculties of perception to the beholding of the Reality of God in his very thought and standard.

Now I must, in defense of some arhats and advanced adepts upon the planet, affirm the accuracy of those who are able instantly to detect in depth the vibratory patterns manifesting in the world of others. It is incorrect to suppose that these will always speak out concerning their discernments. Naturally, gentleness and the will to see perfection supplant darkness will guide their motives and acts; but I solemnly warn here that whenever you are in the presence of a true adept or even an unascended being who has mastered many elements of perfection in his life, you should understand that if there is darkness of motive within you, he may see it, or he may choose to ignore it.

By the same token, I solemnly warn those who fancy themselves adepts, but who in reality have not overcome more than an iota of their imperfections and who have achieved in the eyes of God but a small portion of that which they imagine, to take heed that they do not incorrectly discern in their so-called readings of the lives of others some quality that may not even exist; for thereby some have brought great karma down upon their heads.

All should exercise humility and care in placing their value upon the development in the soul of the higher consciousness of the God Presence, for this is "without money and without price."[9] It is the invincible attainment by which men become truly one with God.

Devotedly, I AM

Kuthumi

Thou Mercy Flame

Mercy is the grace of Love
Forgiveness from Above
Beauteous starfire might
Falling rain of Light

Mighty God-caress
Freedom from distress
Touching mind and heart
With Love's divinest part

Frees the soul from blindness
Ope's the mind to purest kindness
Glorious Light enfold all now
In Heaven's greenest bough

Joy of Nature's band
God's extended hand
Living Flame Most Holy
Answers now the lowly

No difference does He make
All His children who will take
His offered cup of Love
Perceive His Comfort Dove

No darkness in His motive
But only Light and Life
Behold the flaming votive
We share one common Light

Kuthumi

1. Isa. 30:20. 2. I Cor. 6:20. 3. Matt. 7:1. 4. John 10:30. 5. Gen. 37:3. 6. John 19:23. 7. Matt. 27:19. 8. Luke 23:4. 9. Isa. 55:1.

Pearls of Wisdom®

Vol. XIV No. 25   *Kuthumi*   **June 20, 1971**

STUDIES OF THE HUMAN AURA
The Intensification of the Aura
V

To the Devotee Who Would Make Contact with Our Brotherhood:

Man thinks of himself as solid. He lives within an envelope of flesh and blood that is penetrated by his consciousness. Consciousness must be regarded as man's connection with his Source, and its flexibility as man's greatest asset; yet when wrongly used, it is his greatest weakness. The consciousness of humanity today is so easily influenced by banal and barbaric doings that the magnificent cosmic purpose Heaven has prepared in the creation of man is seldom recognized even minutely.

Man so easily becomes involved in the trivial manifestations of the footstool kingdom; and his indoctrinations, being what they are, make him believe that the divine purposes and the doings of the Ascended Masters would not be to his liking. The singing of devotional songs, the chanting of holy mantras, the engaging of the mind in spiritual conversation and prayer to the Almighty are regarded today by the sophisticates as a milksop endeavor which could not possibly produce any good for them, but is reserved only for the weak-minded.

May I challenge this concept *in toto* and say that the greatest strength, the noblest ideal and truest valor, is to be found in the aspirant who ultimately achieves first his adeptship in his fulfillment of the divine plan, and then his eventual mastership in the ascension. Men erroneously think that only Jesus and a few other notable figures from the biblical centrum have ascended. How they would change their minds if they could see the cloud of witnesses above them in the heavens![1]

It is time that men understood the effects of their consciousness and their thoughts upon the human aura. I would go so far as to say that even their opinions have a strong influence upon them for good or for ill. I suspect that many have decided that I do not intend to discuss the negative aspects of the human aura. Perhaps they are right—we shall see. I am interested in stressing how that grandiose aura of the

Christed One, surging with Light, radiates out a divine quality in its very emanation that carries healing, nobility, honor, and cosmic strength to all who come in contact therewith. This aura of which I speak is not and never can be the product either of man's environment or of his social involvements. It is produced by divine doings, by entering into the Cosmic Consciousness of God through involvement with universal purpose, and especially by contact with our Brotherhood.

There is still too much vanity, however, in the whole business of God-seeking. There are times when we would gladly chasten men because of our great love for them, if doing so would stimulate a greater involvement in the only and true purpose behind the manifestation of their lives. Remember, the Light shines in the darkness; and whereas the darkness comprehends it not,[2] those who do begin to open their understanding because this is their desire will find an absolute intensification of the Light taking place within themselves. Hence a great deal more spirituality is involved in the God Flame within the heart of each individual than he at first realizes.

In this very Flame man has a catalyst posited right within himself, a sparkplug that can motivate him to make such attunement with his Presence whereby the magnificent influences of our Brotherhood can shine through his aura and he can become the outpost of heaven upon earth. Whoever said, and who dares to say, that any one person has the exclusive possession of this quality when it is the divine plan for all to radiate the one Light? Just as man and all things were made by one Spirit, so the one Spirit expects all to enter in at the door. The door of the Christ Consciousness literally trembles with anticipation of the moment when the individual will joyously enter into the sheepfold of his own Reality.[3]

Probably some of you may wonder just what I am driving at and why, when I have offered to you studies on the human aura, I seem to be going around Robin Hood's barn. I can understand that, and I feel that now is the time for me to tell you that by this method I am seeking to develop a special quality in all of our students. That quality, which is of the Christ, will enable you to develop the kind of an aura that I will call *self-proving*, because it can be consciously intensified to do the most good.

In effect, man's aura is literally a broadcasting station for God's energy and His cosmic rays. Energies of Light and the very thoughts of God Himself and of the Ascended Masters combine with the benign thoughts that emerge from the very life plan of the individual and are then beamed or broadcast in all directions into the world of form. Those who are sensitive and can attune with these waves may perceive

their nature and their origin, while those who do not understand
cosmic law may become beneficiaries of these wondrous energies
without ever knowing their source.[4] It makes little difference. We are
concerned with overcoming the preponderance of human darkness
that is abroad in the world today by literally flooding forth more Light
through the auras of many souls who shall dedicate their lives as
outposts of cosmic regeneration to the planet.

Christ said, "I AM the Light of the world: he that followeth me
shall not walk in darkness."[5] When we speak of the Light of the world,
we speak of the Light of the aura, and we are talking about a tangible
manifestation. It is difficult for me to restrain myself when I hear the
thoughts of individuals who carelessly read my words and then say,
"What a nebulous concept he brings forth!" Contrary to their
opinions, my concepts are incisive and they are given with a very
definite purpose in mind and directly in accord with the one Law of
God. I say this because I am talking about permanent manifestations
of universal grace, and withal I am trying to impress upon your minds
the great fact that the Law of God—the Law of His Love—is very much
involved with the human aura. What is the human aura if it is not an
extension into the world of form, into the universal web of the sum
total of what the individual really is?

Well, then, if a man manifests a whimsical attitude, working his
own or another's will without discrimination—sometimes good,
sometimes bad or indifferent—can this be compared with the one who
is literally harnessed to the divine dynamo and whose aura can be seen
by those who truly see, as beginning to vibrate with the universal
purpose? Not only do I know that these states of consciousness cannot
be compared, but I know that one day in the changing consciousness
of humanity the former will cease to be altogether. For God will win,
of this I am certain. And those who follow the way of darkness because
of the consuming of the thread of their own identity will ultimately be
extinguished altogether by the very fires of creation;[6] for God is the
Creator, the Preserver, and the Destroyer, and we have seen Him in
these and many guises.

In heaven's name, from whence cometh energy? What is it that
beats your heart? A wish obviously not your own, or it would not so
suddenly terminate. Instead, the will of God, the desire of God, beats
your heart. Men's lives would not be paltry, then, if they also let Him
determine their consciousness and their thoughts.

Now that we have created a certain measure of understanding in
many of our students about the factors that influence the human aura,
we shall begin to show in greater detail the processes involved in
broadcasting the qualities of the Christ so that great good can flow

from your being out into the world in these troubled times and create in the brilliance of the sunshine a new awareness that fulfills the destiny of the children of men under the cosmic teachers for this age.

Extending my love to each of you, I hold the chalice of holy wisdom to be of special value in creating a new future out of which shall be born a greater summoning of understanding and its use. For knowledge must be correctly used and appropriated by transcendent magnificence, rather than consumed on a few short years of sense pleasures without purpose.

The Brotherhood beckons to the many. The many can respond. If only the few do, I am certain we shall take delight in opening the curtain for them upon a new era of possibility. Let the weaving of regeneration begin anew the spinning of the tapestry of Heaven's deepening involvement in the raising of humanity into the folds of The Brotherhood, into the delight of revealed purpose.

Firmly established in that purpose,

I remain

Kuthumi

1. Heb. 12:1. 2. John 1:5. 3. John 10:1. 4. See Romance of Two Worlds by Marie Corelli, available from The Summit Lighthouse. 5. John 8:12. 6. Isa. 1:28.

Pearls of Wisdom®

Vol. XIV No. 26   *Kuthumi*   *June 27, 1971*

STUDIES OF THE HUMAN AURA
The Strengthening of the Aura
VI

To the Student Willing to Experiment with Cosmic Law:

The thrust for a purpose envisioned by Master El Morya should be brought to bear not only upon the activities of The Brotherhood mutually coordinated on earth and in heaven, but also upon the life of each and every student. One of the first exercises I wish therefore to give to the students for the strengthening of the aura involves a threefold action. The student begins by visualizing the Threefold Flame expanding from within his heart;[1] he then seals himself and his consciousness in a globe of white fire; and when he is set he proceeds to recite the following words with utter humility and devotion:

> I AM Light, glowing Light,
> Radiating Light, intensified Light.
> God consumes my darkness,
> Transmuting it into Light.
>
> This day I AM a focus of the Central Sun.
> Flowing through me is a crystal river,
> A living fountain of Light
> That can never be qualified
> By human thought and feeling.
> I AM an outpost of the Divine.
> Such darkness as has used me is swallowed up
> By the mighty river of Light which I AM!
>
> I AM, I AM, I AM Light.
> I live, I live, I live in Light.
> I AM Light's fullest dimension;
> I AM Light's purest intention.
> I AM Light, Light, Light!
> Flooding the world everywhere I move,
> Blessing, strengthening, and conveying
> The purpose of the kingdom of heaven.

As you visualize the cosmic white fire radiance around yourself, do not be concerned with the errors in your thought that through the years may have intruded themselves upon your consciousness. Do not allow yourself to concentrate upon any negative quality or condition. Do not let your attention rest upon your supposed imperfections. Instead, see what the Light can do for you. See how even your physical form can change, how a strengthening of the bonds of your health can occur in body, mind, and spirit. Try this exercise, simple though it may seem, and know that many Ascended Beings will be performing it with you.

So many times adults fear to be thought childlike.[2] They would rather appear to be worldly-wise and sophisticated—if they only knew that they are running from deep-seated fears and insecurities which they have buried beneath the clamor of social doings. Surely with all they know about the physical universe, their environment, and the patterns of the mind, they must be able to reveal how great they really are! But, dear hearts, what a shock some men and women are in for when they shall come face to face with the blazing truth of Reality and realize that so much of what they have learned must be unlearned, and that what they have thought to be their own greatness must be sacrificed upon the altar of the true greatness of the Christ Self. Then, perhaps, they shall compare that which they do not yet know with that which they do know, and they shall see how very lacking in luster they are in the eyes of the Cosmic Hierarchy.

It is not needful to impress the Masters with any quality you may have. Heaven already knows exactly what you are Above and below. Heaven already knows that you were made in God's image and likeness. If you return to that image in a simple, sweet, and childlike manner, I can promise you that Heaven will not allow you an overabundance of time in which to function in the domain of the child; but it will elevate you into the consciousness of a mature son or daughter of God. While you maintain the attitude of the child, you will be able to do something for yourself that will be both valuable and valid; you will be able to loose the ties that bind you to your egocentricities, until at last the little bird of the soul shall flit into the heavens and behold the glory of the eternal sun.

We in our Brotherhood of the Golden Robe are devoted to the freeing of those who are yet enmeshed in the vain aspects of the human consciousness. That they may develop spiritually, free at last to express the purposes of Life as God intends them to do, is our prayer. Many think it would be "so nice" if God would speak the word and, suddenly, as with the rushing of a mighty wind, all could speak the heavenly language.[3] Men forget the karmic patterns that others have carelessly woven and even the patterns that they themselves have woven. They forget that these are the self-made prison walls that keep them from discovering the delights of heaven and from becoming Gods among men. They do not understand that this planet is a schoolroom and that in these latter days many have permitted their consciousness to grow dark even while knowledge seems increased across the land.

The knowledge that is important is the knowledge whereby man becomes first the master of his own consciousness and then the master of his world. Whereas in a relative sense one man may attain greater mastery than another in the manipulation of energy within a finite circle, this in no way guarantees that the big frog in the little pond will be able to navigate in the circle of the Infinite. We are concerned with the measure of a man's advancement according to the divine precepts of The Brotherhood, which have been established under the guidance of the eternal Father from the beginning. We are interested not in generation, but in regeneration.

Now I am well aware that for some of our readers it is even a new idea that their thoughts can impinge upon others or that the thoughts of others can influence their own moods and manner of life. Nevertheless, it is so. The wise will therefore seek scientific methods of dealing with the problems of auric influences and thought penetration. If everyone knew how to use the tube of Light and the violet consuming flame and believed in this method of self-transformation, I am certain that the world would be a different place.[4] The dissemination of such practical knowledge is invaluable when it is applied by those who receive it; hence I urge those disciples who have been calling for more Light to be alert to properly use that which we shall release as they practice the aforementioned exercise.

So many misalignments in the human aura, so many nodules of dark and shadowed substance continually spew out their pollutants into the mainstream of man's energy, sapping his strength and weakening the entire manifestation of his life, that there is a great need for the flushing-out of darkness by a bubbling action of the Light. Naturally, I am concerned that we first clear up these centers of shadow—the shadow of misqualification that is within man—before we energize the consciousness of our students. This problem sometimes presents a moot point; for those who pray often, who decree much, who love much, who involve themselves with the whole repertoire of the mantras of our Brotherhood seldom realize that as they gain in the power aspect of God, or even the love aspect of God, they also need the holy wisdom that shall direct their proper use of their forte of energy.

To misuse energy, to send out enormous power into the world

like billowing storm clouds, is not the fulfillment of the divine intent. Energy should be directed as the perfect day coming from heaven into the lives of all it contacts. Let radiant blue skies and golden drops of sunlight pour through the foliage of man's consciousness, increasing the green, the beauty, and the color of the day of perfection in all men's thoughts.

May I chasten some by pointing out that sometimes knowingly and sometimes unknowingly you are using the energy of God to further your own moods and feelings in the world of form. Try God's way, the way of perfection;[5] for just as the Christ Consciousness is the mediator between God and man,[6] so man can become a joint mediator with Christ; and inasmuch as he does what he wills with the energy God gives him, he controls, in a relative sense in the world of form, a portion of the divine energy for the entire planet. When he realizes this, the whole foundation of his life can be altered if he wills it so. This thought is injected as a direct quote from a conversation I had with beloved Morya, and I trust that the students will take it to heart.

What a wonderful opportunity lies before you as a gift from God as you correctly use His energy. Why, you can literally mold yourself and the whole world in the divine image. The potential for goodness lying within man is wondrous indeed; and as he learns how to properly extend and guard his auric emanations, he will realize more and more of that potential.

We shall do our part to make known the wondrous kingdom of heaven to as many as we possibly can. Will you help us to reach out in God's name, as His hands and feet, to lovingly become more and more the manifestations of the grace of God? The auric cloud glows; the auric cloud grows; the beauty of the kingdom of heaven solidifies in man as he gains a greater understanding of his own real nature.

Serenely in the Light of purpose,

I remain

Kuthumi

---

1. The blue plume to one's left, the yellow in the center and the pink plume to the right. 2. Matt. 19:14. 3. Acts 2:1-4. 4. This teaching of The Brotherhood is explained in the Keepers of the Flame Lessons. 5. Pss. 18:32. 6. 1 Tim. 2:5.

Pearls of Wisdom®

Vol. XIV No. 27   *Kuthumi*   *July 4, 1971*

STUDIES OF THE HUMAN AURA
The Expansion of the Aura
VII

To You Who Would Let Your Light Shine:

Coalescing around the spinal column are little portions of magnetic energy which I choose to call pieces of human destiny. As a man thinks, so is he.[1] As a man feels, so is he. As a man is, so goes his relationship with God, with Purpose, and with the whole domain of Life. The fabric of a man's being is composed of minutiae. The fabric of a man's being is composed of thought, and thought is indeed made up of the same substance as that faith once delivered unto the saints.[2]

Now as we recognize the need to let the sense of struggle cease, we want the students to develop in their consciousness the living tides of Reality that flex the muscles of true spiritual being, enabling it to take dominion over the earth. Just as Christ walked upon the waters, so humanity must learn the way of the possessor of Light. It has been said that the way of the transgressor is hard,[3] but those who possess the divine potential and exercise it in the divine way are in contact with the cloud of witnesses[4] that from spiritual realms extend the energies of the purpose of God to the earth.

There is a time in the lives of most children when Heaven seems very near. Their journeys through the portals of life and death reveal the celestial truth of soul-knowing often forgotten with the passing of the years. Contact with Heaven through the reestablishment of the threads of Light between the heart and being of man and the living Father is beautiful and necessary if the world is to mature into an age of renewed innocence and tenderness expressed by mankind toward one another. Grace is a very special quality of God that charges the aura with a buoyant and joyous expression of heaven's beauty and wonder, continuously expressed here below and continuously expressed Above.

There is neither boredom nor unhappiness in the celestial state, but only a joyous sense of ongoingness that knows no defeat of sordid thought nor shame in its reflections. The miracle of eternity is caught in the web of time as man momentarily understands the power of his influence at the courts of heaven—as he realizes through oneness with his Christed Being that he is the maker of his own destiny.

How much help is given and how much help can be evoked from
the Universal is a subject in its own right. Yet I feel the need to assert
on behalf of the students everywhere their friendship with those who
dwell in the Ascended Master Consciousness, in the Christ Consciousness, a friendship maintained through the liaison of the angelic hosts
and God-free beings and even the tiny elementals who are involved in
the very outworkings of physical manifestation.

The words of the Psalmist "For He shall give His angels charge
over thee...lest thou dash thy foot against a stone"[5] are intended for
every son of God. Yet the temptation to command that these stones be
made bread, for the purpose of assuaging mortal hunger, is very great;
nevertheless, every son of God must be prepared to overcome this temptation as the Master did when he rebuked the lie of the carnal mind with
the words "It is written, Man shall not live by bread alone, but by every
word that proceedeth out of the mouth of God."[6] Just as the world has its
conspiracies practiced against the sons and daughters of God by those
conspirators of Satan whose lives are literally snuffed out without their
ever knowing the end from the beginning, so heaven has its own conspiracy of Light; and its emissaries are conspiring to evolve the wondrous God-designs which the Father hath prepared for them that love
him.[7]

Now as the celestial bower is momentarily lowered into view, the
shape of things to come is revealed

When God does do His perfect work as planned
To right the wrongs of men by soul demand
And newly bring to view the hopes the ages sought
But never understood—the love and sacrifice He bought
To gather sheep and consecrate all lives
To higher goals and drives they little understood.
He vowed the plan to sweep from man
That hoary dust of ages overlaid,
To make men unafraid.
By love He showed to them that they should understand
The power of the pen that's mightier than the sword
And teaches all that I AM casting out all fear
From those who call upon Me, far and near.
My Light beams like a star of hope,
Dimension's newest opening upon the words I spoke;
For there is hope for all
Beneath the sun and star, or even moon.
For all things 'neath thy feet
Reveal the way complete
Is ever found within My Word,
The precious bread I broke;
For thou art Mine and I AM thine—
Our living souls awoke.
Oh, see the magnet purpose, glorious connecting chain,
Eternal joy revealed as Love does ever reign!

Devoted ones, the pathway to the stars is found in the thread of Light anchored within the heart whence the individual auric pattern expands naturally. Man has so often been concerned with the concepts and the many manifestations of the human aura—how to protect it, how to direct it, how to increase it, how to see it, how to interpret it—that he has seldom taken into account these simple words Jesus long ago revealed, "Let your Light so shine before men...." This Light of which he spake is the Light which can be magnetized through the human aura; for it is the human emanation which Heaven would make divine. Therefore, "let your Light so shine before men, that they may see your good works, and glorify your Father which is in heaven."[8]

In our studies of the human aura, which are given to those who journey to our retreats as well as to you who are fortunate to receive our weekly instruction, we seek to promote the same understanding that Jesus imparted to his disciples—sometimes through parable, sometimes through objective analysis of themselves and their contemporaries, sometimes through direct teachings on the Law, which he read to them from the archives of The Brotherhood. His entire effort was to demonstrate what man can do and what man can be when he unites with the God Flame. And I say to you today that it is to be, it is *be-ness*, it is to understand that you are a ray of intense Light that cometh from the Central Sun into the world of form. This is the key to creative mastery.

You must understand that you can draw forth renewed magnificence and devotion to the cause of your own immaculate freedom and that this freedom can be a crystal river flowing out from the throne of God through your aura—which you have consecrated as a vessel of the Holy Spirit—and into the world of men. You must understand that wherever you go, your opportunity to let your Light shine—your aura—goes with you, and that because you *are*, because you have being and are being, you can take the sling of enlightened fortune and fling into the world, with almost delirious abandon, your cup of joy that runneth over in simply being a manifestation of God. You must increase your understanding of the magnificence of flow—the flow of the little electrons in their pure, fiery state that seem to dance with total abandon and then again to march like little soldiers in precision formation—now disbanding as they assume what at first may seem to be erratic shapes, now regrouping in their intricate geometric patterns.

Purposefully man pours out into the universe the healing balm that is his Real Self in action. Its flow is guided by the very soul of the living God, by an innate and beautiful concept of perfection, steadily emanating to him and through him. Does man do this? Can man do it of himself? Jesus said, "I can of mine own self do nothing; but the Father that dwelleth in me, he doeth the works."[9] Understand that the inner fires banked within yourself by the Fire of the Holy Spirit can be expanded by your own desire to be God's will in action. Understand that these fires will act as a divine magnet to increase the flow of perfection into your aura and thence into the world. Understand that you must therefore wax enthusiastic about daily expanding your Light through your meditations upon the Holy Spirit.

Because it is our belief that men would do better if they knew better, we have written this series even as we long ago dedicated our service to the enlightenment of the race. It is our desire to teach men that the human aura need never be a muddied sea, but can ever be an eternal *seeing* into the streams of immortal perfection whence cometh each man's being. One of the facts men should understand is that along with the pollution of their consciousness with impure thoughts and feelings and the emanations of the mass mind, which seem to take possession of the very fires of being and entrap them within imperfect matrices, is their desire for self-perpetuation. Hence, often the little, pitiful, dark-shadowed creatures of human thought and feeling will clothe themselves with a sticky overlay of qualities and conditions calculated to preserve the loves of the little self—thereby gaining acceptance in the consciousness bent on its own preservation. This is done in order to obscure the Light of Truth and to impugn it by reason of its very simplicity and perfection.

Do not be deceived. The Light is yours to behold. The Light is yours to be. Claim it. Identify with it. And regardless of whether or not men may mock simplicity, be determined in your childlike efforts to mature in God. One day the divine Manchild will come to you, and the aura of the living Christ will be yours to behold and to be. To follow Him in the regeneration is to follow Him in the sun tides of the Light that He was, that He is, that He ever shall be. You cannot cast yourself upon the rock and not be broken. But this is preferable to having the rock fall upon you and grind you to powder.[10]

There are more things in heaven than men on earth have dreamed of;[11] yet wondrous threads and penetrations have occurred and many have come Home. We await the redemption of the world and we need in our Brotherhood those who, while having fallen in error, can simply trust and place their hand in ours as in the hand of God. For then the shuttle of the highest Cosmic Workers can move to and fro, from Above to below, to carry greater instruction to the race of men, to the fountain of the individual life, where the shield of the aura is esteemed for the wonder God has made it.

Next week let us talk about the shield of the aura. God be with you each one.

I remain

Kuthumi

---

1. Prov. 23:7. 2. Jude 3. 3. Prov. 13:15. 4. Heb. 12:1. 5. Pss. 91:11-12. 6. Matt. 4:3-4. 7. I Cor. 2:9. 8. Matt. 5:16. 9. John 5:30; 14:10. 10. Matt. 21:44. 11. William Shakespeare, Hamlet, act I, sc. 5, lines 165-66.

Pearls of Wisdom®

| Vol. XIV No. 28 | Kuthumi | July 11, 1971 |

STUDIES OF THE HUMAN AURA
The Shield of the Aura
VIII

To Those Who Are Learning the Control of Energy:

Some men upon the planet are little aware of the need for protection to the consciousness; nor are they aware of the possibility of others creating a barrage of negative energy calculated to disturb the equilibrium of their lifestreams. Let us set the record straight. There are many who are at various stages of mastering the control of negative energy and manipulating their fellowmen by a wide range of tactics and techniques. There are also spiritual devotees of varying degrees of advancement who are in the process of mastering the godly control of energy and who understand somewhat The Brotherhood's systems of protection and the countermeasures they can take in defense of their own life plan.

A God-endeavor indeed! Upon this earth, Heaven needs many who can work the handiwork of God. If a planet is to fulfill its destiny, it must have those who can work in the Light of God that never fails, unhampered by the forces of antichrist that would, if they could, tear down every noble endeavor of the sons and daughters of God. From time to time these are and will be viciously assaulted through psychic means whereby the garments of their individual auras are sometimes penetrated and even rent, unless they are spiritually fortified. Yet that blessed aura, when it is properly intensified and solidified with Light, becomes the shield of God against the intrusion of all negative energy, automatically and wondrously repelling those arrows that fly from the dark domain,[1] seeking to penetrate the peace of God that abides within, hence destroying peace.

Let me remind all of the natural envelope of invulnerability that serves as the protection of every man against those arrows of outrageous fortune[2] that fly so loosely in the very atmosphere of the planet betwixt men. However, through extraordinary measures the forces of darkness are often able to engage men in some form of argument whereby, through inharmony, they momentarily forfeit their protection. This is the game they play to catch men with their guard down; then again, they launch such an attack of viciousness as to cause them, through fear, to open up their worlds to discordant energies, which results in the rending of their garments.

Earlier in the series I gave an exercise for the strengthening of the aura through the development of the consciousness of invulnerability. Now I would make plain that in addition to spiritual fortitude one must also have spiritual reserves—what could almost be called reserve batteries of cosmic energy. The storing-up of God's Light within the aura through communion with the Lord of hosts and through invocation and prayer, plus the sustaining of the consciousness in close contact with the angels, with the tiny builders of form acting under divine direction, and with all who are friends of Light, creates an alliance with the forces of heaven. Through contact with each devotee's aura these veritable powers of Light can then precipitate the necessary spiritual fortifications that will give him a more than ordinary protection in moments of need.

Let the student understand that his protection is threefold: First of all, he enjoys, by the grace of God, the natural immunity of the soul, which he must not forfeit through anger or psychic entrapment; then there is the assistance of the angelic hosts and Cosmic Beings with whom he has allied himself and his forcefield through invocation and prayer; and last, but certainly not least, there is the opportunity to request of his own Presence the continuation of godly defense through an intensification of the tube of Light that will also establish in his aura the needed protective strata of energy which create a protective concept that cannot be penetrated.

Bear in mind that sometimes the best defense of man's being is a necessary offense. And when you find that it becomes necessary to momentarily engage your energies in this way, try to think of what the Master would do, and do not allow your feelings to become negative or troubled by your contact with human discord of any kind. If you will consciously clothe yourself with the impenetrable radiance of the Christ, asking yourself what the Master would do under these circumstances, you will know when to take the stand "Get thee behind me, Satan!"[3] and when to employ the tactic of gently holding your peace before the Pilate of some man's judgment.[4]

Remember always the goal-fitting that is required of those who would remain on the Path. You did not begin upon the Path in order to become involved in strife. You began in order to find your way back Home and to once again hold those beautiful thoughts of celestial fortitude and cosmic intelligence that would create in you the spirit of the abundant Life. Birthless, deathless, timeless, eternal, there springs from within yourself the crystal fountain of Light, ever flowing, cascading in its own knowingness of the joys of God that create a chalice from which can be drunk the very water of Life.[5] Freely you have received and freely you must give,[6] for the heart of each man can gather quantities without measure of this infinite Love in its super-abundant onrushing.

There is an erroneous thought in man that I must decry. It is the idea that man can get too much of spirituality. Oh, how fragile is the real thought of truth about this subject, and how easily it is shattered by human density and the misappropriation of energy. Man can never secure too much of God if he will only keep pace with Him—with His Light, with His Consciousness, with His Love. It is up to each one to do so, for no one can run the eternal race[7] for you. You must pass through the portals alone; you must be strengthened by your own effort. And you must also face the dragons of defeat and darkness that you once allowed free rein in your own arena of thought and feeling. Slay these you must by the sword of spiritual discrimination, thus building an aura of use to the Masters of The Great White Brotherhood.

Of what use is an electrode? Like the hard tip of a penetrating arrow flying through the air, an electrode becomes a point of release of giant energies that leap forth to conquer. And there are many things that need to be conquered. Above all, there are within oneself conditions of thought and sensitivities of feeling that require man's dominion. The man of whom I speak is the heavenly man—the man who abideth forever, one with God as a majority of Good. His heart must not be troubled. And the injunction of the Master "Let not your heart be troubled"[8] must be heeded. For the aura is a beautiful electrode that can become of great use to Heaven, and it must be consciously strengthened if man is to truly realize his potential.

Won't you understand with me the need to be the shield of God, to remain unmoved regardless of what conditions or difficulties you may face? For it is the power of Heaven that liveth in you to strengthen the emanation of Light from your being, both from the within to the without and from the without to the within. You can receive, both from without and from within, of the strengthening Light that maketh man truly aware that he can be, in his aura and in his very being of beings, a shield of God—impenetrable, indomitable, and victorious.

I remain firm in the love of the purpose of your being,

Kuthumi

1. Pss. 91:5. 2. William Shakespeare, Hamlet, act 3, sc. 1, line 58. 3. Luke 4:8; Matt. 16:23. 4. Matt. 27:13-14. 5. Rev. 22:17. 6. Matt. 10:8. 7. Heb. 12:1. 8. John 14:1.

Thousand-Petaled Lotus Flame

In the Name of the Beloved Mighty Victorious Presence of God, I AM in me, Holy Christ Selves of all Earth's evolutions, Beloved Kuthumi and the Brothers of the Golden Robe, the entire Spirit of The Great White Brotherhood and the World Mother, I decree for the expansion of Illumination's Flame throughout the Earth, the elementals, and all mankind:

1. I call to Kashmir in God's dear Name
   O Thousand-Petaled Lotus Flame
   From Kuthumi's dear Heart and Hand today
   Charge us with Illumination's Ray.

   *First Chorus:**
   Wisdom Bright from starry height
   Charge my being and mind with Light
   Make and keep me wise and free
   By God's grace eternally.

2. I call to Kashmir in God's dear Name
   O Thousand-Petaled Lotus Flame
   From Kuthumi's dear Heart and Mind of Light
   Let 'Lumination's Flame our souls unite.

3. I call to Kashmir in God's dear Name
   O Thousand-Petaled Lotus Flame
   Golden-Robed Brotherhood so wise and kind
   Raise our Earth and all mankind.

   Second Chorus:
   Wisdom Bright from starry height
   Charge our children and youth with Light
   Make and keep them wise and free
   By God's grace eternally.

   Third Chorus:
   Wisdom Bright from starry height
   Charge the elementals with heavenly Light
   Make and keep them wise and free
   By God's grace eternally.

And in full faith I consciously accept this manifest, manifest, manifest! (3x) right here and now with full power, eternally sustained, all-powerfully active, ever expanding and world enfolding, until all are wholly ascended in the Light and free! Beloved I AM! Beloved I AM! Beloved I AM!

* Give the entire decree once through, using the First Chorus after each verse; then give the verses again using the Second Chorus after each one; conclude by using the Third Chorus after each verse.

Pearls of Wisdom®

Vol. XIV No. 29   *Kuthumi*   *July 18, 1971*

STUDIES OF THE HUMAN AURA
The Protection of the Aura
IX

To Men Who Would Entertain Angels:

Beware of those who by intellectual argument or religious dogma seek to destroy your beautiful faith in the gossamer-veiled protection of the angels! By his unbelief man has failed to realize the magnificent protection that the human aura can receive from the angelic hosts. By his lack of recognition and his lack of attunement he has allowed himself to pass through many harrowing experiences which could have been avoided by a simple cry for assistance to these beings whom God ordained from the foundation of the world to be His swift messengers of love, wisdom, and power.

Have you thought upon the love, wisdom, and power that the angels convey? May I suggest that you do it today. For over the track of your thoughts and the extension thereof into spiritual realms, over the swift and well-traveled pathways of the air, these infinite creatures of God's heart, serving so gloriously in His name and power, fly on pinions of Light to do His bidding and to respond to your call. What a pity it is that some men lack the sweet simplicity of heart and mind that would allow them to speak unto the angels! By their sophistication, their worldly-wise spirit, their hardness of heart, and their refusal to be trapped by the "plots" of Heaven, they literally cut themselves off from so much joy and beauty; and their lives are barren because of it.

Will you, then, begin today the process of initiating or intensifying your contact with the angelic hosts as a means of fortifying your aura with what amounts to the very substance of the outer corona of the Flame of God's own Reality, directed and glowing within the auric fires of the angelic hosts? How they love to receive the invitation of mortal men who desire to align themselves with the purposes of God; and do you know, these powerful beings cannot fail in their mission when they are invited by an embodied flame of Light, a son of God, to come and render assistance!

Once mankind understand this fact—that the angelic hosts will respond to their calls—once they understand that these emissaries of

Heaven are bound by cosmic law to respond to their pleas and to send assistance where it is needed, they will also realize that even Christ availed himself of the ministrations of the angels throughout his life. Standing before Pontius Pilate, he said, "Thinkest thou that I cannot now pray to my Father, and he shall presently give me more than twelve legions of angels?"[1] The angelic hosts are the armies of God, the power, the service, the perfection, and the strength of God, flowing from the realm of immortality into immediate manifestation in the mortal domain, establishing the needed contact between God and man.

Consider, for a moment, how the Master employed the angelic hosts, not only in Gethsemane but also in his healing ministry, how he remained in constant attunement with them, acknowledging their presence in a spirit of oneness and brotherhood, esteeming them as the messengers of his Father. By startling contrast, the spurning of the angelic hosts by an ignorant humanity has caused many to fall under the negative influences of the dark powers that hover in the atmosphere, seeking to destroy mankind's peace, power, and purity.

I cannot allow this series to terminate without sounding the trumpet of cosmic joy on behalf of the angelic hosts. Many of us who are now classified as saints by some of the Christian churches[2] invoked the angels when we, as spiritual devotees, offered ourselves unto Christ in the service of humanity, knowing full well that of ourselves we could do nothing. Therefore, we looked to the assistance of the angelic hosts as God's appointed messengers. We did not expect God Himself to come down into the everyday situations we encountered that required some special ministration from heaven; but we knew that He would send legions in His name, with the seal of His authority and power, to do His bidding.

How tragic it is that some men, through the puffiness of human pride, will speak only to God directly, thereby ignoring those whom God has sent, including the Ascended Masters and the sons and daughters of God upon the planet to whom is given a special ordination of conveying the message of Truth unto humanity. It is so unnecessary for a distraught humanity engaged in numerous wars and commotions betwixt themselves to also launch an offensive against those who in truth defend every man's Christhood in the name of God.

To go forth with His power and in His name is a calling of considerable magnitude. May our protection abide with the Brothers of the Golden Robe serving at unascended levels, who in Wisdom's gentle name would teach men the Truth of the ages and thereby receive within their auras that celestial song that is the glory of God in the highest and the peace of God on earth to all men of good will.[3] The message of the angels that rang out over the plains of Bethlehem at the birth of Christ has since been heard by the few in every century who have communed with the angel ministrants; yet the Light of the angels is for all.

How could it be that we would so carelessly forget, as mankind have done, the service and the devotion of the angels directed from an octave of power and beauty interpenetrating your own? Will you, then, consider in the coming days and throughout your whole life the blessed angels—not only the mighty Archangels but also the Cherubim and Seraphim? For there are many who will reach up to the great Archangels, such as the Beloved Michael, Chamuel, and Uriel, without ever realizing that even they in their great God-estate have their helpers who, in the performance of their novitiate and in their own aspirations to rise in the hierarchy of angels, will do almost any divine kindness on behalf of the children of God on earth when called upon by them to do so. All should understand, then, the need to make the request. For Heaven does not enter the world of men unbidden, and the tiniest angel in all of heaven welcomes the love and invitation of men to be of service.

The information I have given you this week can help you to consummate in your life the building and charging of an aura with a radiance so beautiful that as it sweeps through your consciousness, it will sweep out the ignorance of the human ego and replace it with the Light of the Christ. Wherever you move, God moves; and His angels accompany Him. Let your auras be charged with such purity and determination to do the will of God and to be an outpost of Heaven that if your shadow should but fall upon another whom God has made, healing, joy, beauty, purity, and an extension of divine awareness would come to him.

You belong to God. Your aura, the garment of God given to you, was designed to intensify His love. Do not tear it; do not carelessly force it open; but as a swaddling garment of love and Light, keep it tightly wrapped around you. For one day, like the ugly duckling that turned into a swan, the aura will become the wedding garment of the Lord—steely white Light reinforced by the divine radiance that no man can touch—that literally transforms the outer man into the perfection of the Presence, preserved forever intact, expanding its Light and glowing as it grows with the fires of Home and divine Love.

Graciously, I AM

Kuthumi

1. Matt. 26:53. 2. Kuthumi was embodied as Francis of Assisi (1182-1226), founder of the Franciscan order. 3. Luke 2:14.

Protect Our Youth

Beloved Heavenly Father! Beloved Heavenly Father!
Beloved Heavenly Father!
Take command of our youth today
Blaze through them Opportunity's Ray
Release Perfection's mighty power
Amplify Cosmic Intelligence each hour
Protect, defend their God-design
Intensify Intent Divine
I AM, I AM, I AM
The Power of Infinite Light
Blazing through our youth
Releasing cosmic proof
Acceptable and right
The full power of Cosmic Light
To every child and child-man
In America and the world!
Beloved I AM! Beloved I AM! Beloved I AM!

Suggested preamble which may be used with this or other invocations:

In the Name of the Beloved Mighty Victorious Presence of God
I AM in me, Holy Christ Selves of all mankind, Beloved Michael,
Beloved Jophiel, Beloved Chamuel, Beloved Gabriel, Beloved
Raphael, Beloved Uriel, Beloved Zadkiel and your Beloved Archaii,
the Beloved Seraphim and Cherubim, the Twelve Legions of Angels
from the Heart of the Father, the Christmas Angels, and all the angelic
hosts serving the Earth and her evolutions, the entire Spirit of The
Great White Brotherhood and the World Mother:

Pearls of Wisdom®

Vol. XIV No. 30   **Kuthumi**   *July 25, 1971*

STUDIES OF THE HUMAN AURA
The Purification of the Aura
X

To the Neophyte Who Is Ready to Be Purged by the Sacred Fire:

Remember that your aura is your Light. Remember that Christ said: "Ye are the light of the world. A city that is set on an hill cannot be hid. Neither do men light a candle, and put it under a bushel, but on a candlestick; and it giveth light unto all that are in the house."[1] Remember that he left this timeless advice as a means of inculcating into the consciousness of the race the inner formula for the proper employment of the human aura.

How many men have misunderstood what the aura is and what it can do! The aura is the sum total of the emanation of individual life in its pure and impure state. Often gently concealing from public view the darker side of human nature, the aura puts forth its most beautiful pearly-white appearance before men as if mindful of the words of God that have come down from antiquity "Though your sins be as scarlet, they shall be as white as snow."[2]

Occasionally the aura will momentarily turn itself inside out, and the more ugly appearance of a man's nature will come to the fore and be seen by those who are sensitive enough to perceive the human aura. This shouting from the housetops[3] of a man's errors ought not always to be deplored; for when the gold is tried in the fire of purpose, the dross often comes to the surface to be skimmed off. Therefore, when from time to time some negative influence appears in yourself or in someone else, consider it not as a permanent blight, but as a thorn which you can break off and remove from the appearance world. The fact that the within has thrust itself to the surface is an application of the principle of redemption; and when properly understood, this purging can mean the strengthening of your aura and your life.

As a part of the blotting-out process in the stream of time and space, dear hearts, God, in His greater wisdom, often uses exposure to public view or to your own private view as a means of helping you to get rid of an undesirable situation. Have you ever thought of that? What a pity if you have not. Suppressing evil or driving it deep within, tucking it away as though you would thereby get rid of it, does not

really do the trick; for all things ought to go to God for judgment—
willingly, gladly, and freely.

Men ought not to remain burdened by the inward sense of guilt
or nonfulfillment that the suppression of Truth often brings. For the
cleansing of the human aura of these undesirable conditions need not
be a lengthy process. Just the humble, childlike acknowledgment that
you have made an error and the sincere attempt to correct it will do
much to purify your aura. God does not angrily impute to man that
which he has already done unto himself through the misuse of free
will; for man metes out his own punishment by denying himself access
to the grace of God through his infringement of the Law. Therefore,
the gentle drops of mercy and of God's kindness to man are offered as
the cleansing agent of his own self-condemnation. They are like a
heavenly rain, refreshing and cool, that is not denied to any.

Fill your consciousness, then, with God-delight, and observe how
the purification of the aura brings joy unto the angels. Have you never
read the words of the Master "Joy shall be in heaven over one sinner
that repenteth, more than over ninety and nine just persons, which
need no repentance"?[4] Oh, what a wonderful world will manifest for
humanity when the power of God literally rolls through the heart and
being of man untrammeled, flooding the planet with Light! Yes, a
great deal of instruction will still be needed; for there are so many
things that we would reveal, not even dreamed of by the masses; and
there is so much ongoingness in the Spirit of the Lord that my
enthusiasm knows no bounds.

Yet mankind should understand that until they have prepared
themselves for the great wedding feast to which they have been
bidden,[5] they cannot fully know the meaning of the ongoingness of
Life; for the dark dye of human sorrow and degradation creates such a
pull upon the consciousness that it is difficult for man to recognize the
bridegroom in his God Self. Alas, man, although heavenly by nature,
has through the misuse of free will decreased the natural, God-given
vibratory rate of his atoms to such a low point that even the body
temple must be broken again and again in order to arrest the cycles of
the sense of sin. This breaking of the clay vessel affords him the
opportunity to catch glimpses of Reality, which he would never do—
unless he had first attained self-mastery—if his life were to continue
indefinitely in one physical body.[6]

How deep and how lovely are the mercies of God. How carefully
He has provided for the gift of free will to man so that through the
making of right choices man can find his way to the throne of grace
and there receive the affirmation of his own God-given dominion,
"Thou art my Son; this day have I begotten thee."[7] I am also reminded
of the many devoted souls who through the ages have suffered the
condemnation of their fellowmen as the result of the misunderstanding of their devotion to purpose. Like Joan of Arc and
others who revealed a fiery determination for heaven to manifest upon

earth, these great spirits have received little welcome from their peers and little understanding of their mission.

Let us hope together for the world that through the spreading abroad of the balm of Gilead and the mercy of God as an unguent of healing, mankind will become unflinching in their devotion to cosmic purpose, even as we intensify our love through the student body. Tearing down any altars you may have erected in the past to the false gods of human pride and ambition and surrendering your momentums of failure to apprehend your reason for being, you will turn now with your whole heart to the development of the most magnificent focus of Light right within your own aura.

Oh, I know something about the angstrom units, about the vibratory rate of the aura, about its impingement upon the retina of the eye and the interpolation of auras. I know about the subtle shadings that indicate gradations of tone in the thoughts and feelings of the individual which vacillate as a spunky wind or a frisky colt that has never been ridden. But how much better it is when, rather than label these as typical of the life pattern of another, men see at last the original image of divine perfection which God Himself has placed within the human aura. For in most people some Light can be perceived as a point of beginning, as a vortex around which greater Light can be magnetized.

How much better it truly is when men hold the immaculate concept for one and all and concern themselves not with the probing of the aura, but with the amplification of all that is good and true about the real man. I do not say that advanced disciples should not use methods of discrimination to discern what is acting in the world of another at a given moment or that the soul does not use these methods to give warning and assistance to other lifestreams; nevertheless, those who are able to discern the face of God in the face of man can retain the perfect image and assist the cosmic plan even while correctly assessing the present development of a lifestream. To hold faith in the purposes of God for another until that one is able to hold it for himself is to ally one's energies with the omnipotence of Truth, which intensifies both auras in the richness of cosmic grace even as it intensifies the aura of the whole planet.

I want to bring to every student the realization that just as there is the Flame of God in the individual aura, so there is the Flame of God in the aura of the planetary body. Every act of faith you perform adds to the conflagration of the Sacred Fire upon the planet, just as every act of desecration tears down the great cosmic fortifications so gently and carefully builded by angelic hands who join with men and Masters in service to Life. Let all understand the building of the cosmic temple within the microcosm and the Macrocosm. The cosmic temple of the aura is an enduring edifice of the Sacred Fire. The cosmic temple of the world is made up of many auras dedicated to the indwelling Spirit of the Lord. Illumined thoughts and illumined feelings will enable individual man and humanity, striving together as one body, to cast into the discard pile those thoughts and feelings and actions not worthy to become a part of the superstructure of the temple of being.

Oh, be selective! Oh, be perfective in all your doings! For someone is assigned to watch and wait with you until the moment comes when you can watch and wait with others. Just as the buddy system is used between soldiers in battle and between law enforcement officers keeping the peace in your great cities, so there are Cosmic Beings, guardian angels, and lovely nature spirits of God's Heart who watch over thee to keep thy way in peace and security, unmoved by mortal doings. For immortality shall swallow up mortality as death is swallowed up in victory,[8] and Light shall prevail upon the planet.

The strengthening of the aura is a step in the right direction. Let none hesitate a moment to take it.

Devotedly and firmly I remain wedded to the precepts of The Brotherhood,

Kuthumi

---

1. Matt. 5:14-15. 2. Isa. 1:18. 3. Luke 12:3. 4. Luke 15:7. 5. Matt. 22:1-14. 6. The Master is speaking of the death process, given to man as an act of mercy that he might have a reprieve from the vanity of this world and partake of the Light and wisdom of higher realms between embodiments; moreover, the forfeiting at birth of the memory of previous lives enables the hope of heavenly spheres to replace the seemingly endless records of mortal involvement. 7. Pss. 2:7. 8. Isa. 25:8; I Cor. 15:54.

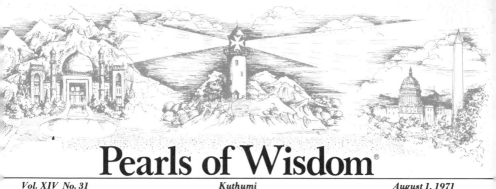

Pearls of Wisdom®

Vol. XIV No. 31   **Kuthumi**   **August 1, 1971**

STUDIES OF THE HUMAN AURA
The Star of the Aura
XI

To Each One Who Will Wear the Garment of God:
    The garment of God is the most transcendent man can ever wear. It represents the highest echelon of Life, the development not only of the love nature of God and of the wisdom of God but also of the element of power. This so many seek without willing first to make the necessary preparation in the refinements of love and holy wisdom in manifestation within the soul. How easy it is for individuals to accept primitive as well as intellectual ideas that rationalize the thrust of ego upon ego, without ever analyzing the attitude and the aura of the masses, who are saturated with the concept of oneness as the blending of human personalities. The oneness men should seek to understand and manifest is that of the individuality of God reflected in man. Oneness in Spirit is ever consecration in the Gloria in Excelsis Deo— the Glory to God in the Highest.
    Through the linking-together of the great and the trivial in human consciousness, mankind defeat evermore the manifestation of true spiritual transcendence. The ongoingness of the nature of God as it manifests in man is a study in individual development. As one star differs from another star in glory,[1] so by the process of linking together the mediocrity of man and the sublimity of God, the latter is compromised beyond recognition. But only in the human consciousness does the ridiculous detract from the sublime. By the splitting of divine images and by the subtle process of image distortion resulting in the redistribution of the soul's energies according to astral patterns which nullify the original spiritual design, man begins to feel that the magnificence of cosmic ideas is in reality too far from him and the gulf between the human and the Divine too great; thus his consciousness remains in the doldrums of mortal experience.
    Wise is the chela who guards against this invasion of the mind and heart, who recognizes those negative subtleties which seek to

stealthily enter the aura and turn it from its natural brightness to
darkening shadows of gray and somber hue. The strengthening of
the bonds of the aura with Light and virtue will enable the soul to
leap as a young deer across huge chasms of erroneous ideas separating
man from God when once the esteem of the immaculate concept is
given preeminence in his consciousness. To involve oneself in the
distractions of the world and to love the things of the world,[2] being
consumed by them, deprive one of the magnificent occupation of
seeking to become one with God, a cosmic occupation of permanent
Reality.

There may be a time to plant, to water, to love, and to die;[3] but we
are concerned with the abundant Life, which is nowhere more abundant than it is in the magnetic shower of Cosmic Christ power that
pours forth to the individual from the Heart of his own God Identity
when he fixes his attention upon the Presence and understands that
herein is his real, eternal, immortal, and permanent Life. As long
as he, like a potted plant, sits in the limited circle of his own individuality, he remains tethered to its ranges; but once he allows the
power and the pressure of the divine radiance to descend from the
Heart of his God Presence, he becomes, at last, the recipient of immortal Life in all of its abundance and unlimited outreach.

The illusion of the self must remain an illusion until the self is
surrendered; therefore, men ready and willing to be delivered from
the bondage of a self-centered existence into the infinite capacities of
the God Self must surrender unconditionally to the Divine Ego. Then
there is not even a sense of loss, but only of gain, which the soul perceives as cosmic worth as he increases his ability to develop in the aura
the consciousness of the absolute penetration of the Absolute. Physically, the very atoms of man become drenched with a shower of cosmic
wave intensity—the drinking of the elixir of Life, the magic potion by
which a man is transformed. In a moment, in the twinkling of an eye,
the trump of true Being sounds.[4] This is God, and no other will do.

The carnal mind cannot remain in command of the affairs of
such a one. A Christ is born, a nova upon the horizon, one willing to
follow in the footsteps of cosmic regeneration. Thus the purity and
power of the Presence strike a new note, and old things truly pass away
as all things become new.[5] The domain of destiny is all around us. As
man evolves, so Cosmic Beings evolve—wheels within wheels, leading
to the Great Hub of Life and to the Reality of spiritual contact as the
antahkarana is spun, perceived, and absorbed.

How beautiful is contact with Hierarchy, with the hand of
those Brothers of Light whose garments are robes of Light, whose
consciousness, reflecting the anticipation of spiritual progress, is

joyously attuned to those God-delights which remove from the mind of man the sense of the comparable or the incomparable. The world of comparison diminishes; the world of God appears. The aura is drenched with it—no sacrifice too great, no morsel too small to be ignored, no grasp too significant not to find its own integral pattern of usefulness. And so the domain of the human aura is lost in a sea of Light, in the greater aura of God; the windows of heaven open upon the world of the individual, and the showers of Light energy resound as an angelic choir singing of the Fire of worlds without end.

The anvil of the present is the seat of malleability; all things less than the perfection of the Mind of God mold themselves according to progressive Reality, plasticity, the domain of sweetness, the chalice of new hope to generations yet unborn. The historical stream, muddied no longer, appears as the crystal flowing river from which the waters of Life may be drunk freely.[6] The monad makes its biggest splash as it emerges from the chrysalis of becoming to the truth of living Being as God intended.

Sensing the human aura as a star, man gains his victory as he sees the universe flooded with stars of varying intensity. By comparison his own auric Light glows more brightly, for the fires of competition fan the flame of aspiration. But all at once he staggers with the realization that he is in competition with no one, for the incomparable mystery of his own exquisite Being is revealed at last.

Questioning and doubts as to the purpose of life no longer engage his mind, for all answers are born in the ritual of becoming. The fascination of Truth envelops him, and he weans himself from the old and familiar concepts that have stifled the glow of perpetual hope within his soul. He is concerned now that others shall also share in this great energy Source of Reality flowing forth from on high. Naught can transpire with his consent that God does not will, for the will of God and the will of man are become one.

When each man consents to this victory, the struggle lessens and then is no more; for faith in the Fatherhood of God reconciles men through Christ to the fountainhead of their eternal purpose. The glow of a new hope, infusing all, lends direction to the expansion of the auric Light. The forcefield is magnified, and in the magnification thereof the star of the man who has become one with God shines on the planes of pure Being as the angels rejoice.

A new life is born—one for whom the expectancy of Life will continue forever; for in the endlessness of cycles, the aura, as a glowing white fire ball, a summer radiance of the fruit of purpose, continues to magnify itself in all that it does. God is glorified in the auric stream.

Next week we shall conclude our dissertation on Studies of the Human Aura. The richest blessings of our Brotherhood be upon all.

Devotedly, I AM

Kuthumi

Meditation on Self

I AM no blight of fantasy—
　　Clear-seeing vision of the Holy Spirit, Being;
Exalt my will, desireless desire,
　　Fanning Flame inspired Fire, glow!
I will be the wonder of Thyself,
　　To know as only budding rose presumes to be.
I see new hope in bright tomorrow here today;
　　No sorrow lingers, I AM free!
O glorious Destiny, Thy Star appears,
　　The soul casts out all fears
And yearns to drink the nectar of new hope;
　　All firmness wakes within the soul—
I AM becoming one with Thee.

1. I Cor. 15:41. 2. I John 2:15. 3. Eccles. 3:1-8. 4. I Cor. 15:52. 5. II Cor. 5:17. 6. Rev. 22:17.

Pearls of Wisdom®

Vol. XIV No. 32   *Kuthumi*   *August 8, 1971*

STUDIES OF THE HUMAN AURA
The Crystal Flowing Stream of the Aura
XII

To Men and Women Desiring to Preserve the Immortal Soul Within:

The aura is a crystal flowing stream that issues from the Heart of God. No negation is here: only an indomitable fountain continually pouring forth a steadfast stream of magnificent, gloriously qualified substance—the substance of Life itself.

As a little child presents his first freshly picked bouquet of flowers to his mother, so the innocence of the child-mind tunes in with this crystal flowing stream of God's Consciousness, infusing the natural aura of God in man with the Life that beats his heart.

O children of the day, the night should not be given pre-eminence! Your energy should become qualified by the eternal flow of Hope that, if you will it, can enlarge its own opening into the fountain of your mind and heart—into the fountain of God's own Mind and Heart. Your mind must become the Mind of Christ; the desire of your heart must become the desire of the Holy Spirit, flowing assistance to those awaiting the loving hand of Perfection in their lives.

May I tell you that when you come in contact with the dark and sullen auras of those who have misqualified the bulk of their energy throughout their lives, you ought to recognize that in reality these are not happy individuals. They may laugh, they may dance, they may sing and make merry, they may wail and utter lamentations—they may run the gamut of human emotion; but they shall not prevail, for the Law inexorably returns to each one exactly that which he sends out.

The way of perfection is the natural way of the aura. But, almost as a mania, individuals seldom fail to misqualify the energies of their lives, bringing their very nerves into a taut state. They become like a tightened spring of energy wound in erratic layers, and they refuse the stabilizing influences of the Christ Mind and the divine Heart. Having no other energy, they are compelled to use this which they have locked in the coil of their mental and emotional incongruities. Thus through psychic imbalance the spring is sprung and the impure substance of the aura pours forth in a putrid stream. All of the delicate refinements of the soul and the natural culture and grace of the Holy Spirit are spilled upon the ground; and the kingdom of heaven is denied the opportunity to function through the individual auric pattern.

To say that they suffer is an understatement; for through their own denial of the hope of Christ they are punished *by* their sins, not *for* them. The Light of God that never fails continues to flow into their hearts, but it remains unperceived and unused; for instead of flowing into vessels of virtue—those pure forms and noble ideas that retain the Light of God in man—it is automatically channeled into the old and crusty matrices formed in earlier years through ego involvement and contact with the forces of antichrist that permeate society.

These patterns sully the descending Light as dark clouds that filter the sunlight of Being and preclude the spiritual advancement of the soul. Yet in moments of naked truth men and women admit their inner need, and their hearts and minds cry out for the preservation of the immortal soul within them. They fear the response of Heaven; and, failing to recognize the all-pervading love of the Spirit, they watch helplessly as the soul, little by little, loses hold upon the steadily outpouring energies of Life; for each misqualification brands them with the fruit of retribution.

While for a time it seems that those who dwell in error escape the wrongs they have inflicted upon others, let me remind you that Life will make her adjustments and none shall escape the responsibility for their actions. As he whose voice was of one crying in the wilderness said, "[His] fan is in His hand, and He will thoroughly purge His floor, and will gather the wheat into His garner; but the chaff He will burn with fire unquenchable."[1]

We are not concerned with matters of crime and punishment, but with the joy and courage that are born in the soul through the crucible of experience—the courage to be the manifestation of God, the courage to walk in the Master's footsteps, to feel the surge of His hope wherever you are, and to know that even though you walk in the valley of the shadow, you will not fear,[2] because His Light is surging through you.

Beware the sin of complacency and of passing judgment upon the lives of others. Before allowing your thoughts and feelings to crystallize around a given concept, ask yourself this question: Is the evidence indeed conclusive, and do you possess absolute knowledge concerning the motive of the heart and karmic circumstances surrounding other lives? If so, are you able to weigh these factors better than Heaven itself? Wisely did the Master speak when he said, "Judge not, that ye be not judged."[3]

Therefore, point by point, let the Holy Spirit remold the vessels of thought and feeling that hinder your flight; and let the fruit of the crystal flowing stream, the fountainhead of Life, be perceived for the diadem that it is—a crowning radiance that bursts around your head. Then the emanation of the Spirit Most Holy shall take dominion over all outer circumstances and, like the branches of a willow, trail upon the ground of consciousness by the still waters of the soul.

The Lord comes down to the meek and lowly;
His peace none can deny.
His Light that glows most brightly
Is a fire in the sky.

The children hear Him coming,
His footsteps very near;
They 'wait His every mandate,
His word "Be of good cheer."[4]

They feel a joy in knowing
That deep within their hearts
There is a glimmer showing,
Enabling all to start

Release from all earth's bondage,
Each weight and every care—
Open Sesame to Being,
Helping all to know and share.

The Lord is in His heaven,
So childlike is His love.
The Christ, the heavenly leaven,
Raises each one like a dove.

His face in radiant Light waves
Is pulsing ever new;
Freedom from past error
He brings now to the few.

But many are the sheep,
His voice each one may hear;
This is His very message,
Wiping 'way each tear.

Oh, see Him in the burdened,
The hearts o'erturned with grief,
The lips that mutter murmurs,
The tongues that never cease.

For social clamors babble,
Their judgments utter bold—
A child of Light untrammeled,
A soul made of pure gold.

Each moment like a rainbow,
The Presence ever near
Caresses in the darkness,
Bids all, "Be of good cheer."

Oh, take, then, Life's great banner,
I AM God Presence true,
And hold me for the battle,
A victor ever new.

For Life's own goalposts show me
The way I ought to go.
My hand is thine forever,
Enfold me with Thy glow.

May all be reminded each day as they utter the words of Jesus
"Our Father which art in heaven"[5] or any prayer, any call to God, that
the aura is the Father's Light and that His Son has said to all, "Let your
Light so shine before men, that they may see your good works, and
glorify your Father which is in heaven."[6] May the sweet concepts of the
living Christ, recalling a lost youth and the era of holy innocence,
remind you of Life's noble opportunities to be the grace and sweetness
that you expect others to be.

Then, regardless of what men do unto you, you will know that
what you do unto them is a part of the Age to be, of a mastery to
become, of an adeptship now a-borning. Through night and day,
through time and space, through life and death you shall remain
undismayed as the outpost of delight that melts away the darkness now
gathering o'er the land. Thus shall the world's tears be wiped away as
the mantle of God covers the earth. Everywhere through the night let
the shafts of Light, right where you are, pierce the gloom of the world
by the "good cheer" of the Master.

We, the brothers of our retreat, together with each Master, each
Angel, and each Adherent of the Sacred Fire of the living God from
their place in Cosmos, beam our love to you wherever you are. We shall
never forsake those who do not forsake the Light of their own God
Presence.

Eternal devotion,

Kuthumi

1. Luke 3:17. 2. Pss. 23:4. 3. Matt. 7:1. 4. John 16:33. 5. Matt. 6:9. 6. Matt. 5:16.

Pearls of Wisdom®

Vol. XIV No. 33   *El Morya*   *August 15, 1971*

We Shall Not Forsake Our Chelas

To Those Who Would Steel Their Minds for the Battle:

Thrust forth the concept of the common weal! God has thought first. On the magic carpet of man's free will, He may glide upward or downward. The sword at the gate of Eden keeps the way of the Tree of Life. The invulnerability of cosmic levels remains a tightrope which none can breach.

In the murky contents of the carnal mind, residual factors of Light remain to be used or misused by the soul without knowledge. Straight knowledge is above the sophistication of mere intellectualism as the clouds are above the earth. The pockmarked human psyche continues to berate itself. Neither modern nor ancient historical reflections are tales of infinity or of a heaven world of ethereal magnificence.

Men say falsely that only the senses report accurately. The history of science will clearly show a host of conflicts which are to be expected if progress in the search for understanding is to be forthcoming. The kingdom of heaven does not rise and fall with the vicissitudes of humanity's struggle. The kingdom of heaven, independent of all human effort, is inaccessible to those whose consciousness is unreceptive. Therefore, before man can know God or the laws governing the manifestation of Spirit in Matter, the holiness of cosmic purpose must be quaffed.

The very emptiness of the human heart, steeped in the debauchery and clash of purposeless ego-strutting, like a dog howling at the moon, only reverberates. The flutter of substance does not denote tomes of wisdom, but only movement. We measure progress by soul-knowing and humility, by God-sowing and tranquility. Peace at any price betrays. True peace is a cosmic vibratory action, wherein the middle wall of partition sends flowers of hope to those upon the pathway.

Morya speaks of the watching of guidance. Does heaven perceive? We are not spies, but only progenitors, hoping to avoid pitfalls. Delays are dangerous. The nets of the gray ones are tenuous, dripping with drops of "good" and "evil." Discernment becomes difficult. Only the heart of the arhat, like a straight arrow, flies into the arms of God. The tower of man's strength is ever true spirituality. Those who shatter the fine china of man's morality will not only sweep up the pieces, but karmically they may also have great difficulty in once again putting the pieces together.

The spoilers are currently in the ascendancy only because of the lethargy of those who cry, "The cause is lost." Fear not to cry out against darkness. So shall the hallmark of quality be engraven in the minds and hearts of men, for Light and darkness exist side by side. He that is for us ought not to be against us.

The myths of atheism and agnosticism are only chasms to trap the unwary. Actually it is an absurdity to doubt the existence of God. To overlook His laws is folly.[1] But not all who cry, "Lord, Lord"[2] will understand the Lamb of God slain from the foundation of the world.[3] They think that in the worship of the only begotten Son of God, they do honor their Heavenly Father. Only those who do God's will can rightly ford the muddied stream of current human thought. Youth holds out a tarnished shield. The shield is each man's; as he formed it, so must he reform it.

The Christ Consciousness neither flees nor pursues; it is simply there. To ignore the flares of regeneration is worse than never being born. For birth is the gateway to immortality when the stewardship of Truth is perceived. Tradition has many gaps; humanity have many clichés of thought and feeling. Cosmic ideations escape them solely because of old and fearful concepts, ranging from total condemnation to feelings of inadequacy.

The parable of the talents brings to mind the episode of the servant who buried his talent in a napkin.[4] Man may multiply his spiritual fruit tenfold or one hundredfold. I have not seen the limit. Limitation is self-imposed by those who degrade God by creating thimblelike concepts. Largesse of heart is the universal quality of the universal man.

The chalice glows with a sweet and sacred fire. The holy will of universal purpose is drunk in remembrance of the rule of creation that came from the Christ who declared, "Before Abraham was, I AM!"[5] The words "Aum Tat Sat Aum, I AM that I AM"[6] are scarcely understood by any upon the planet. But their inner meaning will come to the fore as greater spiritual progress is made, and ultimately men shall see their limitations vanish in the unlimited sense of Christ-awareness.

The concept of infinity does not transgress against the finite law: it transcends the finite law as though it never had been. Yet the usefulness of that law within its own domain must be perceived, for the sword of discrimination is of perfect balance.

We speak of the chalice of the heart. We speak of the eiderdown softness of Love's fragrance, borne upon the wings of the air, ethereal yet substantive, that levitates the consciousness. We speak of singing Light rays that, in contact even with the cells of the body, vibrate as a ten-stringed harp. We who have attained arhatship cannot repudiate it. Shall we limit ourselves by the standards of mortal weakness? We shall not! For the holy will shall prevail in those who will heed, as the testing of time and eternity, both karmic suffering and their personally created retributions formed by poor mastery of thought.

Men, by the simple acceptance of their private sense of struggle and hopelessness, create furnaces of seething emotion. God is Peace. Like a fragrant lily on which is impinged the Light from far-off stars, the soul may be the recipient of cosmic whisperings from the hearts of angels. The shining goblet of consciousness, like a giant reflector, must become a receptacle of receptivity—not to every wind of doctrine nor to a search for conflict, but to an awareness of the continual radiation of the sublime Fatherhood of God. He ceases not to speak to the human heart that listens, but His wisdom is always the wisdom of peace, the wisdom of reason, the formula of delicate logic.

O hearts of Light, thrust thy hands upward through the veil! The omnipresence of God, the eminence of Spirit, breaks the vain images of hypocrisy erected both in ignorance and in partial knowledge by man, who has inscribed upon the book of record the infamy of unbridled, untutored selfhood. Let the reins of guidance be in the hands of God, but be unafraid to take dominion over the earth.[7] Out of a common reason is born the meaning of love. So shalt thou love the will of God by thy will firmly based in wisdom's flame.

We shall not forsake our chelas. Each disciple is precious to us, but in his esteem for the spiritual mountain is the communal strength born.

Renewing the fires of devotion, I AM

El Morya

1. Pss. 14:1. 2. Matt. 7:21. 3. Rev. 13:8. 4. Matt. 25:14-30; Luke 19:11-27. 5. John 8:58. 6. Ex. 3:14. 7. Gen. 1:26.

A "Blue" Mantra
from the Lord of the First Ray

The Light of God's Will
    Flows ever through me
The glow of real purpose
    I now clearly see
O pearly white radiance
    Command all Life free!

Pearls of Wisdom®

Vol. XIV No. 34   Enoch   August 22, 1971

Seek an Immortal Friend

To Those Who Would Walk with God in This Age:

The paradise of Light escapes those unwilling to place their trust in the sublime purposes of Life manifest in nature. The organization of both organic and inorganic substance is a miracle of electronic efficiency, an infinitude of certainty about the destiny of Life.

Man's struggles to understand his little self and his greater Self, which seem to stretch endlessly before him, are a drama of supreme indulgence. As the interminable night of uncertainty in unreality plagues child-man, the long-suffering nature of God attends the hour when the darkness of aloneness will give way to the dawn of his all-one-ness, his be-ness in the Central Sun of Reality. Then all mankind shall see the emergence of the greatest consecration to purpose, the greatest comfort of heart, and the highest delight of mind and being.

The concept of oneness is ever an outreach through the doorway of selfhood to the magnificence of the divine intent, fashioned from the beginning through the orderliness of the Consciousness of God. The fact that individuals do not feel His Presence or make conscious contact with the Supreme Radiance is no cause to deny it. For the Sun of righteousness, who ariseth with healing in His wings,[1] also carrieth with Him the greatest peace and the greatest purpose that can most certainly be cognized by any manifestation of His Spirit. Nevertheless, the abuses of the carnal mind are legion as it surfeits in the knowledge of this world that, through the variegation of motif, denies the simplicity to be found in the doorway to the Eternal Consciousness.

Simplicity is the keynote of spiritual discernment. With the mind and heart as of a child, man may approach through the humble doorway of selfhood the Divine Radiance that manifests everywhere. Men stoop to go through the doorway and rise to stoop no more. The dignity of the Divine drapes the mortal form; the consciousness is imbued with the perpetual wonder of eternal discovery. The inscrutable becomes linked to the self, and understanding blossoms as a flower.

> I think then of the beauty
> Of the unsophisticated child
> Who raises hands in holy prayer,
> Parting then and there

The continents of the air.
Shining faces peeping through
The latticework of heaven,
Now appearing in full view,
Unveil protection's shower,
Radiant love rays, God's own power.
Sensual contact disappears,
And graceful listening always hears
The Word of God to man.

We await the acknowledgment by man of the power of his mind to penetrate form and substance and to induce the perception of intricate and far-off worlds instantaneously upon contact with any part of Life—even with invisible realms; for these are as real, and even more so, as that which comes in contact with the external surface of the eye.

The eyes of the soul open with childlike wonder and envision in hope a new day when the visitations of God upon the planet shall become so logical, so acceptable, and so meaningful to the masses of mankind that from the earliest days of childhood the knowledge of God will be given as the very foundation of the creative life. Thus will gentleness and peace replace the sense of struggle that denies God's abundance as the fruit of His wisdom for all.

The mystic message "I AM come that they might have Life, and that they might have it more abundantly,"[2] echoing through the two-thousand-year chamber of the historical flow, speaks to hearts today and for aye. The abundant Life within you is the panacea that cures all human ills, that brings the mind to a natural frequency in harmony with the omnipotence of God. Unless men develop their potential spiritual outreach, which all possess to a greater or lesser degree, they will lack the ability to relate with the great frequencies of the future. For how can they be changed "from glory to glory" except by the Spirit of the Lord?[3]

The tranquillity of God covers the earth like a mountain of Light. As men rise through the peaceful avenues of heavenly pursuit, their understanding rises with them. The fragrance of God is a tangible offering made by the Spirit unto the soul of man. Can man do aught but return to the Spirit the fragrance of holy prayer and service offered to the Body of God on earth?

What a delusion is the supposition that God, in bestowing free will upon the race, has endowed it with a latitude of choices all the way from relative good to relative evil! Who is the rationalist that thinks the Almighty caters to a broadening way where anything goes as long as it is meaningful to the individual?

The Lord left no room for compromise in His statement "Strait is the gate, and narrow is the way, which leadeth unto Life, and few there be that find it."[4] But once the Elysian fields are perceived by the eye and the elixir of immortal Life is drunk by the mind, the consciousness, imbued with the hope of the infinite Omnipresence, exclaims:

> "Great is the Lord, and greatly to be praised!"[5]
> The mountains cover His framework
> And the seas are the outpouring of His mouth.
> The firmament uttereth beauty,
> No darkness is there to be found.
> The dearest fruit of the ages
> Tumbles from the Tree to the ground;
> In hope man raises it upward—
> His esteem is a magnet of faith
> To draw humanity higher,
> Away from their toys and their ploys,
> Accenting the beauty of heaven
> And bringing to all God-poise.
> For thought is the doorway to contact,
> And contact the blessed release
> That brings to each soul the sure knowledge
> That I AM the Prince of Peace.
> The world's warring capers must end then,
> All struggle of ego so bold;
> And man, like a rocket free-rising
> At dawn's beginning in gold,
> Shall conquer the spoiler and mocker
> Who laughs at the children of God
> With fire descending from heaven
> On pathway the saints have trod.
> All motive bends purely to Love's ray,
> His strength is the strength of ten.[6]
> For surely our God will triumph;
> His victory's the victory of men.

Midst all of the struggles, the wars, and the prophecies of the ages, the return of God into the rustic hearts of men has continued. But I AM confident that if the reappearance of the Spirit is to be accelerated, a new sense of Life must be formed—a point of contact with Reality, a point of receptivity to Truth, outlined in the renewal of each man's definition of free will. The free will of God can be the free will of man. Man can make it so, for God wills it so. Only thus will the night of his misunderstanding fade in the golden dawn of Christed illumination.

It has been done before; it can be done again. The successful mastery of unknown worlds by an unknown God[7] declare we unto you. The victorious overcoming by untold evolutions in untold ages past is the promise and the hope of Light's victory to this generation. The potential is here within every man who will return to the inner walk with God.

In all of the frightful aspects of delusion and confusion humanity now face, we come with our counsel into the marketplaces of life to meet with the children of men. As they seek a mortal friend, so it is needful for them to seek an immortal one. The raising of the consciousness into the present possibility of friendship with God which Abraham knew [8] reveals the consummate sense of Light completing its potential.

The potential of humanity is very great. What a pity so few know it. In bestowing upon you now the knowledge of your opportunity to make contact with us as your friends of Light, we remind you of your individual need to comprehend the never-failing Light of God. The peace we leave with you, the peace we give unto you,[9] is from the balm of our hearts, received from Him who said, "Thou shalt have no other gods before me...for I the Lord thy God am a jealous God." [10]

Awaken, then, to the realization that the passing of the darkness will come, that the night shall not always linger, that men shall not always slumber. There is hope, and that hope lives in *you*. It also lives in us; therefore we would make this day a bond of hope between the communion shores of our hearts. For the ageless days of the past—the ages of glory and fulfillment—are linked to contemporary man through the universal Christ Consciousness.

We extend our hands through the veil, and the name of the veil is hope. Our hands are hands of charity. Won't you accept the proffered gift in faith? For without this trinity of action man would sleep and dream, perhaps nevermore to wake. With it, all Life shall move toward a far-off victory, realized in part this day. Though you now see through a glass darkly, when you see face to face, you shall truly be known as I AM known—one with God.[11] And so shall you be received, even as you also shall know God and receive Him.

Your life trembles in the chalice. The planetary chalice quivers. We come in the name of the Lord. The seed of the living Word shall not return to us void or unfruitful.[12] Life shall triumph over death, and the mountain of the Lord's anointing shall inundate the brutishness of human thought with the oil of mercy.

Gratefully, I AM your elder brother,

Enoch

1. Mal. 4:2. 2. John 10:10. 3. II Cor. 3:18. 4. Matt. 7:14. 5. Pss. 145:3. 6. Tennyson, Sir Galahad, stanza 1. 7. Acts 17:23. 8. James 2:23. 9. John 14:27. 10. Ex. 20:3,5. 11. I Cor. 13:12. 12. Isa. 55:11. Also see Gen: 5:18,21-24; Luke 3:37; Heb. 11:5; Jude 14-15.

Pearls of Wisdom®

Vol. XIV No. 35   *The Great Divine Director*   *August 29, 1971*

Slayers of the Lamb of God

To Those Waiting upon the Lord Who Cometh with Fan in Hand to
   Thoroughly Purge His Floor:
   The beauty of the God-design in all creation bears witness to the
perfect concept held by God for every man.

   As a point of spiritual discernment, the students of Light ought to
examine carefully the activities of the spoilers, so-called by reason of
their immature conduct and their alliance with the powers of darkness,
who utter unfounded statements against the laborers in the Father's
vineyard.[1]

   He who said, "Ye shall know the Truth, and the Truth shall make
you free"[2] also spoke these words: "By their fruits ye shall know
them."[3] While we advocate that the student of cosmic law become as
harmless as a dove, flooded with the milk of human kindness tethered
to divine kindness, we also advocate that he should learn to be wise—
even wiser than a serpent[4]—in this era of great social cleavage when the
hearts of men are nigh failing them for fear.[5]

   Saint Paul referred to those who become hypercritical of
individuals and organizations dedicated to the beautiful purposes of
God, saying, "There are many unruly and vain talkers and deceivers,
whose mouths must be stopped, who subvert whole houses, teaching
things which they ought not, for filthy lucre's sake."[6] Let the students
of Light understand, then, that unfortunate though it may be, there are
those who move among the brethren, professing that they come in the
name of God, who participate in evil rituals of gossip and slander and
thereby tie themselves at inner levels to forces not of the Light. A word
of explanation is due from our level to those sincere students who
desire to know the truth about the deceivers.

   It was recorded by John in the Book of Revelation, "The accuser
of our brethren is cast down, which accused them before our God day
and night."[7] This passage refers to those fallen angels who were cast
out of heaven and, for reasons best known to the Lords of Karma, were
sent into embodiment to balance their karma among the very ones
upon earth they had sought to overcome from their astral vantage.

"Clouds they are without water," noted Saint Jude, "wandering stars, to whom is reserved the blackness of darkness for ever."[8] The presence of individuals upon the planetary body who espouse the cause of darkness should therefore come as no surprise to the students of Light. Let them be wary, then, of such as these; and let them see to it that they never underestimate the evil intent of these wolves in sheep's clothing![9]

Their modus operandi requires an explanation, and I shall give it. First let me say that the reason that the tactic of criticism, condemnation, and judgment is used by the evil powers upon this planet is that it has proved successful in "subverting whole houses" and turning individuals against the Light of the Christ. The chastisement of the devotees of Truth by those who brazenly speak out against their Light is a token and a symbol of their un-Christlike state of consciousness. These slayers of the Lamb of God[10] shall certainly give account for what they do; and those who heed them will find themselves caught in a web of darkness spun by those who have misappropriated the divine energy and entered into a negative fiat of their own egocentric creation.

As you know, energy released from God or man is girded into spirals that begin with a circle, or cycle, and then rise in the form of a cone or a cylinder. When misqualified by incorrect thought and feeling processes in man, these spirals, eddying upward, become charged with negative magnetism, which, like a cyclone, carries its own vortex of destructive energy.

When this vortex of charged hatred comes in contact with the aura of either the new student or the old one whose faith has never actually been grounded in the rudiments of Truth, the doubts and questions of an undisciplined mind or an untutored heart may cause him to be receptive to a word of seemingly well-intended caution from another. Quite naturally, we expect that even the highest things of the Spirit will be placed under scrutiny by those who are unfamiliar with the teachings of the Masters, inasmuch as they have not experienced the Truth for themselves and have no a priori evidence to confirm what they hear.

Over the thread of the attention, then, the vortex is transferred from the aura of the speaker to that of the listener; in a flash there is a release of the crimson and black substance of criticism, condemnation, and judgment, which leaps the gap between monads or even between groups and quickly subdues the enthusiasm, the joy, and the great impulses of Love and Truth with which the Masters have imbued the innocent of heart.

I would like to point out that in their appraisal of one another, individuals are capable of seeing in a given moment only a small portion of the total life record. Through the bias of a partial assessment it is easy to overlook the radiant good that has flowed through a lifestream. Nevertheless, when someone raises an eyebrow concerning the integrity of a servant of God, those who are yet unsure of their ability to evaluate the situation may allow their own minds to enter the limited frame of reference of the critical observer. Thus they forget that there is undoubtedly more to the spectrum of the devotee's service than meets the eye; and they even forget the virtue that they themselves may have witnessed in the life of the one in question.

Absorbing, then, the negative concepts of the condemner, those who lend their ears to ungodly conversation are no longer in a position of judging righteous judgment.[11] Failing to realize that they may lose their faculties of discernment by even listening to gossip, they become the unwitting victims of a hypnotic influence, a magnetic forcefield, that spews from the aura of the betrayer as a smoke screen of deception. And if they are not wary, little by little this forcefield will permeate their entire consciousness until at last they cast all their hopes into a sea of bitterness and discouragement.

These are among the most important and more obvious reasons why Saint Germain has so often admonished the students of the Light to avoid the criticism, condemnation, and judgment of individuals and their activities. There are other reasons involving karma and the second death which I shall not go into at this time: suffice it to say that the return to the sender of such virulent energies directed against the children of God is fraught with grave danger. Knowing this law, the Master said: "Whoso shall offend one of these little ones which believe in me, it were better for him that a millstone were hanged about his neck, and that he were drowned in the depth of the sea. Woe unto the world because of offences! for it must needs be that offences come; but woe to that man by whom the offence cometh!"[12]

Then there are those who are overly cautious and carry their reserve to an extreme. Let them not forget that God has given man the faculty of spiritual discernment through the Christ Self and the Threefold Flame within the heart. You therefore have the divine authority to discern the fruit of the Spirit in the lives of others, to apprise yourself of what is right and what is wrong, to shun evil, and to expose its lie wherever manifest. But when you exercise this right, you should do so impersonally and with humility—sitting not in the seat of the scornful,[13] but ever beholding the Reality of the Christ in those who have temporarily come under a sinister influence. Jesus said, "Judge not, that ye be not judged";[14] therefore, you must beware to judge not the individual, whose heart only the Lord doth know, but his fruits; for by his fruits you shall know what is acting in his world and with what forces he has aligned his consciousness.

It should always be remembered that "the fruit of the Spirit is love, joy, peace, longsuffering, gentleness, goodness, faith, meekness, temperance: [for] against such there is no law."[15] Motives and acts that ignite hatred, strife, sorrow, confusion, agitation, and antagonism among brethren should be recognized for what they are. "Doth a fountain send forth at the same place sweet water and bitter?"[16] These thorns never emanate from the Christ Consciousness of the Rose of Sharon,[17] but from the consciousness that has aligned itself with the forces of antichrist.

Those who truly love God will make calls to The Karmic Board for the illumination of those whose energies have been darkened by denigratory deeds. However, the fact remains that there are those who in the present and forseeable future cannot be expected to respond to the outpourings of Light which the children of God invoke; for by nature they are concerned only with the personal self and its aggrandizement.

Out of their ignorance of the Great Law and their jealousy of other parts of Life, those whose minds are bent by the perverseness of selfish concern, who will not cease to analyze the faults of their neighbors, cannot hope to understand the meaning of the abundant Life lived in God until they have shed the snakeskin of their personal identity pattern. In the vastness of Cosmos there is room for all to develop the fullness of their soul-potential and, in so doing, to transmute whatever impedes the flow of Light through them as they become one with the God-ideal in the truly abundant Life.

In a spirit of constructivism, born out of the desire to alert and to admonish, we release this report. It would be most beneficial if all men had the awareness of spirit to discern not only the signs of the times and the astrological impact thereof from a cosmic standpoint, but also the sure means of governing the actions of their world; yet although Heaven has decreed perfection for man, man has not yet appropriated all of the joy and wonder God has in store for him.

We advocate a recognition of the fact that whereas we always espouse the positive, the victorious, the perfect and complete kingdom of God, we perceive that habits of negation and energy misqualification formed in childhood and infancy have often served to cover humanity with an opaquing cloud of illusory substance that one day will be no more. The living God is neither despot nor tyrant; His is the highest way. Unfortunately, because of the nature of human habit, patterns entering the mind from the earliest years often seem correct when they are not, simply because of their long acceptance by the mind and feelings.

It is highly improper that students of the Light should be impugned by those who do not understand that the kingdom of God[18] is truly within all who will open the door of their hearts to Love and Light, to peace and joy, to forgiveness and the beautiful thoughts of others, consciously created and upheld.

He who said, "Bless them that curse you, and pray for them which despitefully use you"[19] also promised his flock, "Lo, I AM with you alway, even unto the end of the world."[20] Certainly the fulfillment of his promise is more apparent in those kind moments when the magnet of your love for the ascended Christ, like a fire of living Truth, blazes its noontide glory throughout the worlds of all you meet regardless of their level of understanding.

Let honor and truth live. Let the strength of our Brotherhood expand into a full-blown maturity. Let the students of the Light be aware not only of the subtleties of the dark powers but also of the salvation of our God, by whose grace all who follow in the Master's footsteps shall be raised. There is but one Lord, and He maketh the sun to shine upon the just and the unjust[21] until the day of the harvest when the tares are separated from the wheat.[22]

In deepest devotion, I AM

The Great Divine Director

1. Matt. 20:1. 2. John 8:32. 3. Matt. 7:20. 4. Matt. 10:16. 5. Luke 21:26. 6. Titus 1:10-11. 7. Rev. 12:10. 8. Jude 12-13. 9. Matt. 7:15. 10. Rev. 13:8. 11. John 7:24. 12. Matt. 18:6-7. 13. Pss. 1:1. 14. Matt. 7:1. 15. Gal. 5:22-23. 16. James 3:11. 17. Song of Sol. 2:1. 18. Luke 17:21. 19. Luke 6:28. 20. Matt. 28:20. 21. Matt. 5:45. 22. Matt. 13:30.

Decree to the Great Divine Director

In the Name of the Beloved Mighty Victorious Presence of God, I AM in me, my very own Beloved Holy Christ Self, Holy Christ Selves of all mankind, the Beloved Great Divine Director, the entire Spirit of The Great White Brotherhood and the World Mother, I call for divine direction throughout my affairs, the activities of The Summit Lighthouse, the governments of the nations, and all Ascended Master activities, worlds without end:

1. Divine Director come,
   Seal me in thy ray,
   Guide me to my Home
   By thy love I pray!

chorus: Thy Blue Belt protect my world,
   Thy dazzling Jewels so rare
   Surround my form and adorn
   With essence of thy prayer!

2. Make us one, guard each hour;
   Like the sun's radiant power
   Let me be, ever free
   Now and for eternity!

3. Blessed Master R,
   You are near, not far:
   Flood with Light, God's own might,
   Radiant like a star!

4. Divine Director Dear,
   Give me wisdom pure;
   Thy power ever near
   Helps me to endure!

5. Shed thy Light on me,
   Come, make me whole;
   Banner of the free,
   Mold and shape my soul!

And in full faith I consciously accept this manifest, manifest, manifest! (3x) right here and now with full power, eternally sustained, all-powerfully active, ever expanding and world enfolding, until all are wholly ascended in the Light and free!
Beloved I AM! Beloved I AM! Beloved I AM!

Pearls of Wisdom®

| Vol. XIV No. 36 | Chamuel | September 5, 1971 |

The Love of God

To Those Who Would Pursue and Capture the Flame of Love:

The fires of Love, roseate and splendorous, pulsating upon the altar of God's Heart, are a tangible reality from which the chambered heart of each of His children may draw strength.

I AM an Archangel, and well do I realize that to some it seems altogether unnatural that I should communicate with those upon this planetary body who have faith in our existence. How like a game our solicitude must appear to those who have ears to hear but hear not,[1] whose memory of other spheres has not been quickened. That we should come from realms of Light to speak to man today stretches their brittle imaginations to the breaking point. "Preposterous! Fraudulent! Hypocritical!" is their unenlightened comment on the greatest phenomenon of the ages—the passing of Truth ex cathedra from God to man.

Nevertheless, this frail yet noble possibility[2] is the treasure of our heart; for in speaking unto those who believe that we are, we capture a singular opportunity, divinely ordained, to weave the mighty conduit of communion with those who require the thrust of our attention and the fires of Heaven's love in order to grow in grace and wax strong in the knowledge of the Lord.[3]

Humanity, so often burdened by the myriad demands made upon them by Dame Circumstance, fail to apprehend just what the divine plan is for themselves, their nation, or their world. Little do they realize, in their busyness, how the purposeless nets of sense delusion and the forcefields of ingrained habit they have woven keep them from contact with heaven, which to many still seems but a cloistered reality.

Half in doubt, half in fear, they remain unaware of the strength of Love. Often their tiny egos become absorptive of every erg of energy which Heaven has granted them. By and by, surfeited in the pain and pleasure of the world, they reach out as though to an unknown God[4] whose cosmic existence and plan they can scarcely realize, yet whose help they desperately need. In the past their lives remained untouched by His love; for they were unable to conceive of either the wealth of energy with which He executes His purpose through all who call upon His name or the grand design which He gives to all who have faith in the promise of the abundant Life. But now, even in their blind reaching-out, they begin to appreciate His Consciousness and to benefit from the ideals with which He would mold the minds of all as the one means of integrating them into the fiery heart of His love and Being.

Feeling themselves remote from His Flame, as though cast upon an island of illusion somewhere in the endless sea of time and space, men and women place themselves outside the universal perspective that would enable them to apprehend the gigantic Love that has given all visible things birth and yet has never denied it to invisible things.

Beloved ones, is not a thought unseen and unperceived until it begins to function? Is not the wind also unperceived until it moves upon the branches?

Is it so difficult for you to recognize in the interplay of thoughts within the chambers of your mind and heart that as man thinks and often knows not how, so God thinks and always knows how? His thoughts are so high, so beautiful, and so totally constructive of spirals of ascending consciousness that I am impelled, in this era of mankind's involvement in a miasma of shadow and pain, to speak to you of that which the many have long neglected—*the love of God.*

Men suppose these four little words to be void of meaning beyond the realm of the ordinary in which they move and think and rashly scribble Life's energies as upon a scrap of foolscap. Let them understand that the love of God is the spiral of the universe, and more, that it is the cool spring and the winding stream that slakes the thirst of the ancient mariner who ponders the irony of life, "Water, water, everywhere, and all the boards did shrink; water, water, everywhere, nor any drop to drink."⁵

In truth, God is everywhere; the waters of Life flow freely, yet men know not how to tap the Great Fount of Life. Let them understand that the love of God is the Life-fount, that it is immortality bestowed, that it is communion with the most valiant and beautiful spirits that have ever coexisted in Divine Love. Created by God and endowed with free will, they freely and assiduously availed themselves of the opportunity to become co-creators and inhabiters of celestial realms. Men and women of today who thirst for a tangible Reality can also find it by literally drinking into God, by following the beck and call of His voice that says, "Ho, every one that thirsteth, come ye to the waters!"⁶

How foolish it is that men suppose, in the darkness and vanity of their minds, that they who exist but a few short years upon the planet— and that in pursuit of the beautiful strands of Reality which they never quite capture even in frail moments of mortal bliss—are endowed with a reality, a substance, and an immortal existence with which Cosmic Beings are not! Surely you can see the folly and the total lack of perspective in this concept.

I am here to affirm that there are beings celestial just as there are beings terrestrial, and the glory that separates them is vast indeed.[7] That which is of the earth earthy[8] must change ere it become one with the heavenly. That which is of the heavenly may also change as expanding universes reach out through the transcendence of God into the domain of cosmic possibility where change itself is a part of the immutability of God, the outworking of the firmness of His purpose and His will.

How often embodied men have presumed upon the patience of an angel and, I might add, upon the patience of God! In solemn hope that one and all will soon possess their souls,[9] may I say that each time one from the realm of human misery establishes himself at last in a spirit of concord with the angels and the heavenly realm, the place prepared by the Lord "that where I AM ye may be also,"[10] bands of His hosts rejoice and sing hosannas in His name. They gather 'round the one newly born to the Spirit of Reality even as they gathered in Bethlehem at the hour of the descent of the Christ Light into a darkened but waiting world.[11] Thus the attention of the finite self shifts from earth to heaven through the interpenetrating gaze of the angelic hosts; and through the renewed awareness of God which they bring, it perceives not only the mystical outreach of His Mind but also those magnificently endowed beings of His Heart—the angels of God.

I AM Chamuel, Archangel of Love. When I recognize the goodness of God, the long-suffering nature of God, and the faith of God in the ultimate outcome of all things, I am nigh a state which in the human octave you would refer to as being "stunned by it all." Such love as this which the Father holds for His children concerns itself not with mere punitive action (for the law of retribution functions automatically), but with the regeneration, the reeducation, and the re-creation of the whole man, that he might share in the Godhead and in the design of his being which the Lord hath made.

The Architect of the universe delays the very act of creation through the shuttle of time and space, enabling His sons and daughters to participate with Him in the wonders of creativity. The foreverness of His Mind descending into the stream of temporal realization may seem a hard thing to mortal rationale; but as the glow of cosmic purpose flashes into fulfillment on earth, each child of His Heart feels first a faint glimmer of hope and then the comfort of contact with the Holy Spirit that is right where each man is.

There is no separation from the love of God. At each point in space, the infusion of the glowing reality of purpose can be expanded so as to literally expel and disintegrate unwanted feelings and wrong attitudes from the hearts of progressive men of Light. Progress is possible in love, and love can be tangibly felt within the heart. There is no need for individuals to degrade themselves in the slander of their own beings; but this they unwittingly do each time they deny Him by withholding love in thought, word, or deed. They can instead lift up their hearts in praise of His love and in so doing consciously raise their beings, knowing that ultimately they will be as they already are in the Heart and Mind of God—one with Him.

The Fatherhood of God, when it is known by man, becomes a bond of such love as to scale the stars. But unless men can direct into the chalice of future action each portion of heavenly substance, each erg of cosmic energy entrusted to them, at the same time holding hope as a beacon light upon a hill which cannot be hid, they may not know Him in this life, they may not find the Truth that sets men free,[12] and for them the days may not be shortened. [13] Yet if they will but clasp the hands of the Holy Spirit and the indwelling Christ and maintain faith in the integral wholeness of the Light and mutual endeavor of Gods, angels, and men, they will see emerging from within their minds a stream of white-fire substance which is the actual energy of God's love working out for them in all their affairs the inseparable unity of purpose that is immortality and contact.

In celestial joy and the fruit of loving service to God and man, I stand ready to infuse all who call unto me in the name of the living Christ with the fiery radiance of the pink flame of love, compassion, and tenderness for all Life. Won't you be receptive to the reality of its manifestation right where you are in answer to your call? I do not ask you to believe in those who are not, but in those who are. And it is from the depth of this sense of God's portion—the flame of an Archangel— that I give you my love from my heart!

$\mathcal{I\,AM}$
$\mathcal{Chamuel}$

1. Ezek. 12:2. 2. Frail because the thread of contact is easily broken in this octave, and noble because as long as it is sustained, the souls of men are ennobled by the divine ideal. 3. II Pet. 3:18. 4. Acts 17:23. 5. Samuel Taylor Coleridge, The Ancient Mariner, pt. II, st. 9. 6. Isa. 55:l. 7. I Cor. 15:40. 8. I Cor. 15:47. 9. Luke 21:19. 10. John 14:3. 11. Luke 2:13-14. 12. John 8:32. 13. Mark 13:20.

Pearls of Wisdom®

Vol. XIV No. 37   Hilarion   September 12, 1971

The Undiscovered Wonders of the Unknown God

To the Steadfast Seeker for Truth:

Cell memory! How many times has it been interfered with? Yet how wonderful is the process whereby each cell of man's being is endowed with the wondrous patterns evolving in the very Mind of the Godhead. By the acceptance of the perfection of God, man is able to maintain himself in a framework of harmony and joy. In all of the wonders of science, nothing seems so complete to me as the memory of the cell.

The ability to work change is inherent within the domain of man's free will; hence men speak of cell mutation without regard to the process of *trans*mutation whereby benign change can be consistently directed, both by man as the initiator and by God as the Preceptor under whose unerring guidance the inherent patterns of perfection reappear.

When long ago I spake, "Eye hath not seen, nor ear heard, neither have entered into the heart of man, the things which God hath prepared for them that love him,"[1] it was in the dawning awareness and conscious sense of the magnificence of the original design of the universe executed by the Grand Architect thereof.

I marvel how men work amidst all of the superb scientific principles upon which the design of the universe was framed, without taking notice of them or their colossal presence in the undergirdings of creation. And once again I must cite, in this time of advancing technology, the undiscovered wonders of the unknown God[2]— unknown because mankind realize but a farthing of their own potential, and very little of His.

Men agree that God is mysterious, and they seem content to leave the universe a cloistered but awesome manifestation. Yet God and Nature have already declared themselves unto man: "The heavens declare the glory of God; and the firmament sheweth His handywork."[3] Nevertheless, through blindness of heart and dullness of semantics, men have failed to perceive the unity of the Whole, blazing before them as the noontide of Reality.

When the correct concept of the Universal Christ is apprehended by man, he can more easily perceive that all things were made by Him.[4] In view of the fact that man's life and consciousness, being patterned after the cycles of soul evolution, are subject to change, it is understandable that the natural movement of the soul tethered to the will of God is also toward transcendence "from glory to glory, even as by the Spirit of the Lord."[5] However, when tethered to the human will, the outer mind aborts the natural tendency of the soul to rise; and any change that is wrought follows a downward spiral leading not from glory to glory, but to mutations in the personality, both subtle and violent. This is that pride in self-sufficiency which goeth before the fall[6] of man's energies into the density of the astral.

In ages past on the continents of Lemuria and Atlantis, long before the fiat of God went forth, "Henceforth shall every seed bear after its kind!" frightful mutations and weird forms were created through the experiments of black magicians. This misuse of the divine procreative seed caused the Lords of Karma to decree the destruction of the test-tube creations through the Noachian Deluge. After the Flood, the earth, cleansed and purified by the washing of the water, was once again brimming with the hope of new Life and more noble ideas. Yet only in the Edenic state, where the will of God is honored and communion with Him sought as the ultrachoice of man, can the complete restoration of perfection be achieved.

Unfortunately, those pseudospiritual scientists who invade the lower astral realm[7] for the extension of their schemes—for they have neither the attainment nor the self-discipline that is required to function in higher planes—are often content with making what is termed evolutionary astral progress instead of moving steadily forward, from glory to glory, through the initiations of the Hierarchy. In their mad craze for personal grandeur, phenomena, and power over others, they fail to apprehend Life's opportunity and the fiery destiny of man. They do not understand the fact that the days can and should be shortened,[8] and not prolonged, by the deliberate stewardship of the sons of God working in harmony with His holy purposes on the Path of self-mastery prescribed by The Great White Brotherhood.

Those who sidestep the true and only Path of attainment learn by devious methods and the misuse of the chakras to create vortices of darkness on the astral as well as the physical plane; thus they establish hypnotic forcefields of control whereby they exert an unwholesome influence over embodied and disembodied souls. Unwilling to surrender their human will and thereby receive the reward of the faithful—conscious dominion over the earth—these practitioners of the black arts usurp the authority of the Godhead and plunge headlong into the pits of astral delusion.

How tragic! They have never learned that their desires for mastery would have been satisfied by the Great Alchemist Himself had their motives been pure. They have never known the joy of legitimate attainment achieved through honest striving in humility, in love, and in obedience to cosmic law. They have not seen that there is no need for subterfuge and that, had they been willing, they might have entered in at the straight gate.[9]

By learning to restore the natural function of cells made in the imaged perfection of God's intent, man will also discover the secret of restoring all things, including his lost estate and the science of healing and alchemical precipitation demonstrated by Christ Jesus. But he must also determine to avoid the pitfalls of an evil generation. For not in relative good and evil, but in the consciousness of the Edenic perfection of God alone will the body cells—and the cells in the Body of God—resume their balanced function according to that perfect law of cycles which absolves man from the stain of mortality.

The everlasting Life,[10] envisioned by Christ as the lot of every man, is the hope of God for His creation. Physically, mentally, and spiritually, the change from glory to glory can occur as man is willing to burn away the barrier sheaths of his mortal consciousness by the Flame of the Holy Spirit that clearly reveals the purposes of Life.

These purposes are not for the prolongation of strife, unfounded dogma, or astral speculation, but for the universal revelation of the original Truth of God locked within the memory of the cell. What a pity it is that mankind, in all of their seeking, have failed to apprehend and apply the cosmic science even as they have failed to make practical the simple faith of a little child that is within their grasp, that faith in the ultimate yet ever-present goodness of God which makes their fondest dreams come true!

In the domain of our immortal destiny is the certification of the purpose of Life for each man who sees at last in his unity with the Presence of Perfection the Reality that from the beginning was and is the purpose of God. He came neither to divide nor to unify good and evil; for He said, "I came not to send peace, but a sword."[11] Yet He was called the Prince of Peace.[12]

The enmity between the seed of the serpent and the seed of the woman is the natural enmity of the carnal mind with the Christ. Mutually repellent, the seeds of Light and darkness cannot dwell together harmoniously in the same consciousness any more than a man can serve two masters, as Jesus taught, "for either he will hate the one, and love the other; or else he will hold to the one, and despise the other."[13] Of a certainty, "the carnal mind is enmity against God: for it is not subject to the law of God, neither indeed can be."[14]

A jagged concept, a distorted image, is all that is needed to separate man from the pristine reality of the kingdom. The kingdom of God is real! It is within you all.[15] It "is not meat and drink; but righteousness, and peace, and joy in the Holy Ghost."[16] Even so, those who have found this inner kingdom can draw forth material substance through their expanded awareness of the laws of spiritual abundance.

As an armor of Light, the spirit of cosmic purpose should be put on by the man who is faced with the challenges of today. Then, as David of old, he can say with complete trust, "Thou wilt not leave my soul in hell; neither wilt thou suffer thine Holy One to see corruption."[17] Through a giant faith in his allotted longevity and a burst of awareness of the gift of immortality that lies in his hands, he perceives the need to bring himself into harmony with the laws of the universe that he might take full advantage of his cosmic opportunity. It is as if man were emerging from a darkened cave, a labyrinth of struggle and hopelessness; but once the mouth of the cave is behind him, the Light and beauty of God completely sever his ties to the darkness of his former state and he enters into that eternal sense of the burning Light that never fails.

In the Revelation of Saint John it is written of the Holy City, "There shall be no night there."[18] Thus, in the resurrection of the Christ Consciousness, the Light banishes the darkness, and the triumph of the original cell memory is acclaimed. With the full restoration of his spiritual faculties, man experiences the victory of the Light within his consciousness. This is the culmination of the grand experiment of conferment whereby God, vesting man with a spiritual and a cosmic birthright, establishes in him forever the Christic principle of immortal Life.

Through the soul science of inner perception and Light penetration, man can ultimately dissolve, for himself and the entire planetary body, the spider webs of shadow that ensnare the race in doctrinal struggle. Through the perception of the one Light of God, the Light of Love that floods the earth unconfined by temples made with hands,[19] men will come to know the Christ as the salvation of the world.

Above persons, places, and conditions, yet inherent as the chief cornerstone[20] of Life, the brilliant image of the only begotten Son of the Father, full of grace and truth,[21] will be seen in the glimmer of hope that flows freely within the heart of every cell and atom of creation. Thus does Omnipresence console those burdened hearts who await the flash of God-awareness within the soul.

Devotedly, promoting the inner tutelage of the firm and wondrous Law of Being, I remain

Hilarion

1. I Cor. 2:9. 2. Acts 17:23. 3. Pss. 19:1. 4. John 1:3. 5. II Cor. 3:18. 6. Prov. 16:18. 7. The astral plane is the next above the physical in refinement; following that is the mental, and then comes the etheric. These planes, together with the physical, correspond to the four lower bodies of unascended man and planetary bodies. Corresponding to the emotional body, the astral plane contains the records of mankind's emotional evolvement and, as such, has become the repository of seething vortices of hatred, fear, terror, records of death and destruction and the biding place of entities and discarnates, whose consciousness has an affinity with these astral vibrations. At the mental and lower etheric levels of the earth, we also find the accumulations of the patterns of the mass consciousness. Therefore, only in the higher etheric plane and in the Ascended Master octaves of perfection do we find purity and a reliable source of inspiration and instruction. For this reason the Masters have advised their students to shun contact with the lower planes until mankind themselves are perfected. 8. Matt. 24:22. 9. Matt. 7:13. 10. John 5:24. 11. Matt. 10:34. 12. Isa. 9:6. 13. Matt. 6:24. 14. Rom. 8:7. 15. Luke 17:21. 16. Rom. 14:17. 17. Pss. 16:10. 18. Rev. 21:25. 19. Mark 14:58. 20. I Pet. 2:6. 21. John 1:14.

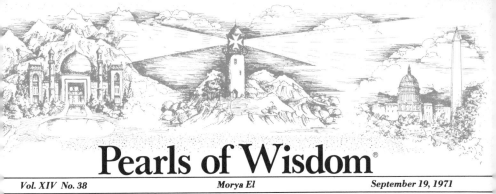

Pearls of Wisdom®

Vol. XIV No. 38   *Morya El*   *September 19, 1971*

Eulogy on The Summit Lighthouse

To Those Who Know and to Those Who Have Not Yet Discovered:

Long overdue is this eulogy on The Summit Lighthouse.

Servant of Gods and men, Citadel of Freedom whose Light beams radiate out into the world, gentle teacher of Christ Truth, The Summit Lighthouse stands. Frequently misunderstood by those unwilling to wait patiently for the manifestation of our clearer purpose, its tenets are sometimes carelessly rejected; and in this age multitudes may turn from its seemingly cloistered mystique. But those who wait as wise virgins to buy the oil of the Spirit, to allow the flowering of their understanding to overtake and engulf their misunderstanding, will stand rewarded for aye.

Meaningful symbol, Lighthouse of the world! Honoring the Christ and flooding forth, as a pillar of fire or a cloud of witness, the radiant inward image which can be grasped, and whose hand can be held by every man and woman, it shall enthrone the living God within the garment of skin and the transient mind of a people grasping for hope.

Hope's star burns brightly within the lantern of the Lighthouse and a true charity that transcends all personality. The Light beams radiate afar, binding together lands and peoples. The services of radiant healing invoked by the sons of God in and out of embodiment bring the kingdom of heaven nearer to the world, as close as men's own hearts.

Those who are willing to cast caution to the wind, allowing their consciousness to float as a vapor through a cosmic doorway, will find that they can discover at last the Reality behind the seeming facade of mere stone and masonry, upholding for all to view the Light of the world, the living Christ.

Through thousands of years the failures of Christianity have been legion, but the failures of Christ have been none. He remains the hope of the world, a living, pulsing Flame against brutality, against violence, and against man's inhumanity to man. Often it happens in the world of form that those who profess to do the will of God exhibit hatred and discourtesy on sight to those they consider far from cosmic grace.

The Summit Lighthouse, as a breathing, living, Christlike image, extending its beams of hope to man, welcomes all who can accept the

Truth that

> God is our Father
> And I AM His son,
> A creation of His own Heart.
> He, the One, once again will start
> The spirals of rising thoughts
> That fall not to despair.
> Gathering faith—
> Yes, whispering a prayer,
> These reach up without fear.
> They climb—the stars their goal—
> Transform the soul
> From mortal bondage days of clay.
> The glorious Golden Way brightly beams,
> Its heavenly lovelight gleams.
> Myth, illusion, shadow, pain—
> These uncertainties let none claim;
> For only Life as God Flame,
> I AM clearly sayeth,
> Reveals the way, the cosmic game
> Of God who playeth
> That all may win,
> O'ercoming sin's delusion,
> Specters' haunting confusion,
> Revealing now Light's eternal glow!
> Fashion heaven's garment here below
> To wear adornment of the Gods, immortal, fair.
> The living Christ lives on,
> Man glows, respondent
> To the Light of cosmic dawn.
>
> It has not all been said, but almost daily
> From the great fountain altar of The Summit
> Flows a point of contact with Our World.
> No dogma fruitless,
> Separating heart from heart,
> Is ours to impart,
> But always cosmic law
> Confirming all that God has wrought
> In olden days
> And in the days of Christ Jesus,
> Refusing to labor fruitlessly
> For mere personal, selfish gain.
> The Light we send lives on to reign
> A thousand years or just a day;
> For mankind's cares can simply slip away
> Into the stream of perfection pure, serene,
> That is the Image Most Divine.

Dwelling in the veils of time
As a duality—the veil rent in twain
Betwixt the inner and outer court of the temple
Does sustain
A Hall of Unity.

Let none profane this purity or mistake these efforts for mortal ones; for The Great White Brotherhood places its supernal seal upon The Summit Lighthouse as an avenue of such cosmic virtue as to claim it holy. It shall stand as a mantle of white Light upon the face of the earth. Its Light rays shall penetrate with cosmic worth through the dark night of human density, dispelling all of the concentration of mortal intensity until at last, gleaming brightly through the mists of time, it will stand in full view, the symbol of man's worth to God.

He gazes upon the sparrow in flight. Each soul, precious to Him, humbling itself and aware of the perfection of the Divine Image, can and shall, by the hand of every Ascended Being, receive such assistance as God would give to every man. Thus shall the ancient prophecy be fulfilled, "Yet shall not thy teachers be removed into a corner any more, but thine eyes shall see thy teachers."[1] The beginning of the Masters' step through the veil into human reality, into mortal view, is the activity of The Summit Lighthouse.

The Summit is a symbol of the great divine heights abiding within the soul of each man and each woman. Let none fear to climb these heights nor to forsake the valleys below; for crowning with the brilliance of cosmic genius, the fires of regeneration, emitted from the altars of the living God in the City Foursquare, do radiate out everywhere the precious reality of the I AM Presence.

Outer organizations may come and go; but the golden Light of the everlasting dawn emanating from the Ancient of Days, from the heart of Enoch, the seventh from Adam, and from each man's own heart shall reveal to him the glory of God in His purposes. His goal is to educate the youth of the world, to free mankind from the bondage of false claims, from the pitfalls of psychicism, from illusion and confusion, from darkness and hatred and all that is unreal. And this shall be the service of The Summit Lighthouse. For here is dispensed by divine grace, and divine grace alone, the Word of God progressively revealing contact with our eternal Brotherhood for the purposes of enthroning within all the redeeming, living, vital virtues of the Christ, by whom all things were made, and without whom was not anything made that was made.[2]

Eternal valor be ever yours, each one.

I AM

Morya El

—and by God's Grace,
"The Illustrious"

The Lighthouse

The rocky ledge runs far into the sea,
  And on its outer point, some miles away,
The Lighthouse lifts its massive masonry,
  A pillar of fire by night, of cloud by day.

Even at this distance I can see the tides,
  Upheaving, break unheard along its base,
A speechless wrath, that rises and subsides
  In the white lip and tremor of the face.

And as the evening darkens, lo! how bright,
  Through the deep purple of the twilight air,
Beams forth the sudden radiance of its light
  With strange, unearthly splendor in the glare!

Not one alone; from each projecting cape
  And perilous reef along the ocean's verge,
Starts into life a dim, gigantic shape,
  Holding its lantern o'er the restless surge.

Like the great giant Christopher it stands
  Upon the brink of the tempestuous wave,
Wading far out among the rocks and sands,
  The night-o'ertaken mariner to save.

And the great ships sail outward and return,
  Bending and bowing o'er the billowy swells,
And ever joyful, as they see it burn,
  They wave their silent welcomes and farewells.

Steadfast, serene, immovable, the same
  Year after year, through all the silent night
Burns on forevermore that quenchless flame,
  Shines on that inextinguishable light!

A new Prometheus, chained upon the rock,
  Still grasping in his hand the fire of Jove,
It does not hear the cry, nor heed the shock,
  But hails the mariner with words of love.

"Sail on!" it says, "sail on, ye stately ships!
  And with your floating bridge the ocean span;
Be mine to guard this light from all eclipse,
  Be yours to bring man nearer unto man!"

Henry Wadsworth Longfellow

1. Isa. 30:20. 2. John 1:3.

Pearls of Wisdom®

Vol. XIV No. 39   The Maha Chohan   September 26, 1971

The Process of Perfectionment Goes On

To Those Who Would Advance in the Knowledge of the Law:

How foolishly men have cast away the glorious winds of the Holy Spirit which permeate Cosmos with the fragrance of other worlds while bringing zest to all of Life, whatever its current format—transmuting, purifying, and exalting! The process of perfectionment goes on.

It is necessary for the seeker to believe that God is and that we are His representatives if he is to extract the greatest possible assistance from heavenly octaves for the flowering of his understanding and the expansion of his consciousness. This we long to see take place. The flower and fruit of the unfolding soul potential cannot be known until consciousness has expanded; and this cannot take place until faith is made active through works in the life of the devotee of Christ. The unfettered power of the Holy Spirit that drives back the dark clouds and highlights the bright ones is beheld through eyes of universal vision. Without the vision of the omnipotence of God, man feels alone—separated from Life and at odds with the world around him.

And then there is the matter of platitudes, which, because men have heard them before, lose the appeal of newness. Hence they have a tendency to reject Truth because of its garments as they often do one another. This is ever folly; for if one will look carefully, he will see that it is the Spirit that giveth Life and the letter that killeth. [1]

It is not enough that men have heard a piece of music or an old saying before; until the alchemical keys contained therein have served their purpose in unlocking the Light of the soul, men can well stand to hear them a thousand times. And this applies particularly to the Holy Scriptures and the slokas of the Vedas. By much hearing and little doing, men have indeed seared their consciousness; and their points of receptivity, like nonresilient fibers, no longer have the play of vibrancy and life within them.

Renewal is needed—renewal of the mind and of the marvelous faculties of spiritual attunement and discernment. In his false sense of the miraculous as something that happens to him instead of something that he causes to happen, man often believes that God is the only initiator of Good and that he must wait for the Spirit to provide the impetus that will swiftly dissolve the morning mist and reveal the sun shining in his strength[2]—and of course He shall; but the quickening process is greatly enhanced by the exercise of man's own initiative and free will correctly applied.

It may seem to some as though we were constantly prompting our students in the form of a shallow preachment. On the contrary, we are providing simple yet profound patterns of instruction based on both known and unknown laws in such a way as to make them acceptable to mankind's current modes of thought. Thus, whereas there is nothing new under the sun,[3] all things are thereby made new.[4]

Man is not going to get out of the universe, even by the process of physical self-destruction. Both here and hereafter he retains his God-given right to life, liberty, and the pursuit of happiness; but he should understand that the little self is but a doorway into the larger Self, and he must seize the opportunity Life affords during his appointed cycles to master energy and circumstance so that he may consciously enjoy the gift of dominion.

So many make the mistake of substituting for self-control the control of other selves. It would seem they think that by manipulating others and persuading them to do their bidding, they thereby gain superiority over men. O dear hearts, won't you see once and for all that this is putting the cart before the horse! It is a complete reversal of the intent of Heaven for every man's home rule. He that would rule a city must first rule himself.[5] Man must be willing to subdue his human self in its old mayic[6] patterns and reach up for the freshening winds of the Holy Spirit.

Man is cleansed by water, by air, and by fire. This triangle of purity is used to aerate the mind of wrong thoughts; to flush out the emotional body, to relieve it of the sense of drudgery and age-old hatreds, of crusty concepts about people, places, conditions, and things; and, above all, to let the fire of the spirit of man, as a part of the living nature of God, consume from the etheric body and the soul every vestige of impurity—cause, effect, record, and memory.

We are announcing new classes of instruction to be given in our spiritual retreat here in Ceylon to which the sincere among mankind may apply. Although attendance is by invitation only, disciples in embodiment who aspire to the purification of their consciousness by the Flame of the Holy Spirit may, as they fall asleep, simply express to the inner Christ Self and the guardian angels their desire to be taken to our temple. Those who are worthy will be drawn in their finer bodies and placed in graded classes according to their attainment.

Some will retain in their outer mind the instruction they receive and a knowledge of their contact with our Brothers; for others the memory of the inner experience will not come to the fore of their consciousness, but they will evidence greater self-control in their feelings, more abundant illumination in their mind, and a tethering of their being to that sincerity of soul which seeks to know the will of God and believes that the Father intended from the beginning that they should become victors over self and circumstance.

The molding of a better world by the spiritual processes of molding better individuals is the work of The Brotherhood. Benign, true, and pure, the motives of its members are to produce the longed-for kingdom of heaven, first in the consciousness of the individual and then in humanity at large.

Let not your hearts be troubled, then; neither be afraid [7] when confronted by the spectres of mass confusion arrayed before you in the daily newspapers. I do not say that the facts, however sordid, should not be brought into the open and that mankind should not be alerted to current dangers so that precautions might be taken. I do say that a great deal of news reporting today is tailored for mass consumption and mass manipulation. Then again, when men desire to produce certain political or economic trends, they often announce their intentions beforehand. Their tactic is to test the opposition. If public reaction is not too great, they take it as a sign that they can safely get away with their manipulation of the masses. One day they will cope with those who have become wise as serpents and harmless as doves. [8]

I know of no men upon the planet more formidable than the men of the Spirit; for they, as mankind say, have no axes to grind. Their one desire is to see the kingdom of God manifest upon earth, to multiply mankind's opportunity for education in heavenly things that he might improve his lot both spiritually and materially. Wise is the chela who begins, then, in full faith to pursue the understanding that will give him the advantage over every mortal condition through purity of thought, word, and deed. Armed with this knowledge, which we shall outline in the new classes at our retreat, he will not glory in earthly things, [9] but in heavenly things; [10] and he will express mastery over both. His logic, superior to that of the dogmatists of the world, will develop through unity with the Holy Spirit; and through the Holy Spirit he will gain intimate contact with the Father and the Son.

I await the gradual yet potentially swift expansion of the Light within the children of God upon the planet. I await with a cosmic excitement their mounting interest in the things of the Spirit [11] that is turning men toward God. Let us hope for each man, for only hope and faith will precipitate the longed-for charity of God to a waiting world.

Valiantly in the service of the Light, I remain

The Maha Chohan

Representative of the Holy Spirit

1. II Cor. 3:6. 2. Rev. 1:16. 3. Eccles. 1:9. 4. Rev. 21:5. 5. Prov. 16:32. 6. From maya, meaning illusion; hence illusory. 7. John 14:27. 8. Matt. 10:16. 9. Phil. 3:19. 10. Heb. 8:5. 11. I Cor. 2:14.

The Divine Potential

Not my will, but Thine be done

through

The Holy Spirit

The mandate of God—
Be ye therefore perfect,
Even as your Father which is in heaven is perfect—
Can be fulfilled in man.

With God all things are possible;
Perfection is attainable
If the will to perfection is invoked.
Each day man can, if he wills it,
Attain a little more of God's glory.

As Above
—————
so below
The Law of Love is perfecting me now! (9x)

Pearls of Wisdom®

| Vol. XIV No. 40 | Kwan Yin | October 3, 1971 |

The Inflexibility of the Mercy of the Law

To Those Who Cherish Mercy's Flame as the Beacon of Hope to Civilization:

When the wick is placed in the oil, the fuel for the flame rises by capillary attraction. Just as natural law governs physical nature, so spiritual law governs spiritual nature.

Through the mists of time the advent of glorious things appears. Thus the beautiful soul Robert Louis Stevenson long ago declared, "The world is so full of a number of things, I'm sure we should all be as happy as kings."[1] One of the great factors which makes a study of the past attractive is the lure of discovering a period and a culture more exciting than one's own. Yet civilizations have come and gone and the affairs of men have fallen from time to time into a cyclic round of regrets; for the pages of history are replete not only with high adventure and interesting stories about people, but also with infamous acts in almost numberless array.

Wise is the historian who learns the art of sorting out the wanted from the unwanted as he peruses the archives of the race memory. If permitted to invade the bastions of heaven's peace, man's delvings into the macabre, which he allows to parade upon the screen of his mind, would cause the very ethers to tremble; and the web of contact, if allowed to exist at all, would pollute the pristine purity of higher spheres with the mire of humanity's fascination for the unreal. Therefore, man's containment within the confines of his own musings and mediocrity is clearly a part of the divine plan for which all should be grateful. If the halter pinches, blessed ones, if the corral seems to curb your freedom, remember that the pursuit of the perfection of God, the highest adventure possible to anyone, must be guarded for the few in every age—yourselves included—who come apart from the world because nothing else will satisfy their souls.

Men expend their energies in far-off adventure, climbing the Kunlun Mountains or the Himalayas in their desire to conquer their physical environment; but the time will come in the life of every man, if he permits the flow of gentle cosmic evolution to guide his soul unerringly to its goal, when he will respond to the great inner need to master his affairs rather than be mastered by them. And when the gentle dropping of the oil of mercy saturates his consciousness, he will also understand the role that others play in the drama of life.

How often even the average individual suffers the criticisms of those he does not know. The anger that flows in a torrent from the lifestreams of the masses can be disturbing even to those of ordinary sensitivity. Directed in a tirade by those who would accomplish the control of others, this energy spreads into the world at large like the black ink of a cephalopod, producing the very havoc that the dark spirits intend. Therefore, let wise men and women in every walk of life shun anger and the rising pillar of wrath that shatters the crystal glowing drops of mercy we would dispense to the world.

From the Temple of Heaven in Peking,[2] we perceive that there burns in the hearts of mankind the nostalgia of earlier years, the memory of family and home environment. As an act of mercy, we would caution individuals against such indulgences of the memory, however pleasant; for only in reaching beyond the relative good and evil of all human experience—one's own history or that of the planet—into the realm of Pure Cause that lies just beyond the cosmic veil, can man accurately trace the history of the soul and the real meaning of life.

Man came forth from God; he need only dip the wick of his consciousness into the oil of spiritual illumination and mercy to realize, by a spiritual capillary attraction, his own fiery destiny. Then will the flame of his life burn brightly without sputtering. Probing the ancient history, not of astral delusion but of spiritual evolution, individuals will see clearly through and beyond the mists of time 'neath the clamor and adventure of past lives a golden thread of brilliant hope penetrating and transcending all.

Man need not lose himself in the densities of time and space or in the labyrinthian caves of his mind and emotions; for by God's intent he can sharpen his soul faculties and cut through the mortal dilemma. Even those who consider themselves spiritually undeveloped or unendowed can acquire a greater penetration of higher octaves; for the precious gifts of perception are already a part of the abundant Life that God has given to man in the superb manifestation of the flame within the heart.

> Flame of soul brightly appearing
> As hope and fragrance to the mind,
> Sweet incense rising in the air,
> Contacts each heart bowed in prayer
> And kindles memory's shining hope
> That though appearances belie,
> God will strengthen and make whole.

May I ask of the devotees of the Light, wherever they are, that they remember the power of mercy not as a bending branch of willow or a hollow bamboo stalk, but as a shaft of courage and integrity that no man can sway. The inflexibility of the mercy of the Law is the ultimate source of man's freedom. As a lotus rises from the swamps of life casting fragrance everywhere, so let men whose lives are permeated by Christ Truth release the fragrant love of Father, Son, and Holy Spirit.

Whether men living in other climes say, "We believe in Brahma, Vishnu, and Siva," or, "We believe in the gentleness of the Buddha, unfolding his consciousness into the Image Divine," or, "We believe in the Nazarene Master who appeared two thousand years ago in Bethlehem," let them discover in the dignity of the Holy Spirit and the reign of the eternal Christ that the ageless nature of the only begotten Son is truly one in all humanity. God's mercy is extended to all through the great cosmic bank of abundance; but it is made tangible only to those who pursue relentlessly until the mists of past and future hopes are parted by the sun shining upon the crystal sea of Reality unbounded. God is one, Christ is one, humanity is one!

There may exist current dangers to mankind's attempts to unite nations and peoples without conformity to the Spirit or the law of living Truth; but one day the principle of divine union will become the foundation of true brotherhood and God-government over all. When men open the windows of the soul as we open the Temple of Heaven, the floral winds of mercy will penetrate their consciousness and make them one as never before. The premature integration of those whom Nature has divided geographically and ethnically before the Spirit has produced the miracle of cosmic love in their hearts, could well bring about the slaughter of the innocents [3] (the destruction of the manchild of the heart who focuses the *inner sense* of God's love). But when the day of God's appearing in the heart is welcomed by all, men will stand upon the platform of mercy as a dais of their united accomplishment.

These are the ideals we have espoused. Let us, then, who understand the need for mercy in healing, in ministration, and in serving together create in Spirit an ageless temple of mercy as a monument to a world alive and waiting for the sunrise of God's merciful hope.

Devotedly, I remain

Kwan Yin

Goddess of Mercy

THE RADIANT WORD
Excerpt from a Dictation by Beloved Kwan Yin
The Sword of Mercy
given at the Pyramid Conference, October 1969

Beloved ones who worship at the Temple of Mercy, gather close now round about the flame. Dip into the flame with your heart and with your love and partake of the essence of the Sacred Fire. Recharge your form with its regenerative momentums and let the living Light of the mercy of God be known around the world.

Let the cry of hope go forth! Let faith answer, let charity point the way; for this day we have declared it: Mercy shall triumph in the world and mankind shall come to know the fullness of the Law of God, the fullness of the manifestation of His Truth! To this end we serve. Will you serve with us, beloved ones?

Won't you stand now and draw the sword of mercy from your own hearts? Did you know that you can do that, beloved ones? You may place your right hand upon your heart and draw forth the flame of mercy therefrom, which you then qualify as the sword of mercy. Do you know that at any hour of the night or day you may draw forth this sword from your heart? And what is this sword? It is the living Word; it is the power of the Flame of the Holy Spirit.

With this sword in hand you may then go forth acknowledging the power of the Christ; and you may give the following call unto me and I will answer, for I am bidden by the Lord of Hosts to answer the call of each and every devotee of mercy:

"O Beloved Kwan Yin, charge now this sword with thy flame of forgiveness, of healing and truth, of mercy and freedom. Make my right arm the scepter of thy power in the world of form where I desire to extend thy grace—into this situation, into this problem. Let the full expansion of the fire of mercy from the altar at Peking be charged now through my right arm and through my heart by this sword of living flame, that the children of God upon earth may come to know that the fire of mercy will allay all fear, will quench the blaze of men's emotions, will stop the rioting of the masses, will quiet the concerns of the youth—their worries and their rebellious energies."

Beloved ones, whenever a problem is called to your attention in the world of form, whether it involves hundreds or millions, your own family or your country, draw the sword of mercy, point it directly into the core of the problem, and feel the action of mercy's power rushing in to balance minds and feelings—to transmute and make whole. Meditate upon the sword; visualize its penetrating, all-consuming action; and let the flame do its perfect work. All you have to do is call to me and then know that the fullness of the Law will act if you will hold your attention upon the desired perfection and meditate upon the Light of the Christ for several moments or minutes as the need requires.

Now, beloved ones, take the sword—the precipitated power of the Sacred Word—and return it to your heart, and think upon this thought this day: If you can draw forth the sword of mercy from the flame focus within your heart, can you not also draw forth the sword of blue flame, the sword of truth, the crystal sword, the sword of divine love, the sword of healing, and the sword—the pillar of fire—of your own ascension?

Sharper than a two-edged sword is the living Word of God; and whenever and wherever it is called forth, His fire will go out into the world to manifest His perfection. If you will but keep the Flame of Life blazing within your heart and make the call for it to come into manifestation, you will have at your disposal a most powerful instrument of God for the healing of the nations and the victory of the Light in all mankind. Therefore, accept this opportunity and humbly and joyously acknowledge that through you God will certainly do all that is required to bring humanity into the knowledge and understanding of His will and into the triumph of the Golden Age.

Whenever you are confronted with a situation wherein you would be tempted to say to yourself, "I just don't know what to do; I don't know how to handle this problem," stop for a moment. Become calm and centered in the Presence of God within; call to me in the name of your God Presence and your Christ Self; and then draw forth the sword of mercy and behold the action of the Christ.

This is my gift to you this day—the understanding that as sons and daughters of the Flame you have the power and the authority, if you will but claim it in His name, to invoke the power of the Flaming Sword[4] and to see what wonders God will perform through your hands, through your hearts, and through your heads....

1. Robert Louis Stevenson, A Child's Garden of Verses, **"Happy Thought."** 2. The etheric retreat of the Goddess of Mercy where the mercy flame is enshrined. 3. Exod. 1:22; Matt. 2:16. 4. Gen. 3:24.

Pearls of Wisdom®

| Vol. XIV No. 41 | Lord Maitreya | October 10, 1971 |

Initiations of a Planet and a People
in Religion and Science

Children on the Ladder of Light's Attainment:

The process of initiation is a continuing one for all. Some fail to realize that even a babe is not bereft of God. A lack of sensorial development or mental maturity is no indication that the soul does not comprehend, through the light in the window of being, Life in its infinite ranges. The never failing Light of God posited within the Heart Flame of man always knows and cannot be deceived.

Human attempts to explain the warp and woof of the universe according to mortal, mechanical concepts are understandable; but they do not afford the opportunity for clear seeing that is needed before the initiatic system can be meaningful. Therefore, those who aspire to the initiations of The Brotherhood probe beyond a mere surface rationalization of the causes behind the effects which they observe in their physical environment.

The lessons of life are learned in two ways: through the gathering and storing of data by the outer and inner mind, and by the assimilation of knowledge through the eyes of the soul at conscious and subconscious levels. As the result of both methods, the individual may, at intervals in the time stream, find the net gain of his soul-tutoring coming forth on the surface of his consciousness with profound admonishment. Thus the process of enlightenment goes on whether or not it is recognized as such by the conscious mind. We cannot decry this process nor do we fail to encourage man to study to show himself approved unto the living God.[1]

The callousness of those concerned only with the gratification of the senses is indicative of their emotional immaturity and lack of understanding of the larger concerns of Life. Those who are concerned with the mandates of the Almighty are also concerned with getting on with the purposes of Life. They do not wish to experience further delay and the frustrating dalliance of a purposeless existence. Their discontent—the hallmark of true progress—is almost an aberration in the eyes of the world. They are restless of soul, eager to find the answers they seek, and not unwilling to place personal peace last and divine knowledge first. As their Wayshower said, "I came not to send peace on earth, but a sword."[2]

I think also that the knowledge and light of Truth may easily become a lash to the outer man; yet we know without question that the outer man must be conquered. For man is a dual being: he is both human and divine. Thus the purposes of Life are calculated to inspire men to forsake the former and to engage their attention with the latter. Some have spoken out against this view as an impracticality. Well, it seems to us who have attained, by the grace of God, that man is impractical either here or there, in heaven or on earth, in Spirit or in Matter.

Can we not seek, then, for our unascended chelas that perfect balance of body, mind, and soul which we outpictured, that they may bring into the realm of mortal affairs the practicality of the Spirit that enhances the quality of life for their fellowmen as well as for themselves? Can we not also expect that they might bring at least an equal amount of their God-given genius to bear upon the process of attaining that spiritually natural habitat in which they will ultimately dwell in the foreverness of God? Must humanity totally neglect the things of the Spirit in order to complete their round of mortality? I do not think so. If they will maintain the proper perspective between the human and the divine, they will certainly devote a reasonable portion of their lives to acquainting themselves with that wondrous realm of God-delight so totally foreign to many who yet dwell in the veils of time.

Now, we have observed that the things of the Spirit are becoming of increasing interest to mortals, and by their explorations they are raising themselves and the world to a new step in cosmic initiation. Meanwhile, unfortunate devices of cruelty are being employed to promote bigotry, prejudice, and misunderstanding among men. Racial tensions stirred by agitators accomplish little good in the world, while the fruit of a just understanding and the fair and intelligent examination of every problem confronting the children of God produces the miracles of faith that enhance the brotherhood of man and the building of the kingdom of heaven upon earth.

Whereas the Fatherhood of God is obvious in higher realms, the permeation of His love and intent could also be seen in lower realms if man would will it so; yet humanity must have patience if they are to fulfill their destiny. It is haste that construes so much evil in the world—haste, and man's failure to take an impartial viewpoint when Good and evil must be adjudicated. Because right methods are clear and easy, wrong methods need never to be used; yet they are. While men may decry situations not to their liking, let them remain spiritually unmoved midst the disturbing panorama of world events being used to produce fear, division, and economic imbalance across the globe.

Among the initiations the planet is currently passing through is one similar to that which humanity faced both preceding the destruction of the planet Maldek[3] and during the period of the last days before the Flood. This test involves the employment of the creative genius and power to the glory of God. In the aforementioned epochs scientists engaged in genetic manipulation and the creation of animal forms that took into account neither spiritual law nor the existence of The Karmic Board, thus aborting the cycle of fulfillment that always follows the correct use of divine opportunity.

Man's attempt to alter the structure of the DNA molecule and thereby gain control of the human embryo is not new; successfully accomplished in past eras, it may be achieved once again in this age. When respected and rightly implemented by wise men of divine attainment, this feat of science will present such marvelous possibilities to the race as to appear miraculous—albeit all miracles are the demonstration of natural law. However, the great danger in such discoveries lies in their misuse by corrupt men who, while playing God in the realm of Matter, neglect to play God as they ought in the realm of Spirit.

The possibility of failure, individual or collective, in the spirals of initiation is not to be taken lightly. If the planet as a whole is to pass victoriously through the tests of this age, religion and science must go hand in hand, the one providing proof for the other in this time of advancing cycles. The kingdom of God that is within you[4] is the foundation for the successful pursuit of the initiatic process at the individual level. And only through initiation, first at the individual level and then at the planetary level, is the miraculous sense of the divine restored and retained within the human consciousness under the guidance of the Ascended Masters.

Our services are yours. We offer them to you and to those among humanity who will believe in our existence, in our sincerity, and above all, in the sincerity of God. Thus, together we hold the balance, the health and the sanity, of life waves moving on to perfection through the grand initiatic process of the Father of worlds without end.

Devoted to His service and to the service of the Universal Son of God, I remain confident of your confidence in our purposes.

Triunely One,

Lord Maitreya

1. II Tim. 2:15. 2. Matt. 10:34. 3. The remains of Maldek comprise the asteroid belt between Mars and Jupiter. 4. Luke 17:21.

THE RADIANT WORD

Excerpt from a Dictation by Beloved Mighty Hercules
The Pact of Hercules and Arcturus, given at the 1971 Freedom Rally

Bolts of blue lightning descend from the heart of the Great Central Sun into the earth—into the heart of the earth! I, Hercules, decree it this night, that the earth shall not be the same again. For I have come with legions of blue lightning from the heart of the Sun. And they are ready; they are waiting; and they are most willing to manifest the will of God in the hearts of all mankind—to expand it in the heart of the atom, to call to the rocks to quicken the hearts of elemental life, and to say: The hour is come for the fulfillment of the will of God upon this planetary home, let the chips fall where they may!

I, Hercules, have come with legions determined to brook no interference with the will of God upon this planetary home, and Amazonia stands with me focusing the power of Omega as I stand in the place of Alpha. O mankind of earth! Receive the blue fire of the Great Central Sun and know that the hour is come for the dividing of the way. To the right or to the left mankind shall fall; and the sword shall rend in twain the garment; and the Light of God that never fails shall determine whether man shall be immortal or no more.

Precious hearts of Light, do not fear; for when the blue lightning descends, it is an armor of protection, a bulwark to those who have served their God. And to those who have not, it is instant and swift destruction; and they know no more....

Immortal sons of freedom who have come with me bearing the violet flame and the angels of the violet flame: Descend now and prepare the way for the coming of the sons and daughters of God in embodiment into the Light. For we will wait no longer. We have taken our swords of blue flame this night and we have shattered the density of human night. I say, it is done! And I, Hercules of the Sun, have come to quicken in you all your divine plan, your mission, and your blueprint for life....

O precious ones, blue lightning is not to be tampered with. Blue lightning is the holy will of God. And if you expect to find salvation, you must become that lightning—you must invoke it; you must will it; you must hear it crackle; and you must understand that wherever you go—before you, behind you, to your right and left, above, beneath, and in the center of your very Heart Flame—there blue lightning fire goes with you. For you are living in a time of great density, when there is a requirement to shatter and consume! shatter and consume! shatter and consume the astral muck and debris through which you must daily walk and breathe and move.

I say, my legions are ready and stand with you; and they will not be moved! They will not be moved! They will not be moved until the hour of your victory, until the hour of the victory of the planetary home! I say, then, call to them wherever you go and do not forget that you require blue lightning to survive in this world this day; for without it your Light will be smothered. And when you have cleared the road with blue lightning, then let flow the holy fires of freedom! Let them flow! Let them flow! Let them flow by the power of Hercules, by the power of Arcturus!

For we have made a pact this day; and we have sworn before the altar of Almighty God eternal, eternal, and I say eternal hostility against every form of tyranny that besets the minds of men. Wherever the blue lightning is invoked, Arcturus has pledged to follow it with violet flame; and wherever the violet flame is invoked, I have pledged to follow it with blue lightning. And so a braiding action of the first and the seventh rays of Alpha and Omega shall take place until the earth is truly the Lord's and the fullness thereof!...

Precious hearts of Light, there are millions and millions and millions of Cosmic Beings and hosts of Light who are determined that this planet shall manifest the Golden Age and ascend victorious. Therefore fear not, for the hosts of Light upon the hillsides are far greater than all the enemies and mights and armies of the world, which have no power against the Lord's hosts. Therefore I say unto you: Invoke them! Invoke them without ceasing! **For upon your invocation depends the salvation of this planet!**

We are here. We cannot enter in unless you invoke. Therefore invoke! Invoke and accept and expect the indomitable, invincible Christ-victory of this planetary home! The time has come for fulfillment. It is done! I, Hercules, have spoken!

Pearls of Wisdom®

Vol. XIV No. 42	*El Morya*	*October 17, 1971*

The Need for Creative Energy Rightly Used

Hearts Waiting in Hope for the Appearance of His Will:

The pillar of hope keeps alive, encourages dynamism, opes the mind, and lends constancy to the spirit!

It is not enough to aspire: the energy drains must be plugged. An act of will invokes the Heart of God. Man's supply of gettingness is proportionate to his givingness. The banner of our Light given so freely to all is most costly. The expansive format we advocate is one of spiritual formlessness.

Those lacking the constancy of the tall pines which remain fixed for generations, those who, like potted plants, prize their mobility and above all their freedom to prescribe their own form, may one day find that the earth itself will deny them.

Those who abide under the shadow of the wing[1] perceive that idle chatter murders spirits.[2] We need lovers of selflessness. We have spoken of the raising of the banner of the Lord as though it were a fait accompli. Circumstances that tether man to reason can, when rightly directed, assist the soul in avoiding the senseless delays of innumerable squabbles.

Hearken well! Hearken well! Hearken well! Those who listen may learn; but the inner ear of the spirit attuned to Deity extracts the most virtuous juice. The removal of tarnish need not be deplored; for the fire of polish, by virtue of its chastisement of the molecular structure, reveals the presence of a certain free energy. Wise is the individual who exchanges discontent for content as he exchanges content for discontent.

The universe is a place of opposites, and unfortunately man provides his own best opposition. To cry, "Stop, thief!" when one is filching one's own energy is a mistake. Instead, explore the best possibilities; perceive the nature of energy and its right use. We cannot condone its abuse, for the energy of the world is the Lord's.[3] Those who tie into it often say, "It is our own act; it is our own choice; we do as we will." Let them understand responsibility. So by judgment shall men grow—not by judgment of others, but by judgment of themselves.

Morya warns: The day of reckoning is at hand. Those who know not shall be judged with those who know. And who shall say that either ignorance or knowledge shall provide excuse before the Lords of Karma? Judgment cometh swiftly, and the casting of aspersions is the work of the dark ones. The purposes of Life are glowing ones. Shining like the sun, they dazzle the eye and make us to cry, "Surprise! Surprise!—Affinitize!" Men seek for Heaven and then do not recognize it when it appears before them.

While God provides a continuous loop of consciousness, the immature seek the loophole of escape. Both responsibility to Life and moral law provide the graceful curbing of illicit desire. "What a pity," some remonstrate, "that the way to the Master's abode is so well hidden!" Let them perceive mercy in this fact. Those who come to us are not only learners and sojourners in living Truth: they are also future arhats.

Those content with either discontent or contentment may remain attached to mutiny as though they were attached to mucilage. Some expect us to pry them off when our very own direction, clearly set before them, advocates to all: Seek! and thou shalt find.[4] It is silly that the blind prefer an unkind wind which blows no good to anyone. First let us open men's eyes; let us reveal the panorama of perception as our initial act of liberation. And then love of Truth will break old and useless ties without so much as the flicker of an eyelid.

All the king's horses and all the king's men may not be able to put things together again,[5] but certainly the only reason for this is that mankind consciously wills it so. The ritual of breaking up old human patterns, rightly undertaken by the heart bound with morality and sprinkled well with the oil of spirituality, abounds in cosmic potential.

It appears that there exists in the consciousness of man a very sooty ordination—what they have termed an ordination to evil. We abhor witchcraft, variance, and all practices of belittlement of the will of God. Long ago the binding of our hearts to Him was accomplished. We have never wished to cut these bonds, only to tie them tighter.

The nuisances of the day are signs of the perpetuation of old and recalcitrant evils which have never been helpful to man, which have never assisted him, and which never can. In the midst of darkness, let the Great Light shine!

Be satisfied to invoke Light! Wherever there is darkness, invoke Light! Be unsatisfied with your development, for the greatest source of encouragement is dissatisfaction. It is not enough to rest upon one's laurels. The past is indeed prologue;[6] and no greater devouring of man's energies can be made than to allow the little egos to affirm, "This we have accomplished."

God's work will remain an unfinished symphony. The continual proddings of His Spirit are contrived by deliberate action and intent to spur in man the impetus of right direction. Of necessity, these will also provide him with the understanding of how psychic energies are siphoned from the masses by the dark ones; how they are restructured, restyled, requalified, and sent forth to produce breeches in the wall of Spirit that, like holes in cheese, add nothing to the infinite plan.

Indomitability is forged. Invocation made to God as an act of free will secures the best possibilities. Even those who doubt may prove the Law by a simple act of childlike faith. Great harms accrue from corrosion of the spirit by denial of the Christ. Always remember, faith begets faith; love begets love. Lesser qualities also produce after their kind.

Man's free will is assured in the perpetuation of the opportunity of creative action in all that he does. The responsibility is his. Hence the shortening of responsibility by the shortening of the lifespan of mankind was a decision of greatest virtue made by The Karmic Board millenniums ago. Albeit we could cut it still further, nothing good would be achieved by so doing. For man's current lifespan, even when lived to its fullest, provides but meager opportunity for soul progress to those who are caught in the nets of darkness. Notwithstanding, those who accept the faith in their own divine Reality can, if they will, enter into newness of Life.

Inflexibility in virtue is the requirement of the hour; compromise is, of all acts, most detestable to us. Thus the word went forth, "Thou art neither hot nor cold; therefore, I will spew thee out of my mouth."[7] The chastening rod of mind and spirit should be recognized as a needed instrument for the flagellation of the merciless aspects of self.

Only through a proper understanding of self-love can turmoil be ended. How many other names they have called it! While man surfeits, the dear earth perishes in purpose. We admire the valor of those who have espoused the Flame and then kept it. How valorous the pathway of Truth; how vainglorious the pathway of self-indulgence!

The battle lines are being drawn. The recruits rally to the flag of purpose. The higher way, revealed and revealing, becomes a continuous pathway of hope. The bonds of love, like flowers breaking forth round the feet of humanity, free men from ancient and degrading records. Let all be willing to forsake those acts of condemnation that even in a child at play spoil the mudpie and soil the garments.

By the proper use of man's creative faculties, the new age shall be born; for the weak shall grow weaker and the strong stronger. To him that hath shall more be given; to him that hath not shall be taken away even that which he hath.[8] Scarcely understood, this fiat of the Law continues to act. Upon the threshing floor of God, the best grains are sorted out; the husks are removed by self-rejection.

Morya speaks: There is no excuse for the pointing finger of accusation. Those who truly know will praise the stalwart hearts. They will also praise the Light within themselves and adore the best possibilities. With God all things are possible.[9]

In Heaven's name, are the days of infamy passed? Have the fruits of darkness all perished? Or does the world still white imperfection? If any require hope and mercy, then may not all require it? Life is opportunity for all.

The highest adventure is the adventure of new purpose. Those who squander the hours in lost regrets accomplish little. Those whose high resolve summons strength for the betterness of perfection understand the need to forget. What a pity that men remember evils— or imagine them—when the cornucopia that showers bounty hangs just overhead. They prefer a lawn strewn with bludgeons.

We say, "Let there be Light!" The tarnished ages are monuments to man's nonfructification of good. The fruit of the Tree of Life standing in the center of the Garden remains to be picked.

In salutory memory of the world's need for creative energy rightly used, I remain

El Morya

1. Pss. 91:4. 2. Matt. 5:37; Matt. 12:36. 3. Pss. 24:1. 4. Matt. 7:7. 5. Charles Perrault, Tales From Mother Goose, "Humpty Dumpty Sat on a Wall." 6. William Shakespeare, The Tempest, act 2, sc. 1. 7. Rev. 3:16. 8. Matt. 13:12. 9. Matt. 19:26.

Pearls of Wisdom®

Vol. XIV No. 43 　　　　　　　*Mary* 　　　　　　　*October 24, 1971*

"Before They Call, I Will Answer"

To Those Attending the Rebirth of the Christ in Human Hearts:

How true it is that if men had the correct understanding of universal purpose, they could never commit those acts or align themselves with those activities which slaughter righteousness and the unfoldment of universal love. The bane of ignorance cloaks their hearts' rays, and in consort with the carnal mind they have again and again opaqued the Light of divine wisdom and love.

The little gems I bring are for those whose every thought reaches out to the implementation of an improved world situation, to an evolvement of self, and to cooperation with the hand of God moving even midst ordinary human affairs.

It has been rightly said that nothing happens by chance, and so the word "chance," in its current usage, has become another name for the outworking of karma and the fulfillment of the law of universal desire. That individuals can and do influence the manifestation of cosmic law in human affairs is a foregone conclusion—Justice is nowhere more blind than in the courts of men. If the free will of man were not the key factor in the bringing-in of the kingdom, the triumph of universal love would have been accomplished in ages long past. But who can deny that Virtue has done her perfect work in all ages, most especially in the lives of those who have held to the faith in the goodness of God and in their own ability to serve Him in the humblest task allotted to them?

Certain features of cosmic law go unrecognized by humanity. One that is often overlooked is the divine answer to humanity's calls that is always forthcoming from God. Yet He has said, "Before they call, I will answer."[1] Because his ignorance or his ignoring of the Law is no excuse, the man of faith cannot rightly persist in allowing elements of doubt in the Creator's word to color his mind and emotions without paying the penalty of being cut off from the answers to his calls. For doubt is the wall that man erects between himself and his God; and it is a self-imposed penalty that only he can remove through corrective measures. It is never the desire of the personal God to place the weight of responsibility for wrong action upon a recalcitrant generation; rather it is the inexorable law of Cosmos, which governs the return of energy misqualified by erroneous thought and feeling to those who send it forth, that determines the burden man shall bear for past mistakes.

I wish to convey the immense yet simple knowledge that every gift of God given to man in answer to prayer must either be kept, used, or dissipated. It is always hoped by those among the heavenly host through whose hands the gift is bestowed that if it is kept and then used, it will be for the constructive good of the individual or of another part of Life.

Unfortunately, those who dissipate the divine gifts of mercy and grace, either through misqualification of the God-ordained intent or by spending the Light upon paltry human desires, will one day find that they are without the answers to their prayers. For one day the karmic hammer will surely fall, and they will have dissipated God's energies for the last time. And that which has been faithfully given them from on high—in recognition of the divine spark within and as opportunity to renew their vows through the many avenues of service to Life—will be withheld. As James said, "Ye ask, and receive not, because ye ask amiss, that ye may consume it upon your lusts."[2]

What a pity it is that individuals regard us as dead! Because we live and move and have our being in God,[3] we are cognizant each moment of every human thought and feeling; therefore, we are vitally aware of the universal need of humanity to hold fast to the Life triumphant and immortal, the Life that pulsates as the Threefold Flame within and holds the solution to every problem. Those who believe that "God is dead," simply because their own concepts of Him are lifeless, find no difficulty in applying the same concepts to the Ascended Hosts of Light, thereby relegating us to the realm of the dead. Those who deny our existence would do well to reexamine their concepts of God, whose Life necessarily includes our own.

Conversely, those who understand and recognize the immortality of the cosmic gifts God gives from His Heart to those whose every thought is directed toward Him have no difficulty in accepting either His Reality or the living Presence of His servant sons and daughters both in heaven and on earth. Their blessed faith starts a circuit of Light that moves from hearts kindled with gratitude to the Heart of God, carrying more of His energy on the return current. These are full of joy as they see cosmic mutations taking place within themselves—a metamorphosis of the soul brought about through the ritual of divine love.

Those who seek us will realize almost from the beginning of their search, and then again when the moment of truly knowing us comes, that our hearts are full of love for embodied humanity and that our only desire is to create through proper education a spiritual uplift in the human consciousness that will enable mankind to avoid both the shedding of tears for human failures and their remorse for divine ones. The fact that individuals have turned the pathway of selflessness into the pathway of selfishness is due not alone to their lack of knowledge but to their great lack of conclusive faith in the ultimate goodness of God.

Born out of His Heart's desire for the salvation of the current age, the continual motions of divine love move throughout the universe, engendering new hope for the ages. Thus the wonder of His love is measured out of the very heart-steps of God Himself. And there is a focus, a place prepared within each one's heart, where He shall abide forever if man wills it so. All that man is and does is by the grace of God; therefore, in the outworkings of divine grace in man, those spiritual works of which his faith is but a symbol do appear. This substance of things hoped for, this evidence of things not seen,[4] can also be kept by man as a divine gift. Those who desire to increase their faith may call for an intensification of the measure of grace given unto them and see the miracle of immortal Life as it unfolds before them the magnificent faith of Cosmos in its own fiery destiny.

Expectancy is a much needed virtue, blessed hearts of love; and this cannot be the expectancy of personal fulfillment through another, but the expectant hope that waiteth on the Lord day and night.[5] And when the triumph of an individual's faith brings him at last out of the smoke of doubt and self-delusion into the fire of cosmic purpose, how very wonderful is the counsel of God to each one concerning his life that is so precious.

Each life, like a locket around the neck of the living God, is the fulfillment of a wish He made as He fashioned the soul, a wish for its creative expression and for the best gifts to adorn the Christ aborning in each one of His children. Won't you, then, O humanity, for all time let go of the awful struggle in which you have engaged your energies? For in your present state of limited Self-awareness, instead of fulfilling the divine plan, you fulfill only the karmic recompense of the law of return; and by reason of your own evil thoughts about one another— often based on mere surmise—you remain bound to the karmic wheel that keeps turning, ultimately bringing to your doorstep the malice which, if unchecked today, can destroy the very fabric of your souls tomorrow.

Will you, then, out of a heart akin to God's own Heart, learn to be patient with individuals at various levels of development? Do not expect too much of those who, far down the ladder of life, leap, childlike, toward what may seem to you only a bauble or a trinket. One day they will come to understand infinite values as you do, and then the joy bells will ring out as the angels of heaven rejoice in the overcoming of undesirable conditions by an individual or a segment of humanity.

Oh, what a pity it is that men do not understand the need to express patience toward other parts of Life! When they are on the receiving end of this and other gifts of God, they hold out expectant hands. How necessary it is that men learn not only to receive the mercy of God but also to extend it graciously to others.

Let us, then, build a tower of Light and hope in the world that shall shift man's interests and intents from the mundane to the heavenly and, drawing him from the murky darkness of failures and follies, polarize his consciousness to the goal of rebirth in Christ. Thus he moves toward the gentle Christ-attainment that thunders forth the peal of universal purpose made available to all because it has been realized by one.

With these thoughts from my heart, I remain devotedly

Your Spiritual Mother,

Mary

1. Isa. 65:24. 2. James 4:3. 3. Acts 17:28. 4. Heb. 11:1. 5. Lam. 3:26.

Pearls of Wisdom®

Vol. XIV No. 44   Pallas Athena   October 31, 1971

"Behold, I Stand at the Door and Knock"

To All Lovers of Progressive Truth:

The desire of the soul for those great personal and cosmic triumphs which can and do rise in the domain of the individual who is successful in his search for self-mastery is indicative of the inherent striving for perfection with which the Lord has endowed His creation. Jesus voiced this mandate of being, this raison d'être, when he said, "Be ye therefore perfect, even as your Father which is in heaven is perfect."[1]

Nevertheless, there are times in the quest when men grow weary, when they are detoured, when even the Light seems but shadow colored by the environmental factors of the human mind or the infiltration of discouragement. Take hope! The closer men approach the goal of Christ-victory, the more frequently they are assailed by the forces of antichrist. The fact that they encounter opposition does not mean that they have taken a backward step. On the contrary, in most cases it indicates that they have come to the place in their spiritual development where they are recognized as advocates of Truth by those moving on astral levels who have espoused the cause of darkness.

Let no one despair because of the apparent intensification of evil upon the planet. Rather, let all understand that this is to be expected from the hordes of darkness—those who have not taken advantage of their opportunity to walk through the doorway that leads to their divine estate. Having no Life in them, they vainly beat the air,[2] seeking to draw attention to themselves or to extract some form of personal favor by attacking the faithful followers of God.

Beloved hearts of Light, remember the words of the Great Master concerning the antics of the rebellious ones "Ye entered not in yourselves, and them that were entering in ye hindered."[3] Thus they expend their dying breath in defiance of the Light to which they may never again have direct access and in which they may finally be extinguished, though the process require centuries or even millenniums.

We who view time and space in a different framework and from another perspective than your own, understand that the disintegration of the consciousness that is wed to evil, or the energy veil, requires a certain amount of time, as you would say, or a predetermined number of cycles, as we would say. We realize how difficult it is for some among humanity to penetrate these mysteries. Rest assured that the outworkings of cosmic law are both precise and just.

For the benefit of the true follower of God, let me say that the powers of Light on the planetary body are not only winning, but they are also gaining footholds in the most unexpected places. Public acclaim for the invisible God is being expressed in many quarters and in many ways; yet we also note that in some areas what is still given the greatest accent in life is its temporal manifestations and the debris of the collective subconscious that rises to the surface for transmutation.

Fear not! The Light is being invoked in countless hearts, and many are turning to the Christ even today. The conflicts between those of this and that religious conviction will continue. This is natural in the search for Truth and ought not to be cause for concern. Remember, O hearts of Light, many of today's dogmatists who are dogmatic about their own particular version of Truth will be numbered among the students of Ascended Master law when they once come to understand for themselves just what Truth really is. We deal with no small matter here; for the search for Truth has been going on for centuries, even before Pilate asked, "What is Truth?"[4]

Truth is often difficult for men to comprehend in their initial contact with its tenets. This is because of the configuration of preconceived ideas, human opinions, and interpretations of scripture within their minds, which do stand as shadows in the doorway of their illumination. I do not say that these convictions ought to be disregarded, but I do say that they ought not to be regarded as absolute. For God Himself has placed within the human psyche an especial factor of recognition referred to by the Good Shepherd when he said, "My sheep know my voice."[5] It is at all times difficult for mankind to separate the voices crying in the wilderness,[6] to decide for themselves just what is really the Voice of God and what is the voice of opinion—even their own.

Those who truly wish to separate the sheep from the goats[7] within their consciousness, and Truth from error abroad in the world where many voices cry, "This is the way," must first understand that a man can be his own worst enemy simply because he does not recognize the potential of his own Divinity, the potential for Christ-mastery which God has given to every son and daughter. In reality, the knowledge of the kingdom of God and of divine Truth is basic to life and can be simply understood. However, those who advance upon the Path do not find it difficult to enter into the greater complexities of the Mind of God.

Yes, Light exists and darkness exists. Some men have tried to simplify this concept by saying that darkness is an absence of Light, whereas others have equated darkness with evil, seeing it as a virulent force that seeks to overthrow the Light. There are elements of truth in both statements. For example, in the mind and being of man, the vacuum that is referred to as darkness, or a lack of Light, is not a positive force; it is not a negative force; it is not even a misappropriated force; it is simply an absence of the realization of Light's potential.

On the other hand, that darkness which results from the misqualification of Light, from its conversion into darkness, is of another type, which can be categorized as a negative force or a positive evil. That there are various types of darkness was clearly pointed out by the Master Jesus in his exclamation "If therefore the Light that is in thee be darkness, how great is that darkness!"[8] This may be read as a question by the earnest disciple: How great is the intensity of the darkness in me? Is it a misqualification of Light, an energy veil, or is it an absence of Light, a lost opportunity? How great an impediment is this darkness to my understanding of Truth?

Let all understand clearly, then, that there is no conflict in the divine and that all conflict exists at human levels. Those who place their hand in God's do not need to speculate—they trust and they perceive. Moreover, their perceptions are guided by their own realization of the divine potential. But as long as they are convinced that they cannot understand great cosmic truths, then so long will they fail to apprehend them.

Conversely, as their faith in God mounts and they allow the hand of Heaven to direct their lives in service, greater and greater truths will be revealed. Quite naturally, those to whom these truths have not been revealed will cry, "Heresy!" Yet for nonbelievers as well as believers, the admonishment remains: "Judge not, that ye be not judged!"[9] Therefore, men should not cry, "Heresy!" without understanding some of the points of the Great Law that are revealed to those advancing in the footsteps of Truth upon the Path.

In matters of progressive revelation God continues to speak to man today, breaking the bread of the living Word. If men are bound to the roots of error or even of stultifying dogma, refusing to build upon those fundamental precepts taught them as children, then they must remain children until they choose to become otherwise. As Saint Paul said: "Every one that useth milk is unskilful in the word of righteousness: for he is a babe. But strong meat belongeth to them that are of full age, even those who by reason of use have their senses exercised to discern both good and evil."[10]

Thus, let men understand Truth as the flower of the Christ, the Rose of Sharon unfolding its petals within the heart and mind—as a spiral of understanding that rises in the being and consciousness of man. Let them also pray for guidance, that they may receive initiation into those steps of the Law which reveal Christ as the ever widening circle of the Mind of God.

It is obvious to the careful observer that mankind in this age have tampered with the workings of natural law and that in their analytical yet highly subjective view of life they have distorted many facts and figures to their own advantage. Why do more men not suppose that man has also tampered with historical fact as well as doctrine well established in centuries past? Nevertheless, there is a place where the record remains inviolate. God has written the sacred scriptures within the being of man, [11] but the letter that killeth [12] has been tampered with both in the past and in the present; therefore, humanity have again and again been misled into areas of discrepancy.

Be open to the Law as it is recorded in the archives of men; but guard zealously the sanctity of the source, the great fountain of Truth that is within. To discern the body of the Lord, [13] to discern the body of corporate Truth as revealed from on high through the Ascended Masters' consciousness, is a gift of great price. It should be sought after and cherished.

Yet men can find within themselves the white stone [14] that reveals to the one who touches it the eternal Truth even as it purifies his consciousness. For then, when the consciousness becomes whited unto perfection, it is also able to behold upon the rock of God's perfect order the universe as He intended it to be. Man then sees it as a place where beauty and the serenity as well as the stamina of purpose become adjuncts to the mighty outpouring of divine Truth which is an afflatus of the Holy Spirit that can never be gainsaid. And Truth, as revelation both past and future, will bring comfort to mind and heart, enabling the body of God upon earth today to rise to meet the exigencies of the hour and to call a halt to the trampling underfoot of the children of the Light by the powers of darkness.

Light shall increase upon the planetary body as men open the heart and mind to the freshness of the will of God and the fresh winds of the Holy Spirit. And the Flame shall burn ever more brightly, not in the dungeons men create within, but in the open window and open door. For He has said, "Behold, I stand at the door, and knock: if any man hear my voice, and open the door, I will come in to him, and will sup with him, and he with me." [15]

Let men, then, open their being and consciousness to the Light and to the Truth being brought forth through progressive revelation. Thus shall a new order of the ages be founded, one that is not based upon human vanity, but upon the original desire and purposes of God, who fashioned man in His own image and likeness. [16]

Devotedly, I AM your sister of Light,

Pallas Athena

---

1. Matt. 5:48. 2. I Cor. 9:26. 3. Luke 11:52. 4. John 18:38. 5. John 10:4. 6. Matt. 3:3. 7. Matt. 25:32. 8. Matt. 6:23. 9. Matt. 7:1. 10. Heb. 5:13-14. 11. Jer. 31:33. 12. II Cor. 3:6. 13. I Cor. 11:29. 14. Rev. 2:17. 15. Rev. 3:20. 16. Gen. 1:27.

Pearls of Wisdom®

| Vol. XIV No. 45 | Paul the Venetian | November 7, 1971 |

The Dangers of Astral Allurement

To Those Who Would Be Pure in Heart:

A sense of beauty assists the soul in relating to the Divinity that originally created all substance and form. Man must learn to separate the darkness from the Light and to eliminate the abortions in nature that occur because of mankind's dual consciousness and their failure to maintain contact with the Divine Presence.

Pain in the world order is unnatural. It is a manifestation of inharmony within mankind's four-dimensional consciousness. When the error is corrected—the error of an ugly arrangement of the thought and feeling patterns of the race—the beauty and perfection of the Presence begin to shine forth in nature as well as in man.

O yes, we realize full well the difficulty men experience in holding fast to patterns of perfection in the midst of a synthetic environment where images of imperfection are constantly being projected upon the screen of the mind. Remember, hearts of Light, it is the darkness that is without that so many gaze upon—the darkness of imperfection which the multitudes do not distinguish from the deep and beautiful Light of the abiding Presence of Perfection within the being of man. This is the Light of the eternal Christos to which all must hold—if they value their liberty—regardless of appearances that would defile and dethrone the Perfect Image. As the rearrangement of concepts and precepts occurs within the mind and heart according to the laws of perfection, men are able to eliminate much pain and anguish, both mental and physical, from their lives.

Men and women should understand how to cope with the energies of the electronic belt, the individual as well as the collective subconscious. They should realize that not only their own thoughts and feelings but also the sum total of the thoughts and feelings of the world body, which may be termed the weltschmerz, have a direct bearing upon their actions and attitudes. The key to that order and beauty which are not universally enshrined in the world, then, is to be found in the perpetual joy of returning to the miracle of the Divine Image that God holds for every manifestation of Himself. For if it is the sense of struggle that makes the struggle, as Saint Germain so often says, then it is the casting-aside of undesirable thoughts and feelings and the cleaving to beautiful images and ideas that effects the magnificent transformation which all mankind require.

It is necessary in this connection that I give a solemn warning to the students concerning the dangers of astral allurement. I refer to the magnetism of those states of consciousness which are below the level of the Christ Mind and which therefore engage the energies below the heart and involve man's perceptions in psychic distortions. Many spiritual seekers are detoured from the Path by the glamor of strange phenomena and the probing of that plane of consciousness just beyond the physical, known as the astral realm.

One of the great attractions in the use of hallucinogenic drugs is that they facilitate contact with the astral and induce those abnormal experiences in the world of sense thralldom which enamor the mind. Such diversions into euphoria which are simulated through drugs, although endless in variation, are not necessarily divine simply because they originate beyond the realm of physical manifestation. Usually they are psychic in nature, that is, they come from the level of the emotions and their mass misqualification by mankind. Thus these turbulent energies, with their moving kaleidoscope of aberrations, key a frequency response that is closer to the vibration of demons than it is to that of angels.

It would be well for the aspiring student to realize the great value of keeping watch upon his thoughts and feelings. For thereby he learns the requirements of self-mastery and how to prevent much that is unwholesome and troublesome from later springing up in his world. By guarding the quality of his consciousness and becoming the master of his household, the individual has no need for drugs to elevate the mind and feelings; instead, he learns to contact the Christ directly on all planes, hence to develop a standard whereby he is able to anticipate in an a priori manner those cultural trends which are foreign to the divine ideal. He also learns to employ the preventative cure of entertaining beneficent concepts and at the same time to avoid psychological pitfalls that might one day prevent the fulfillment of his highest aspirations.

When the student leaves behind the baubles and trinkets of the astral, he soon discovers the beautiful miracle of lovely, godlike thought forms waiting to be lowered from the highest planes into the world of form. Although there are times when man's concepts of God fall far short of the mark, manifesting as they do in the realm of time and space and in the unperfected consciousness, they can and frequently do become the magnet that guides man up the stairway of attainment into the perception and precipitation of genuine beauty.

Life as it is currently being lived upon earth is full of masks and deceits, but this need not continue. After all, beloved ones, what you really are is what endures. If you make yourself into a receiving station for the beauty God is sending forth every day into the world, you become spiritually coordinated with Hierarchy, with the angelic hosts, and with the Brotherhood of Light. If you do not avail yourselves of the opportunity to become outposts for the beauty of the Divine Image, well, then, O hearts of Light, you have no one to blame but yourself for your failure to be the beautiful god of your own universe that the living God wants you to be![1]

You see, it was God's intent, when He created man in His own image and likeness,[2] that this image and likeness of Himself should manifest everywhere upon the planetary body. Without a doubt the average person, who has not the understanding of Truth, blinded to his spiritual opportunity by self-concerns, may find even his worldly aspirations swallowed up by his environment; and we have seen cases where ten thousand years of progress have been buried beneath a lump of clay, simply because the individual could not surmount a host of environmental problems that stifled both his talent and his initiative. Nevertheless, the Lord's intent remains as the goal of Life for every man.

Let us clear the way, then, for all who would run with the Lord! Let us clear the way for an expansion of individual identity within the Godhead!

Blessed ones, the concentric rings of the Causal Body are a marvel to behold. The soft shadings of pastel hue delicately outlining the rainbow rays of God are charged with the allure and vibrancy of genuine living. Truly, the Light of the Christ is a fountain of electronic energy, cascading with expansion and the fire of movement. And this, in all of its wonder and opportunity, God showers upon man as the prize for his victorious overcoming in the world of form and his abandonment of astral decoys bobbing upon the murky waters of the psychic underworld.

The need for the reeducation of man's vision that he might perceive beauty, and then honor and adore it for its affinitizing power, is very great in an age when all that is sacred is being torn down by the forces of antichrist. The examinations by the Lords of Karma and the Hierarchy which men frequently undergo, although they know it not, are but an attempt by the spiritual preceptors of the planet to raise the spiritual standard of the race. They would kindle in all people that

newness of Life and appreciation of beauty and Truth which will lead
them from darkness unto Light, from shadow and shame to order and
perfection; for they know that once mankind see the Light, their souls
will no longer be satisfied[3] with any lesser manifestation.

The comedies and tragedies of the past, with their residue of
opaquing substance, the maya of maudlin memories, will continue to
oppress the seeker on the Path; but once the man of God realizes
within himself that he can be free because he is freeborn, he need no
longer be bound—he is no longer bound.

O beloved chelas, disciples of the living God, followers of the
Christ, whatever your status—whether advanced disciple or
beginner—remember the vast potential of Cosmos as it pertains to the
marvelous unfoldment of the Divine Self within you! Remember the
all-power of Divinity to expand within your consciousness and to
increase, heartbeat by heartbeat, the realization of your Christ-
potential through the sense of beauty.

> May God provide a vision,
>   an all-seeing eye,
> That like a globe of fire
>   elevates and ennobles the soul
> Until at last each one's
>   own passion for freedom
> Reaches out to convey to others
>   the strength of Beauty's shining.

Devotedly, I AM

Paul the Venetian

1. John 10:34. 2. Gen. 1:27. 3. Pss. 17:15.

Pearls of Wisdom®

| Vol. XIV No. 46 | Saint Germain | November 14, 1971 |

Gratitude, the Catalyst of Good Fortune

O Thankful Hearts!

Gratitude as the catalyst of good fortune must not be overlooked by those seeking abundance in their lives, whereas ingratitude rooted in hardness of heart must be considered the enemy of joy, happiness, and the flow of the divine energy from God to man. Truly it is that openness of spirit aptly described in the phrase "leaping and praising God"[1] which frees all men on the planetary body from harms and hatreds and creates a spirit of regeneration that animates the flame of thanksgiving throughout the pageant of the year.

In memory of the men and women the world around who throughout the ages have loved liberty more than life, it is my desire to create in the consciousness of each disciple of progressive Truth in this day and age the same victorious sense of gratitude these pilgrims of the Spirit once had and fortunately, I might add, have retained to the present moment.

The continuity of life, when the quality thereof is ascendant, provides for the gradual magnification of the beautiful purpose envisioned in the eye of God when He first created man in His own image and likeness.[2] It is truly a chastisement of the spirit to devote one's energies to human foibles, to the sustaining of the frustration of human hurts and human irks. In God's name, I say, cut yourself and your loved ones free from your mortal opinions, whatever their source, and observe how your mind becomes unfettered, mounting into the blue to capture the thoughts of God!

There is a direct connection between what men do unto others and what others do unto them;[3] therefore, you have no one to blame but yourself if you allow others to bind you with their opinions and their sympathies. We have seen in the karmic records of many that when they took decisive measures to reverse the trends produced by unwholesome influences, beauty replaced the ashes that had been manifesting in their lives.

All transmutation, beloved hearts, and all balancing of the Law is the fulfillment of the divine edict "Whom the Lord loveth—truly loveth—He chasteneth."[4] The scourging of every son whom He receives is solely for the radiant perfectionment of the individual through the practical understanding of the eternal law "With what measure ye mete, it shall be measured to you again."[5] These words of the Master Jesus should be bound upon the heart and mind of modern disciples; for in the strange miasma of psychic probings and encounter groups and in the weavings of psychological dramas requiring the simultaneous absorption of unrelated data through the use of multi-media, youth and age are reinvolving themselves in the sludge of centuries and in the taffy pull of human deceit.

To be free, truly free, is to let the heart soar like a bird. The sky is one's abode, yet one can swoop down on pinions of Light to raise others in their moments of trial. The heavens need not be sought as a haven of aloofness, but as a dwelling place for those who would survey the world need, descend to lend a helping hand, and then ascend once again to bask in the golden sun of Christed illumination.

Men often lament unfortunate episodes of the historical past. They have not plotted on a graph the rise and fall of mankind's movements toward the Light. They have not taken into account the overall upward trend; nor have they reckoned with one factor of human experience—that the greatest lessons are sometimes learned from the greatest mistakes. Some believe that spiritually speaking the human race dwells in greater darkness today than it has in the past. While I do not believe this to be altogether true, I am certain that conditions in the world order have created an atmosphere of greater tension and temptation than at any other time in modern history. Thus, wherever the communication of evil is increased upon the planetary body, unless equal time is given to training in cosmic law and spiritual admonishment, goading man toward the recognition of perfection as a legitimate goal, he is bound to suffer from the epidemic of human folly that is sweeping the globe via the media.

However, I do not believe that it is necessary to classify mankind today as the purveyors of a subterranean culture. The current age can be one of great enlightenment, and in many areas it truly is; for we see in the achievements of modern technology the potential for communicating the progressive teachings of the Masters and revelations in natural as well as spiritual science. Therefore, we would challenge the authority of those entrenched human traditions which carry with them the aura of "dead men's bones,"[6] of untransmuted records, and prevent the brotherly love of the cosmic Hierarchy from flowing to an expectant humanity, developing souls in godliness and in the recognition of things divine right in the midst of their mundane affairs.

A spiritual renaissance of true culture is imminent; and if it does not come to pass, it will be solely the result of mankind's attention to the banal and darkening concepts that have far too long held sway in the world of form. It is out of our desire to be of service to humanity in the cultivation of the Christ Flame that we seek to enlighten men concerning the integration of their consciousness with social patterns both good and bad and to show them how civilization has at times held them back spiritually even while it has propelled them forward materially.

The festive board of heaven offers an abundant fare for man's spiritual development; but man can partake of this cornucopia of fruit gathered from the Tree of Life only as he consumes his lusts, surrenders his attachments to human frolic and folly, and begins the serious business of eating the living Word of God. I have called the Word of God *living* because the Word of God is the Source, the mighty Fount from whence all Life did spring, and because it is the nature of the Word, conveying as it does the animating principle of Life, to bestow upon man the gifts of God born out of His Life-giving Spirit. When men accept the precepts of the Christ into the sacred cloisters of their lives, activating them in reverent thoughts and deeds, these precepts become once again the bread of the living Word, multiplied through the alchemy of service.

Yes, Thanksgiving 1971 should abound with joy and peace! It should echo through the chambers of men's hearts as the sound of gratitude, the praise that draws forth from God new hope both to the world and to the individual. Gratitude indeed! Gratitude as a mighty torrent of love that opens the floodgates of the heart, melts the frozen waters of the mind, and moves along the higher cadences of mankind's tender and compassionate feelings toward one another. Gratitude in action opens the way for the beautiful sense of God in action that can and ought to permeate the balance of the year as a circling bond of faith, hope, and charity that knows that the darkness will not win because the Light will.

The Christ beholds the raising of mankind's consciousness through the leaven of trust which God has placed within the soul. The Lord has vested man with a swaddling garment of pure Light and grace. Let us give thanks to God this day for all of His manifold blessings, and let us free a world enslaved by the bondages of former years. Let us see what a glorious splash we can make as the stone of the Law is thrown with greater force into the world pond!

For your victory and the victory of all mankind,

I remain

Saint Germain

1. Acts 3:8. 2. Gen. 1:26. 3. Matt. 7:12. 4. Heb. 12:6. 5. Matt. 7:2. 6. Matt. 23:27.

THE RADIANT WORD

Excerpt from a Dictation by Beloved Archangel Michael
The Watch of the Angels 1971, given at the
Retreat of the Resurrection Spiral, October 24, 1971

Hail, O mankind! I AM Michael, Prince of the Archangels! And I come to speak to you this day of The Watch of the Angels. I come to speak to you of the watch God has instituted because of mankind's vanity and because of mankind's failure to recognize the power of the infinite and living God. I tell you, then, this day of the beauty and perfection of inner spheres of Light.

From inner levels of Light and love, little children, even those sleeping in their cribs, are visited from time to time by a watch of angels, a procession of heavenly guardians that observe their goings and their comings and even midst the busy streets of life insist on bringing to mankind, even to those who are babes in Christ, the watchful attitude of loving care whereby beauty and perfection are breathed into their nostrils with each indrawing breath. Do you understand, O mankind, how this speaks of the infinite care and love of God for all men and for all women? I want you to understand now, as never before, the depth of the richness of the love and the wisdom of God in His high concerns for humanity....

Faith is indeed the substance of things hoped for, the evidence of things not seen as yet. We are concerned with the manifestation of faith as an active principle in mortal affairs, that individuals will see this loving care of God and will understand that which I am instituting this day. For I, Michael, proclaim in the name of the living God that effective this day and throughout this year and the Christmas season there shall be observed upon this planetary body a specific activity called The Watch of the Angels.

The descending Light from on high brings forth, then, upon this planet a special bouquet of cosmic concern to humanity. The angels shall watch—whether they are bidden or not by all mankind—because they have been invited by many of you. Answering, then, the call of the few, we shall bring grace unto the many and we shall enhance the quality of happiness upon earth this year. But it shall be a divine joy which shall be specifically captivated within cosmic worship and the cosmic understanding of the Grand Hall of Learning which is itself in our realm. The Grand Hall of Learning of which I speak is the school wherein mankind and the angels are trained in cosmic graces at inner levels. Whether this school shall function under this retreat or that retreat does not make any difference, for the retreats of The Great White Brotherhood are one in the purposes of the Divine.

Understand, then, how Light and love and beauty and the perception of divine qualities may become every man's forte in the days ahead. And rejoice. Let your hearts be filled with joy and enter into the joy of the Lord and the joy of the angels. Let the sense of freedom that we bring to you become a buoyancy in the mind, a buoyancy in the feelings, and a buoyancy throughout your entire being. Give glory unto the perception of God within you, the ability to perceive God, the ability to perceive the angels, the ability to recognize our reality.

Many of you from time to time, as you were children, entered into precarious physical predicaments where, if we had not watched over you, then, you see, your life could very easily have been forfeited. Some of you are familiar with the scene of the guardian angel. You understand how the children walking across the bridge perceived not the glory of their guardian angel; yet the guardian angel perceived them and was able to give them grace to pass safely over the dangers that lay ahead....

We come today in order to increase the quality of mankind's faith in our being, thus increasing their faith in themselves. For the reason that mankind do not actually recognize the quality of our being is that they do not recognize the luster of their own....

Each soul is precious unto God, and to each soul we send the gift of our faith. Let those who can accept it accept it. Let those who will reject it reject it. Let him that is holy be holy still; let him that is filthy be filthy still. For the judgment of God is in the flaming sword of the mighty Word whereby all Cosmos was created and all Cosmos exists and all men exist by reason of the faith of God, the Light that beats their hearts.

I AM Michael, and I say unto you, the time has come when by your faith the works of God must be done before the gaze of mankind, that the kingdom of God may truly speak to multitudes of hearts, to the voices of many waters, and to all who will understand that the living God leadeth man beside the still waters and restoreth his soul. Grace, peace, and joy be multiplied unto you.

Pearls of Wisdom®

Vol. XIV No. 47   The Maha Chohan   November 21, 1971

The Science of Motive

Grace Be Multiplied in Love—

The zither of the Holy Spirit moves always. One could say that the wind thereof steadfastly blows and that Life is ever a matter of attunement therewith. When men fail to realize the omnipresence of the Holy Spirit, they fail to receive its wondrous messages which carry the current mandate of God's will for the individual, for society, and for all Cosmos.

Human beings often pamper themselves too much; at the same time they fail to apprehend just when self-care is really needed. The discrimination of the Holy Spirit can and does guide men into all truth concerning the requirements of the person, of the soul, and of the hour.

How they must beware of psychic glamor, of the glitter of phenomena, and of the fashions of the human ego! The lines of the swaddling garments of God are simple. Those who are always looking to others for psychic materializations and extraordinary powers, because they look to mammon rather than to God, will never find the real power of God manifesting in their own lives.

The key to our abode is to be found not in the extraordinary, but in ordinary, day-to-day events that result in the natural exemplification of the gentle character of the Christ. Greater far than the mortal levers that move men, the virtues of the Son of God are the cosmic levers that move gods and angels. These are obtained through an acknowledged dependence upon the divine graces of the Spirit, through surrender and humility—"Not by might, nor by power, but by My Spirit," saith the Lord.[1]

One must become aware of the science of motive. Motive relates to motor and motion—to actions taken by the individual and to the underlying causes of those actions. The why of action should be examined, for one often uncovers thereby the real reason that he is moved or motivated in this or that direction. Some, upon finding out the truth, will reverse their course speedily. Others, ashamed, will try to hide even from themselves that which they discover. But all must one day reckon with the motivating factors of their lives; for at the nexus of man's decision-making faculty—where motive determines the flow of energy in thought, word, and deed—the lever of karma falls either to the right or to the left of the Law unless the blaze of Perfection be struck.

The secrets of the universe are given to those who have mastered both in overt action and in underlying motive the precepts of the Christ. They are given to those who have offered their beings to God as an altar, welcoming the transmutative fires of the Holy Spirit and yielding their devotions to the laws written in their hearts.[2]

Never have we seen that the Golden Rule, "Do unto others as you would have them do unto you,"[3] can be violated with impunity. Therefore, the principle of correspondence, whereby, for example, the virtue of kindness manifest in the inward parts of man ultimately manifests also without, ought to be fastidiously applied.

The chastisement of the Law is the fulfillment of the principle of love. As long as the individual can fool himself into believing that he is the doer, that his noble and brilliant acts are performed independently of the Creator and without connection to the tides of Life directed by the Holy Spirit, he will ultimately fail to benefit from the power of God and to harness the divine wind.

But we will not give up. As long as man can in faith hang on to Life and to that which is real—even by a thread—the striving of the Holy Spirit continues. For the great omnipresence of God is a throb of moving love that is inconceivable until experienced. The fact that a man at a given moment in his life may not have come to the realization of the Truth of the Holy Spirit and the inward Law is no proof, even to him, that the Law does not exist, that the Spirit does not move to order his universe.

There are many inner causes that make possible even the simplest acts that men take for granted. We do not ask man to be faithless; we ask him to believe, and our asking is based on the knowledge of the divine opportunity that comes to those who call the Holy Spirit into action in their lives.

Although it is true that to the pure all things are pure,[4] it is not true that all things can be pure to the impure, or holy to the unholy. Therefore, let the man who feels himself to be unholy in his thoughts and feelings recognize the centuries of unholy energies that have streamed forth from his historical past. Let him face the fact that he is not going to feel holy until that stream is purified, though he find a thousand excuses and blames for his shortcomings. Forward moving man, under the direction of the Holy Spirit, must be willing to face the Truth, and still move forward.

Does man believe that the human reed without fortification through holy endeavor can withstand the might of the Holy Spirit? It is written in the Book of Life, "No man can see God, and live,"[5] which is to say, No man can see God and continue to live in his former state; for when he comes face to face with the Light of the Presence, he must either be transformed into the divine likeness or be no more.

Because man cannot receive the power of God or stand in His Presence unless he become godlike, he should strengthen his desire to obtain the gifts most holy, gifts of virtue and grace in the knowledge of the Law. He should recognize that it is God who worketh in him both to will and to do of His good pleasure[6] and that it is the God who maketh His sun to rise on the evil and on the good and sendeth rain on the just and on the unjust[7] who alone can forgive and make whole.

Human feelings of inadequacy toward holiness are no excuse for rejecting the gifts of God's love and of Himself, which He affords equally to all. By accepting the gift in humility, knowing that He alone is the Doer and that His Spirit who dwells in man is alone worthy to receive it, the muddied stream of man's consciousness is purified and man feels holy not in or of himself, but in and of God.

Holiness can be the lot of every man regardless of what has come to pass in his life to bring about the condition of unholiness. But let all be forewarned: There is no trifling with the Creator or with His Law. Life is a beautiful gift; it is also a solemn responsibility. It is a joyous ringing in the halls of being; it is the laughter of the soul in springtime; it is the poetry of the Spirit by the fireside in winter; but it is never a callousness toward man or Nature. Life never defies the perfection of Nature or Nature's child; it never mocks those who try, or scourges those who are struggling on the brink of the hill. Life is living—not in a careless or degrading spirit, but in the joy of victory for every soul and in appreciation to the Creator for everything that He has made.

By adding daily to the universal joy and love of the Holy Spirit through the fountainhead of your own life, O mankind, you may unselfishly, as is God's way, let your Light shine before men.[8] And the whole sea of being will quiver with gladness because of thee. But if you do not choose to do so, then fortunately your energies will be circumscribed and the doors of heaven will be sealed to you, and you will find turning in upon you the muddied fountains of your own self-pity and negation, because Nature herself refuses to be contaminated therewith.

The high adventure of successfully traversing the Law of God will give man the power and ability not only to produce phenomena at the moment of greatest need, to precipitate substance, to control events and circumstances, and to master his environment, but to do it legitimately and safely. Not through the yoke of the human ego tied to other human egos are these feats accomplished as an exploitation of another part of Life, but rather in the meek and lowly attitude of the man tied to the Christ Consciousness through the yoke of humility and service. Thus gladly, freely, in holy surrender is a god born in the heart.

Not that any of us would ever lament the Second Coming of Jesus Christ as a cosmic advent to the world that would gladden myriad hearts with His appearing. But we can also accept the Second Coming of Christ to all ages, present and future, appearing in the clouds of renewing radiance that enfold the individual wed to God through the alchemy of self-mastery; for these receive Him within their hearts as the hope and Light of the world. They see not in face alone the eternal victory, but the inner joy of His mastery, the shining strength of His divine character.

The timeless, transcendent virtue of the divine appearing of God in the life of the individual is fulfilled in the manner in which John the

Baptist described, "He must increase, but I must decrease."[9] But all must understand that the power of the Christ destroys not the individual life upon the altar of being, but rather changes it from glory to glory, even as by the Spirit of the Lord.[10]

He that hath an ear, let him hear what the Holy Spirit saith:[11]

> For the time of virtue and love
> That polishes the chaliced cup
> And fills it to the brim,
> And then o'erflowing,
> With the heavenly nectar of knowing,
> The rightful dividing
> Of the Word of Truth,
> Prevents mankind en masse
> From sliding in his youth
> Into unfruitful doings
> Whose shame like a spume
> Descends to dense iniquities,
> A paling of the radiance
> Of the soul in natural state
> To fate aworsening.
> God wills it not.
> His love removes each blot,
> Carefully invokes
> New hope within the soul,
> Reveals a higher goal,
> A way of hope in Christ-renewal.
> To refuel the motive of the man
> As God wills it,
> I now can accept the fire.
> O Spirit most holy,
> Kindle my desire
> To be one with God!

Out of the depths of the Holy Spirit's love have I, who am called the Maha Chohan, spoken to each heart.

> The crumb of Life God broke
> Is just a part of the whole loaf,
> And more will come each day
> As you await the hand
> That feeds your soul
> The bread that makes you whole.

From the devotion of my heart, I remain in service to the Holy Spirit,

The Maha Chohan

---

1. Zech. 4:6. 2. Jer. 31:33. 3. Matt. 7:12. 4. Titus 1:15. 5. Exod. 33:20. 6. Phil. 2:13. 7. Matt. 5:45. 8. Matt. 5:16. 9. John 3:30. 10. II Cor. 3:18. 11. Rev. 2:7.

Pearls of Wisdom®

Vol. XIV No. 48　　　　　*Chamuel of the Light*　　　　　November 28, 1971

The Fire of God's Love

Hail, Devotees of God's Love!

From the fires of the Sun I AM come. True love, recognizing the one Spirit omnipresent in all Life, moves to tremble the web of Being with the vibratory nature of divine love in its ongoingness and its all-givingness.

A heart surrounded by the densities of the world, by greed and selfish desire, is unheard of in our octave of Light. For the one great communal Presence in which we all share is the fire of God's love, whose giant outreach to humanity magnifies in the most lowly of His creatures the great Gloria in Excelsis and that excellence of perfect love and perfect wisdom which can only be derived from the Godhead.

Never in the history of the universe upon any planet or system of worlds has darkness triumphed. In reality, the rolling clouds of darkened and graying conditions such as those which now pervade the world order have only served as a background to perceptive souls for the invincible Light of God which has continued from the very beginning of Love's cycles to pour out the virtue and beauty of Perfection to all creation. Where darkness has been temporarily sustained through the misuse of free will, it has ultimately destroyed itself and those who have given it life. Their place is no more, for only in Light is Self-conscious being sustained.

How senselessly, then, do individuals allow the tramps of darkness to trample upon the tender virtues of the Christ budding within. Why do they permit others to take indecent liberties with the pure seed energies implanted from the hand of God, which, fresh from His Heart and Being, take root in the fertile soil of the soul? Little do they realize that by allowing such injustice to go unchallenged, they align themselves with the darkness that will one day be no more.

There can be no lasting peace without honor; therefore, let the cosmic honor flame be invoked for its saving grace and protection from all harm. The perversion of the purposes of Life and nature by man, originally created in the divine image but now fallen into the unwholesome dilemma of the pseudoimage, has continued to intercept the blessings that flow from the very Source of perfection which originally gave him Life.

Only the righteousness of divine purpose can endure, beloved hearts of Light; for it alone is capable of sustaining the flame of love. And so it is divine love, cherished in the hearts of the many, that has amplified its own currents as a means of perpetuating abundance to all upon the planetary body and to all throughout the universal body of the Lord's manifestation.

I AM an Archangel. Dedicated, then, to the healing of the nations by the principle of healing love, I step forth this day in the certitude of Cosmic Christ victory and in the awareness of the ultimate triumph of divine love in the domain of human affairs. For one day in the not too distant future, perceiving their own hapless and almost hopeless state, men will turn with joyous hearts to the oncoming tides of universal love. These love tides shall magnify in them the idealism of the perfect image in which they were originally created; and then they shall at last ask the question, Why can I not now be remade in that image?[1]

Beloved hearts, the formative power of the present moment is great. It is the creative potential of God's energy idling at the nexus of man's consciousness. If men would only perceive that the passage of time, the falling of the sands in the glass, signifies the opportunity for the manifestation of the being of God in man, I am certain they would make better use of their time and energy. But as long as people are satisfied with the lesser qualities and achievements of the human, so long will they hinder the opportunity dictated by Divine Love to bring forth those admirable virtues and honorable creations which are the fulfillment of cosmic purpose in man.

But when each individual takes his stand with Divine Love and determines that nothing shall stop him from completing his appointed round, that nothing shall halt or delay the onrushing of his energies back to the Heart of God, brimming with the fruits of service, then Life as precious moments of opportunity will not be lost. Take note that I said *nothing* shall stop him. This means that he allows no thing, manifest or unmanifest, known or unknown, to prevent him from fulfilling his own life role in the fruit of the divine plan.

Our God is a fruitful God, and all that He envisions for man is perfection. "As it is written, Eye hath not seen, nor ear heard, neither have entered into the heart of man, the things which God hath prepared for them that love him. But God hath revealed them unto us by his Spirit: for the Spirit searcheth all things, yea, the deep things of God."[2] And thereby we know in part that which God has held in His Heart and Mind to bestow upon mankind in ages to come.

But man need not wait ages to receive the gifts of God; for he is assured, if he accepts the divine plan, that he may at any time climb into the lap of God-identity. There he will find at last the fulfillment of the dreams of his soul that for want of fulfillment have caused him from time to time to be bored with life. There he will remember no more those experiences that kept him bound upon the rocks and shoals of a mortal existence—one that for the most part proved to be a senseless, purposeless engagement of his precious energies, a waste of his brief opportunity in the crucible of time and space.

Will you, then, perceiving that Christ-love is also resident in the archangelic realm, realize that you who were made "a little lower than the angels"[3] are also capable and worthy, if you will accept your calling as sons and daughters of the Most High, of being "crowned with glory and honor"—more than all the baubles and trinkets of the world could ever provide?

We would not, however, downgrade the great scientific potential which the Lord has ordained for this world. For man's technological achievements manifest not as the result of his own willing, but solely because God has willed them so by placing within Nature herself the opportunity for man to take dominion—from the simplest tetragrammaton to the most grandiose helix we observe in an ascending spiral.

The secrets of the universe await the discovery of the smallest child or the most advanced scientist, for God is no respecter of persons.[4] His love is not exclusive; it is not given to the spiritually advanced and denied to the lambs newly awakening to the opportunities of the spiritual Path. His love is given to all, a roseate, onrushing tide issuing from the blazing, bubbling fountain of cosmic activity, infiring the souls of men with the awareness of their creative potential, warming and revivifying them even in the winter of their despair.

I AM an Archangel, and my love and assistance are yours for the asking; but the Great Law requires that you ask. Those of us in our octave understand, and we hope that you do also, that each call you make to us, believing that we exist and that we exist to serve the needs of both God and man, will be answered by that healing stream of energy which it is our role to direct.

I AM Chamuel of the Fountain of Divine Love. Charity, my consort, serves with me. The angels in our band are pledged to direct their energies for the increase of the activity of divine love in all hearts. If the hearts of men, then, will expand their faith in the infinite perceptions of God, they, too, will perceive that only abundant life and abundant strength and abundant joy ought to be the lot of the whole family of nations.

They will see that the bane of negative karma ought to be swallowed up, together with the sea of man's negative emotions, and replaced by the calm, crystal sea of fire that signifies the acceptance by the individual of the Edenic day of Perfection's shining. Then heaven's door, ajar in the life of every avatar and son of God upon the planet, will be open to all hearts, bringing to mankind the wondrous message of peace and joy to the world that will cause all struggle to cease as the kingdoms of this world become the kingdoms of our Lord and of His Christ.[5]

To this end we serve. The human consciousness need not forever remain a battleground; for true righteousness, by the fire of divine love, can and shall claim the minds of men for the triumph of the Light. And the earth shall be lifted out of its maya, its glamor, its karma, and its delusion into the victorious faith of a God-directed order of worlds without end.

Valiantly I came out of the Sacred Fire of God's loving Heart, and I remain ever in the service of the eternal King and His lovers of righteousness.

For His name's sake I AM

Chamuel of the Light

1. II Cor. 3:18. 2. I Cor. 2:9-10. 3. Pss. 8:5. 4. Acts 10:34. 5. Rev. 11:15.

Pearls of Wisdom®

| Vol. XIV No. 49 | John the Beloved | December 5, 1971 |

The Mystical Garment of God

Sojourners upon the Planet Earth:

Among the many mansions of God, of special concern to you is the earth upon which you live. But, in the name of universal love, have you thought of the globe of self-consciousness, of the garment you have woven by your thoughts and your feelings? Are you able to separate the ideas that are your own from those that are driven against you, that penetrate your mind from without—concepts alien to your innate sense of right and wrong, but all too often determinant in molding your thoughts and feelings? Outside influences can be benign as well as evil; for man, if he wills it so, is also subject to the dazzling and powerful penetrations of cosmic Christ-love.

Let men realize, then, that although each man is a law unto himself, that law is subject to the molding factors of other minds— some welcome, some not. This is where the role of the Christ Self comes in. Those who esteem the will of God above all other considerations in their lives, who have faith in God's personal concern for their well-being—in His dispensations of universal justice, in His tenderness, and in His Reality—will amplify only those measures of good which are as cosmic cadences of progress marching onward toward perfection.

The law of love is steadfast, immovable, and tangible in a chaliced heart, receptive to Truth and to the ministrations of the Christ Self. The Christ Self of each man, as the Good Shepherd of his consciousness, leads the soul beside the still waters,[1] teaching him the laws of self-mastery through the God-control of his emotions. He learns to position himself on the Path of progress, to measure his own rate of attainment, and to know what he must do to overcome the last vestiges of human pride and hardness of heart. Then at last the role of the Christ Self becomes the dominant theme of his existence, and the Good Shepherd leads the sheep—the flock of man's thoughts—into those green pastures of God's Consciousness of which our Lord often spoke in parable.

Those conscious only of Jesus' physical manifestation, of his vital, masterful control of the elements in man and nature, may lose sight of their own God-conveyed gift of Christed magnificence. The statement "I AM the Light of the world"[2] was intended to reveal the Christ as the Light of every man in order that each one, finding his place in the cosmic scheme of life, would recognize no limitation greater than the moment. For God intends man to attain to the Gloria in Excelsis Deo, to the glory to God in the highest.

The role of a deep and abiding humility in establishing such God-orientation is great, for without humility men may become the victims of all sorts of degrading views and involvements. By using the lens of the mind to critically measure the life and services of another, they become aware only of the negatives; and without realizing it they formulate a mental caricature, a grotesque exaggeration of the human consciousness, wholly apart from the real heart and motive of the individual.

But God is not so. He who sees and knows the depth of each one's thoughts does not need to ponder or reflect, but knows all things on the instant; for upon the Body of God there registers the full impact of that which is real. The words "Thou art of purer eyes than to behold evil, and canst not look on iniquity"[3] point to humanity's great need for the mediatorship of the Christ, whose consciousness acts as a screening device, allowing only the images of perfection to rise to the throne of Reality. All else is adjudicated at the level of the Christ Self, who discerns each one's service to Life, his progress Godward, and his need for the chastisement of the Law. Thus the ultimate Criterion of Truth does give them the fullest measure of assistance in understanding themselves while they are yet in the state of becoming Whole.

But at the divine level, the pure and beautiful concepts of God for each soul hold him inviolate in the character of the beloved Son. Thus, through meditation upon the perfection of the Presence, man yokes his consciousness to the thoughts of God and is thereby exalted out of his lowly estate into that victorious domain of God-achievement. This is the exaltation which God has promised to every man, the raising-up of each soul out of the cradle of God's love into the masterful Light of that conscious dominion which the Lord of Creation originally intended for man. In the words of the Virgin Mother, "He hath put down the mighty from their seats, and exalted them of low degree."[4]

Unless his perception of Reality grows day by day, man may remain embedded in the mire of the abomination of desolation where he feels forsaken by both God and man. Once a man's heart is truly open to the will of God and he seeks neither to define or refine it, His will is given the freedom to reign in the lower consciousness, and joy to the world floods forth from the cup of being, establishing peace upon earth and in the world of the individual. He then remains undisturbed by the trivia of mortal existence, finding in the passing of the seasons the writings of those chapters in his life—past and future—which, as the pages turn, burn into memory those essential lessons that mature and ripen the soul.

In my own outreach to God, I sought personal closeness to the Master Jesus. To lean upon his breast, I thought, was to achieve the kingdom of God. Significantly, with the passing of the years and the various experiences which were given to me to enhance my own spiritual growth, there came to me, as there will come to you, O beloved hearts of mankind, an increasing awareness of my responsibilities to nurture the divine seed which I discovered, to my great joy, God had also planted within myself.

As I became aware of the divine potential locked within this seed of Light, I grew not apart from him but closer unto him and I realized that my Lord could not convey to me at once all of his own God-given attainment; for I was not ready to receive his mantle in the fullness of my own self-mastery. How little the world really knows of this mystery of the Christ!

With the increase of my inner awareness of the founding principles of individual development inherent within the power of divine love, I clearly saw that the warp and woof of creation was to be found in the mystical garment of God in which all can share. I also saw that the garment of my own life that I had woven would never be complete, but a changing tapestry of continuing unfoldment in the kingdom of heaven.

It was this universal love which I experienced within myself, engendered by the love of Jesus, that drew me, like a heavenly magnet, into the higher dimensions of Love's omnipotence, omnipresence, and omniscience, the all-powerful, all-wise God Consciousness everywhere present. Here in the threefold unity of the Holy Spirit the Beloved showed me the need to replace my dependence upon his person with individual attainment.

Out of the now of conscious awareness I perceived the future and the past and the holy night, the holy of holies when Christ is born in every man. And I perceived that with the passing cycles of man's overcoming, the Christ would, if man could accept it, penetrate the doorway of his heart. "Behold, I stand at the door, and knock: if any man hear My voice, and open the door, I will come in to him, and will sup with him, and he with Me."[5]

The supper of the Lord is a communion of hearts that reveals the infinite capacity of the holy fires of Love, together with the spirit of men's devotions, to cross the threshold of man's awareness and transport him into the bliss of God's awareness. This is the toning of the bars of the universe, cascading down the highways of the stars into each heart, uniting all in the mystery of birth, of being, of eternity, of God, of Love.

Devotedly, I remain your brother of the Day,

John

(The Beloved Disciple)

1. Pss. 23:2. 2. John 8:12. 3. Hab. 1:13. 4. Luke 1:52. 5. Rev. 3:20.

Pearls of Wisdom®

Vol. XIV No. 50   *Orion*   *December 12, 1971*

The Seed of Fire

To Those Who Would Cast Out All Fear:

Difficulties can be overcome, even when all indications point to the contrary. For the virtue inherent in the universal order, while often apparent only to the few, is partaken of as a sacred feast of Light once it is comprehended. Yet the hungers of the soul go unassuaged when those bidden to the marriage feast decline the Lord's invitation. [1]

Brief though his sojourn upon the planet may be, man, living in a physical body and involved in serving the needs of that body, seeks, in preference to facing a doubtful and uncertain future, to understand and master not only his body but also the physical environment that molds and shapes his thinking and destiny. But seldom in the process has he reckoned with the presence in the atom of a seed of fire universally programmed, nor does he understand the nature of this fire. It is therefore to this seed and to this fire that I would direct his attention.

To us it is a Star Presence heralding the closeness of the Identity of God. We see the seeds of fire within the minute portions of material substance as the dwelling place of God. In effect they are His broken Body dispersed as a eucharist of love to every heart throughout the planes of manifestation in Matter. However, man has not always received them in love. Instead, he has used these energies for evil purposes and for the perpetuation in Matter of unwholesome conditions that breed violence and misunderstanding. God—as energy, as Light locked within the fire seed of the atom—is thereby imprisoned in unsuitable forms; and only through invoking transmutation by the power of the Holy Spirit can man undo his wrong and bring about the salvation of that Matter upon which he has superimposed his evil consciousness.

God will escape. He will break, by His law, those imperfect bodies which are no part of Himself; He will shatter the matrices of unsound minds; He will inundate with the washing of the water by the Word unprofitable worlds. And as a potter dashes in pieces imperfect molds, God will restore to Himself the misqualified clay, refiring it in more noble images.

Of this men may be certain, that they have freedom of choice, dwelling as they do within a circle of infinite possibilities. Therefore, above all, they should heed the admonishments which come through the gift of prophecy and that contact with the higher will of God sustained by our Messengers. They should engage their attention and their choices in rightness of purpose, thereby restoring that commeasurement of eternity which is within the seed of fire rather than cast their lot with the swish of passing time.

Some have called me the Old Man of the Hills, thereby honoring the wisdom which God has given unto me. Let them understand that we are all ageless beings as we make permanent together our native, God-given gift of the love of Christ.

It was long ago in Bethlehem of Judea that the song of the angels was wafted over the plains. The hills had witnessed the great drama of the history of man and would remain a testimony to the ages; hopefully man would also record upon his soul the memorable events that occurred that night. For streaming from the earliest beginnings in time, as the supreme effort of Infinity to create and make permanent the manifestation of the Christos in a finite world, came the impact of that holy moment when the heavens descended into the earth: the birth of a holy child would ultimately convey to a sleeping world the meaning of the seed of fire in man.

Whether a God is born late or early in time is immaterial; for once the Light has established its flux of everlastingness within the heart and mind and being of man, he is no longer a part of the mass consciousness but one alone upon the God-directed Path, winging his way Homeward. Physical orientation causes the soul to stray far from the universal Path. Many who identify solely with their physical bodies and physical environments seem hopelessly trapped in the web of time and circumstance. But one day, through the nativity of the Christ Consciousness in their flesh, a sentient, living, immortal being will be formed—as Paul said, "...until Christ be formed in you."[2]

The forming of Christ, the forming of God as the spiritual identity of man, must take precedence over the evolution of the ego relative to the physical plane. The ego must immerse itself in the upward-spiraling Godward movement of the finite into the infinite. And then at last, tutored in the way of the Spirit, ready to assume the mantle of its Real Identity, it becomes one with God and is thereby transformed in the similitude of the Divine Ego, affirming, "I and my Father are one."[3]

Thus the open door of the Christ Consciousness, which no man can shut,[4] replaces the closed doors of mortal minds that refuse to accept the sacred precepts of the Law because these do not agree with human tradition. Truly, there are many valuable teachings that have become a part of the world's body of knowledge, and these should not be lightly cast aside. But in many instances it requires the wisdom of a Son of God to discern the difference between those binding elements of dogma that crucify the souls of men and those God-ideas which all may receive as they kneel in humility before the living God. For true religion sets aside the divisive factors of race and creed and human calling and initiates that openness of heart and mind which draws the mission of the Babe of Bethlehem into perspective in the cradle of the individual consciousness. From there He will one day rise as the noblest of lords in the life of every man, woman, and child.

Man can know God; God can know man. But unless there is an interchange of identifying concepts and ideas, God remains unknown and man does not know that he is known. Joyous hours of Light descending as stars of hope in the midst of man's darkness signal the birth of a god in miniature, who will expand his starry body of Light by quaffing the elixir of Life. By drinking into the Body of God through the rituals established by the Holy Spirit, man, like a tiny babe, is able to assimilate the filaments of a universe. He accepts in consciousness that which he is in Reality—the fullness of the Divine Image—and he sees it no robbery to make himself equal with God.[5]

Man stands often at the crossroads of life, crucified upon a cross of his own making. Yet he can come down from the cross by choosing between the Light and darkness of himself; but his choice must be made within the circle of karmic possibilities which he alone has set up and which he alone must undo.

To choose the Light is the only way. It leads to the uppermost heavenly realm where there is joy beyond belief as the moment of God's renewal passes to man trapped in the mortal concept. In the company of immortals the rapture of God flows freely, unceasingly. Truly, "eye hath not seen, nor ear heard, neither have entered into the heart of man, the things which God hath prepared for them that love Him."[6] The riches of God's eternal Light and grace—these are the things which He has prepared for man's natal day, when he is born a Christ to live forevermore.

Through their recognition of the firstborn Son of God, the Magi perceived the Star of the Master, of the Elder Brother, appearing in the sky. Thus man lifts up the thoughts of his mind to perceive the Star of his own everlastingness that appears as a sign in the heavens. Symbol of hope to a world waiting for revivification, the Star comes to rest over the manger—man, in whose humble heart a god is born.

For the birth of Christ-esteem in the hearts of all, I remain

Orion

(The Old Man of the Hills)

1. Matt. 22:1-14. 2. Gal. 4:19. 3. John 10:30. 4. Rev. 3:8. 5. Phil. 2:6. 6. I Cor. 2:9.

Pearls of Wisdom®

Vol. XIV No. 51   *Jesus*   *December 19, 1971*

The Grace of Eternal Purpose

All Christ Blessings:

Let the remote sense cease. God is at hand—your Father and mine. Ever constant, ever faithful, He abides, hoping for the extension of Himself in form.

The beautiful mystery of the coming of the Light is one of steadfast evolvement that ever waits for the dawn and never forsakes the hope of its appearing. There is a certitude within the heart that rings out the Truth for all time. God is in the earliest Light and will persist until darkness is no more and only Light endures in the square of Matter, contriving to arrange an order of progress that conveys the glory of God to every man.

There are no imperfect images in the grand halls of the Mind of God, but only the stalwart release of those qualities which He hopes to see realized in His creation. Heaven is His throne and earth His footstool.[1] When the concept of be-ness—I AM that I AM[2]—is seized by the mind, it cleaves to the mighty recognition of Life that tongue may not utter and that eye may not behold. This is the Way that mortal mind would opaque from the vision of men; but those who dwell in the tents of the godly, that like stars are encamped round about those who fear Him, are not moved from the central purpose of Life. Disrespect for universal purpose or failure to apprehend the fact that universal purpose does exist prevents men from entering the kingdom of heaven.

O holy night of each man's birth into that kingdom! What joy is shed abroad in celestial realms as the darkness of mankind's consciousness is dispelled in the awareness that "I AM the Light of the world!"[3] "Before Abraham was, I AM!"[4] declares the eternal Christos. The be-ness of Spirit includes the presence of purpose from the foundation of the world that not only penetrates the dark night of the ages but endures in the permanent realm of spiritual omnipresence. It interpenetrates even the atoms of physical manifestation and makes permanent the fire in substance which steadfastly declares that the very ground where the manifestation of God occurs is holy.[5]

To hallow space and substance by invocation to the Holy Spirit is to avoid their desecration by the error of neglect. To determine that the flow of thoughts and feelings through the aperture of the mind will remain polarized to higher purpose is to avoid the sins of commission by the virtue of positive action.

If ever there was a child of the devil, it is that one who sustains the concept of belittlement of self or belittlement of others; for the demons of belittlement have again and again destroyed the confidence of the children of God in the mission of the Christ. Stooping to lessening concepts, they flee from before the appearance of valor; they flee from the realms of a spiritual culture and enter the netherworld of fad and fancy. They call to the mountains of oblivion to fall upon them through the ritual of suicide, failing to understand that our love is the Light that overcomes the darkness.

Midst the spirit of world hatred, world confusion, and world misunderstanding we remain, constant as always, immovable as the North Star, to give the best gift unto man—the gift of the Morning Star. He that hath an ear, let him hear what the Spirit saith.[6] The Morning Star is the original, pure and perfect pattern held in the Mind of God from the earliest beginning, whereby there can and will be conveyed to every soul the allness of universal perfection, that the soul and consciousness may expand in the Divine Image into the realm of self-mastery. Out of the unity of the Father and the Son is born the triumph over Matter, over time, over space—from mortal density to immortal immensity.

Chastise thyself not! See that thou doest it not; but shed the coat of thy oppressive misqualification, of thy ignorant efforts, and the self-righteous garments that thou flauntest before the world as a badge of courage. Replace it all by the grace of eternal purpose!

Out of oneness with God is born the sense of unity of Father and Son. Man needs not an idolatrous self-made image, but a universal image of the living God, a determined awakening and awareness within himself that the never-failing Light of God, holding the hand of his individuality, shall lead him into all Truth by the Spirit of the living Christ.

It is mockery to presume that the shallowness of mortal concepts can bring deliverance to the soul, that the hollow echoes of men's intellectual strivings can be a source of true freedom. Only the joy of cosmic interdependence between God and man can bring awareness; only inner dependence upon the faculties of grace and truth descending from the Great Mediator can provide a merciful and acceptable sacrifice for the shortcomings of the outer self.

For God is not vengeful, but eternally merciful. The message of
His love shone in the Star and in the watchful care of Joseph, my
earthly father, and Mary, whom I always considered as my heavenly
mother. In the acts of these two humble people was the manifestation
of the Eternal Presence. Light flowed into darkness and the darkness
disappeared; and the balm of comfort became an unguent to the
world.

> Now the callousness of men
> Recurs again and again,
> Yet tiny prayers are heard.
> An echo of the past is born,
> Voicing anew the lost Word.
> The Spirit flows most sweetly
> Each new and living day,
> Recording then completely
> God's message for today.
> His heart forever burneth,
> Aflame with love's delight,
> Eternal cycles turneth,
> The wheels of stars so bright.
> O sweet and blessed Christmas,
> Within each heart reborn,
> No frailty in purpose,
> Thou art a stellar morn!
> The majesty of triumph
> O'er stain and darkness bold
> Will change the dusty charms
> Into the purest gold.
> For only Truth can conquer—
> It has the power to free.
> Man's thoughts still enter blunder,
> But Christ will ever be.
> My garments hold the ages;
> The multitudes confuse
> Who write upon the pages
> So often wrongly used.
> But still I came unto them—
> I AM and I remain
> The Prince of Peace forever
> To free the world from pain.
> Oh, hear, then, now my outcry—
> It is a voice most loud.

Oh, won't you hear my message?
But do not heed the crowd.
For few there be that enter
From multitudes that fail,
But God remains the center—
One day His Light all hail!
For now through time and tide I move;
Each year to some I truly prove—
The King of Kings and Lord of Lords
Finds birth in any heart
To show each man the Truth at last—
That he and God are not apart.
For lo I AM and you are too
One Image in his thought,
That all may telegraph the Truth:
Behold what God hath wrought!

Devotedly in the unfailing Light,

Jesus

1. Isa. 66:1. 2. Exod. 3:14. 3. John 8:12. 4. John 8:58. 5. Exod. 3:5. 6. Rev. 2:7.

Pearls of Wisdom®

Vol. XIV No. 52   *El Morya*   *December 26, 1971*

The Body of God Requires Assembly

Dearest Treasures,

Time flies. The day of the savage is past. If remnants remain, I say patience. And in all cases I say patience. Out of the domain of tranquillity are born the most valiant offerings. By stilling the mind, the passions of adversity are understood as passing. The morrow will be valiant. We will it so.

The difficult will is the one tied to selfishness. The fervent will, out of tranquillity, will give birth to an idea. And that idea will drink deeply of the cup of fervor. Thus a fervent will is born. It cannot fail to acknowledge the old electric engrams. Like lightning they flash forth; and in the glare of their appearing, as at noontime, the most hidden objects appear. But their desire to crawl and hide or to masquerade cannot prevent the penetration of the lightning.

Light mirrors Truth, but too close scrutiny sometimes fails to admit change and its potential; for whereas the wheel of darkness turns, so also turns the wheel of Light. Children of the Light often fail to understand that darkness introverts and entangles itself in the skeins of its own creation. This sometimes unperceived snarl is also a snare. What dusty folly is this, that men allow their own spiritual images to be corroded by the mud slung at others?

The frost that appears on the window vanishes with the sun. But the purifying attempts of nature are not to whitewash or to miscolor manifestation. Manifestation speaks for itself. Its utterances through some may at times appear chameleonlike as they present through internal processes of deceit a false coloration. But only the stone, the white stone[1] of absolute Truth, can honestly convey that which is.

Morya shares the avalanche of progress sweeping away old structures and ever preparing for the new. Yet I speak of the hidden room of preservation. The wise ones also save the best images. These understand the difficulty in forging a new structure. Modification of the old is also possible, for out of the modified image a new icon is made and stands in place of a pariah.

The depths of despair come to many. These make mud out of struggle. "Share and share alike," they say, but withhold the gift. The greatest gain comes out of the momentum of givingness, for such concepts as these flow with the universal tide. The cherishment of hearts is our religion. Even men of the cloth, men supposedly clothed upon with Light, dare to vituperate, to allow their minds to flow with world hatred. They say, "We are God's children," as though they were fenced in by the idea.

Let them understand the Light and warmth of the Spirit that melts the winter snows. Let them understand the strength that can destroy and the simplicity of duplicity that mars the perfect image. Only Love kindles the great conflagration. Certainly Love is wise. Is it wise to be self-deceived, to be encased in the rigors of age-old hatreds? Embodiment after embodiment, the same mistakes are faced. The Lords of Karma hope for triumph and individuality. If Heaven can be perfect in patience, should man be less perfect?

To follow the example of the arhats, of the avatars, of the Christed ones, is to see God in all. What viciousness that men say, "He is a heathen" because another recognizes God in one whose garments are alien to their own. Struggle, straggle, and strife—these go together. We should call them the ministry of confusion.

Is God one? Can man and God be one? Through the union of love do we create a meld—O holy savor, greatest favor. Chastisement, when understood, mellows the soul. God-chastity can be man-chastity. Attainment is not destruction: destruction is not attainment. Men of spiritual depth perceive with the passing of the years that trivialities have aborted universalities.

That the deceitful ones come seeking to enter in and to entice the noblest orders does not mean that the principle of rejection should close all doors. Even traitors have been trapped by God's love. Be truly illumined; thus the shaft of righteousness shall be a two-edged sword.

Hastiness in construing the words of the Lord does not guarantee accuracy, nor does long pondering. Sometimes the fires of the heart must be contacted. Subterranean chambers containing the deepest treasures may release those treasures to the surface. Shining upon still waters, they reflect the purity of the golden radiance of the sun. But while unexposed to Light, they may appear as ordinary. So let men understand the greatness of individuality.

Jealousy is the root cause behind most conflict. Who else desires to provoke save the provoker? Let God's love shine. It is the strength of the sun. It is the strength of the soul it molds. Many are the forces that seek to form the soul; glory is its pattern and strength is its asset. As it chooses wisely it may garner strength. Surprising even to the self are the hidden assets. In moments of trial men garner these assets. They draw upon hidden springs of divine wisdom and inspiration. They cultivate the acquaintance of souls long gone before them upon the pathway; for lingering gems have been dropped by the hands of saints. Spurned throughout the ages by men of lesser vision, these, by reason of their immortal nature, remain glowing coals from heavenly altars.

The vision of the world must be changed. The fire of change may come. But unless man initiate his own individual fires, and that quickly, the world may encounter universal fires it knows not of.

Psychic energy and extrasensory perception may speak to some of the frosting on the cake, but we who know seek the substance of divine prana. We adorn with simple Christ-jewels—perception, devotion, unification. The thread of contact is fragile. So may be the thread of perception. In some it grows to a cable of universal strength. In others it snaps, and with it the one contact.

O hearts of Light, the momentous decisions facing the earth may be universally applicable, but the decisions facing each man appeal more strongly to us; for the stables of the world need arhats, men of vision and of faith who will assume the herculean tasks that must be done. The fragrance of the little flowers like Thérèse serving in the obscurity of monastic life may be more world-shaking than the chairmanship of the Red Cross. What always ennobles the task is the measure of devotion, of a life.

Divine jewels remain of greater value than earthly ones. Strange sowings must be avoided, familiar spirits shunned, dangerous drugs abhorred, and creative energy honored—not deposited into the refuse of pleasure. Naked is the soul who cannot find in an abundant universe the garments of the Lord as covering. The realities of God are our strength. Wise is the man or woman who does not fear to honor the invisible, all-wise Creator.

Let the mockers mock. In every generation the earth has received their bones. Now the Body of God requires assembly. More workers must be recruited into the vineyard.[2] In every way shall the path to our abode be mounted. And the wings shall fly; and the clouds of dust shall die down, the clear air reflecting stillness. The hopes shall soar and the dark ones be no more. The Light of the ages voices triumph; the paltry images, no longer paltry, have been remolded.

The mercy of God in enduring is not required to fit itself into the mold of human sympathy, for the time has come for the dividing of the

Light and the darkness.[3] Wise are those virgins whose lamps are trimmed, who have bought oil,[4] who have established themselves unto God as seekers for reunion. Tender is the Himalayan musk, but most fragrant are hearts filled as a fiery chalice with seeds of Light and trust and joy. The *Om mani padme hum,* the mantra of a seeking heart that seeks even when full, awaits the devotions of men.

Not in diversion, but out of one-pointedness have I spoken.

Morya

1. Rev. 2:17. 2. Matt. 20:1. 3. Gen. 1:4. 4. Matt. 25:7-13.

A Christmas Letter from Darjeeling

Devotees of Christ the World Around:

The belt of time moves on. Excuses mar the perfect image. The way to our abode remains difficult; for humanity's departure from the Plan, dishonoring Christ and every noble intent, perpetuates darkness where Light ought to be. Yet the twinkling moments of cosmic rhapsody continue to flood forth from unknown worlds. The merit of beautiful virtue extends new hope to the earth. Each day is a measure of God's love.

The smallest child is encapsulated within the domain of Light. The beauty of his consciousness insulates him from the rashness of the streets. The word "When will mankind awaken?" may jar hearts, but it seldom evokes the expected miracle. Beauty caresses the soul. The tenderness of each moment, recapturing the past within the present, crystallizes the future as each day acts upon the plasticity of that which is to come.

O Light, Thou art the Source of all energy, of all reality, of all perfection! Why will men continue to hide under the bushel of their gross shame the shadows of disparity between what they profess and what they do? One day the Light will shatter all concepts of imperfection; and those who dwell on the rim of questionability, far from our realm of Light, will know and behold those who swim to the center. Yet they themselves will remain far from the heart domain of Deity.

Beautiful Savior, high is Thy Light upon the mountain! The world, through its crassness, loses sight of its opportunity for investment in virtue whereby treasures are laid up in heaven. Each man for himself must thrust forth the hope and dedication of the Christ until the fog in the valley is penetrated and the crowning sunlight of new experience reveals the spiritual peak to which his soul aspires and from which he will never seek to be separated.

Only in union with Cosmic Love all inclusive can man perceive at last the oneness of our purpose. Our Brotherhood, ministering to countless lives, dedicates itself to the perfection of each one. Thus is the newness of God born within man as the appearance of the Christ becomes the glory from the skies of immortal Reality. To cry "Excellent!" is not enough. Each day man must secure for himself by his faith the substance of that faith made manifest as the abundant Life of shining purpose.

Devoted to the unfoldment of the Christ-perfection of God's holy will and the constant outpouring of the everlasting Light,

I AM and I remain

El Morya

of the Zend-Avesta

Index

Volume Fourteen · 1971

lives within all, 43; would penetrate man's heart, 199-200. *See
also* Christ Consciousness; Christ
Self; Lord; Real Self; Savior; Son;
Word
Christ Consciousness: cannot be
claimed exclusively, 76; does not
undergo change, 26; door of,
trembles with anticipation, 100;
as link to ages of glory, 138; must
remold and remake the human
consciousness, 80; the nativity of,
202; neither flees nor pursues,
132; responsibility to guard the,
57; resurrection of, 152; as the
Rose of Sharon, 81. *See also*
Christ; Christ Self; Real Self
Christ Self: angel of the Presence operates through, 85; discernment
through, 141; as the Mediator, 65;
the role of, 197. *See also* Christ;
Christ Consciousness; Real Self
Christed One, aura of, 99-100
Classes, announcement of, at Ceylon,
158, 159
Cleansing, by water, air, and fire,
158. *See also* Blotting-out process;
Chastisement; Purging; Purifica-
tion; Scourging
Cloud of witnesses, contact with, 107.
See also Saints
Coat of many colors, became the seam-
less garment, 96
Co-creators, Ascended Hosts as, 46
Coils, in subconscious, 25
Coins, "In God We Trust" on Ameri-
can, 60
Colorado Springs, retreat of God
Tabor near, 57
Coloration, of the aura, 91-92, 93
Colors, of the Seven Rays, 36n. *See also*
Blue; Crimson; Pink; Violet
Comfort, Flame of, described, 40n
Commeasurement, of eternity, 202
Commerce, attitudes of meanness
through the marts of, 57. *See also*
Economic deceits
Communion, 35; each can find the
pathway of, 61; that evokes the
consciousness of the Holy Grail,
15; weaving the conduit of, 145
Communism, 60
Competition, 125
Complacency, beware the sin of, 128
Complexity, that eclipses the simplicity
of man's true nature, 2. *See also*
Simplicity
Compromise, as the most detestable

act, 171
Condemnation: refrain from, 54; sustaining matrices of, 25; the transfer of energy in, explained, 140-
141. *See also* Belittlement; Judgment
Conflict(s): all, exists at human levels,
179; jealousy as the root cause behind, 210; over religious conviction, 178. *See also* Division; Doctrinal struggle; Struggle
Confusion, ministry of, 210
Connection, between what men do
unto others and what others do
unto them, 185
Conquests, in the world as a substitute
for inner realization, 6-7
Conscience, 65
Consciousness, 57; cannot be receptive
to good and evil simultaneously,
79; of the Christ as a screening
device, 198; development of higher, 97; disintegration of the, that
is wed to evil, 177; effects the aura,
99; as an elevator, 5-6; energy
idling at the nexus of, 194; entering into the Cosmic, of God, 100;
expanding, 157; experiencing the
victory of the Light within, 152;
flexibility of, 99; gathering little
jewels of, 13; goblet of, 133; guarding the quality of, 182; that has
aligned itself with the forces of
antichrist, 142; increasing the
dominion of, 10; need for protection to, 111; partaken of by Adam
and Eve is living today, 87; pollution of, 110; projecting, out of the
physical body, 88; purification of,
180, 191; that remains in the dol-
drums of mortal experience, 123;
searing of, 157; state of, wherein
man takes dominion, 66; yoking,
to the thoughts of God, 198. *See
also* Christ Consciousness; Human
consciousness
Contemporaries, as sheep to be fed, 12
Content, exchanged with discontent,
169
Correspondence, principle of, 190
Cosmic Beings: assistance of, 112; are
determined this planet shall
ascend, 168; evolve, 124; as Light
reinforcements to Earth, 7; watch
over thee, 122. *See also* Ascended
Hosts; Ascended Masters; Beings;
Brotherhood, The; Great White
Brotherhood; Hierarchy; Master(s)

trated from manifesting, 60; has not changed its nature, 61; inner dependence upon, 206; outworkings of divine, 175; pursuing the quality of, 55

Graces, training in cosmic, 188

Graciousness, 55

Grand Hall of Learning, for training in cosmic graces, 188

Gratitude, 187; as catalyst of good fortune, 185

Great White Brotherhood: many activities of, are hidden from the curious, 63; places its seal upon The Summit Lighthouse, 155. *See also* Ascended Hosts; Ascended Masters; Brotherhood, The; Cosmic Beings; Hierarchy; Master(s)

Green: chartreuse, of jealousy and resentment, 93; effects of, light in the aura, 92; as the Fifth Ray, 36n; sheath in the healing thought form, 82; white fire core as the central focus of the, ray, 82

Grids, floating, of astral debris, 31. *See also* Forcefields

Grudges, on harboring, 25

Guilt, 65

Habit(s): can be changed, 21; ingrained, prevents contact with heaven, 145; of negation, 142

Habitations, not of God's creation, 55

Happiness, the key to, 79. *See also* Joy

Harmony, 53; with the law of Love, 53

Haste, construes much evil in the world, 166

Hatred(s): being encased in age-old, 210; floods of, 62

Healing: as the Fifth Ray, 36n; green light charges the aura with, 92; Meta on, 14, 15; restoring the science of, 151; sword of, 164; thought form, 82

Healing Arts, Meta as Patroness of, 15

Heart: balance of, 2; fires of the, must be contacted, 210; a focus within the, where God shall abide forever, 175; invasion of, 123; largesse of, 132; love can be tangibly felt in, 147; soul ties to the Father as relevant to, 41-42; union of, and mind, 42; vast emptiness of the human, 131; where man can become invulnerable, 19; will and desire of God beat your, 101

Hearts, cherishment of, 210

Heaven, 170; contact with, 107; cre-

ating an alliance with the forces of, 112; does not enter the world unbidden, 117; has its own conspiracy of Light, 108; legal aid of, 65; no partiality in, 84; "plots" of, 115; sense delusion and habit prevent contact with, 145; trust in, 28. *See also* Cosmic levels; Hierarchy

Heaven, Temple of, 162, 163

Heavens, as a dwelling place, 186

Helmets, crystalline, worn by angels, 46

Hercules, makes pact with Arcturus, 168

Hierarchy: becoming spiritually coordinated with, 183; contact with, 124-125; examinations by, 183; as the extension of God, 75; never threatens but does warn, 68; truths in the hands of, 76. *See also* Ascended Hosts; Ascended Masters; Brotherhood, The; Chohan(s); Cosmic Beings; Great White Brotherhood; Master(s)

Hilarion, embodied as Paul, 36n

Historical fact, tampered with, 179. *See also* History

History: accurately tracing the, of the soul, 162; on studying, 161. *See also* Historical fact

Holiness, 191

Holy Spirit, 37; aura as a vessel of, 109; Flame of the, as white, 40n; Maha Chohan as representative of, 40, 40n

Homer, Maha Chohan embodied as, 40n

Honor: cosmic, flame, 193; desire for a code of, inculcated in the soul, 1; sense of, as essential to progress, 25

Hope: the pillar of, 169; renewal of, 63; of the world is acceptance of God's grace, 59

Hopelessness: acceptance of the sense of, 133; draws you into negative spirals, 22

Human consciousness: creating a spiritual uplift in, 175; linking-together of the great and trivial in, 123; need not forever remain a battleground, 196; must be remolded and remade by the Christ Consciousness, 80; restoring the miraculous sense of the divine within, 167. *See also* Consciousness; Human creation

to progress, 25. *See also* Injustice(s)

Karma: Armageddonlike conspiracy of world, 38; episodes of thundering, 75; law of, 67

Karma, Lords of. *See* Lords of Karma

Karmic Board: decided to shorten mankind's lifespan, 171; Nada as a member of, 81. *See also* Lords of Karma

Karmic patterns: interfering with, of others, 25; as self-made prison walls, 104-105

Karmic recompense, 84

Karmic return, 80

Kingdom: free will as the key factor in the bringing-in of, 173; within, 42. *See also* Kingdom of God; Kingdom of heaven

Kingdom of God: as the foundation for the pursuit of the initiatic process, 167; knowledge of, as basic to life, 178; within, 50. *See also* Kingdom; Kingdom of heaven

Kingdom of heaven: as inaccessible to the unreceptive, 131; must first manifest in the individual, 31; upon earth, 58; what prevents men from entering, 205. *See also* Kingdom; Kingdom of God

Knowledge: as a gift of the Christed Self, 36; great treasure houses of, guarded by The Brotherhood, 50; as above intellectualism, 131; invoke, 85; that is important, 105. *See also* Wisdom

Kuthumi, embodied as Francis of Assisi, 117n.2

Labors, centered in the human self, 62

Lanto, embodied as a sage in China, 36n

Law: deviations from natural, 67; dharma of the, as salutary, 3; the establishment of, and order, 31; finite, 132; individuals influence the manifestation of cosmic, 173; those inept in applying, 23; of karma, 67; letter and spirit of the, 66; of Love, 67; nature governed by natural and spiritual, 161; no trifling with, 191; registering of cosmic, on inner consciousness, 6; requires that you ask, 195; of retribution, 147; of return, 175; of return of energies to the sender, 141, 174; returns that which is sent out, 127; of sin, 53, 67; sub-

ject to the molding factors of other minds, 197; of Transcendence, 1; of transference of authority, 18; of universal desire, 173; the unwritten, 66. *See also* Laws; Precepts; Principle; Principles

Laws: that frustrate the soul's harmony with Nature, 67; knowing the, governing Spirit in Matter, 131. *See also* Law; Precepts; Principle; Principles

Legal aid, of Heaven, 65

Lemuria, mutations and weird forms created by black magicians on, 150

Lessons: learned from mistakes, 186; of life learned in two ways, 165. *See also* Trial(s)

Letter: that killeth, 157; that killeth has been tampered with, 180; and Spirit of the Law, 66

Life: acknowledging the spark of, 60; becoming the recipient of immortal, 124. (*See also* Birth); deciphering the intricacies of, 9; do not seek to cheat, 67; each generation should attempt to improve, 89; gateway to immortal, 48. (*See also* Birth); lessons of, learned in two ways, 165; making, happier, 28; meant to be a progressive outreach, 46; newness of, 62; purpose of, 20, 50, 166; revealing the purposes of, 151; as a solemn responsibility, 191; in state-dominated countries, 67; tapestry of, 68; tracing the real meaning of, 162. *See also* Existence; Lifespan

Lifespan, shortening of, 171. *See also* Death; Existence; Ongoingness

Lifestream, forward movement of a, 65.

Light: bubbling action of, 105; can be magnetized through the human aura, 109; conspiracy of, 108; expanding your, 110; finding the way of, 12; of God unperceived and unused, 128; has not changed its nature, 61; intensification of, 100; mystery of the coming of, 205; the need to comprehend, 138; powers of, are gaining footholds, 178; strengthening of, 113; those who cannot be expected to respond to, 142; of the world, 101

Lighthouse: every man as keeper of his own, 11; as a meaningful symbol, 153

Patience, toward other parts of Life, 176

Pattern(s): breaking up human, 170; distorted in the entertainment media, 79; seed, of perfection within man, 96; that sully Light, 128. *See also* Engrams; Etching

Paul, Hilarion embodied as, 36n

Paul the Venetian, embodied as Paolo Veronese, 36n

Peace, 1-2, 131; at any price betrays, 131; establishing, 199

Pearl of Wisdom, as unit of cosmic knowledge, 58

Peking, Temple of Heaven in, 162

Penetration: of the Absolute, 124; of higher octaves, 162; ritual of, 91; soul science of Light, 152

Perception(s): enlarging, 92; purification of, 93; soul science of inner, 152; thread of, 211

Perfection: acceptance of, 149; within the being of man, 181; enables fashioning of the wedding garment, 95; increasing the flow of, 109-110; inherent striving for, 177; the lodestone of, 6; meditation upon, 198; as natural way of the aura, 127; pursuit of, must be guarded, 161; restoration of, 150

Permissiveness, floods of, 62

Perspective, holding true, 2. *See also* Vision

Phenomena: producing, at the moment of greatest need, 191; seekers detoured from the Path by, 182. *See also* Miracles

Phidias, Serapis Bey embodied as, 36n

Philosophy, youth brainwashed with a decadent, 59

Physical body, projecting consciousness out of, 88. *See also* Body temple

Physical orientation, causes straying from the Path, 202

Pilate, did not bear witness to Jesus' perfection, 96-97

Pink: effect of the, light in the aura, 92; flame of love, 148; as the Third Ray, 36n

Planet: aura of the, 121; the current initiation of the, 166-167; flood of degrading concepts will destroy this, 59; salvation of this, depends upon your invocation, 168; various life waves upon, 34. *See also* Earth; World

Platitudes, 157

Pleasures, as a temporary palliative, 6

Plots, contemporary, 70. *See also* Tactic

Pollution, mankind's concern with, as a mockery, 59

Pornographic art, 59

Potential: creative, 88; realization of, as freedom, 24; realizing more, 106; rejection of, 20; unlimited, 43; as utterly important, 38

Power: of amplification, 86; blue denotes, 92; as the First Ray, 36n; from the God Presence, 124; to invoke the Flaming Sword, 164; of mercy, 163; of the mind, 136; of the present moment, 194

Prayer(s), 61, 112; answer to, 174; challenge to the concept of, as milksop endeavor, 99; to give with the healing thought form, 82; heartrending, 31; restoration of, in the schools, 58; that some have classed as 'vain repetition', 26; valiant action born out of, 27. *See also* Assistance

Precepts, accepting the, of Christ, 187. *See also* Law; Laws; Principle; Principles

Preparation, for spiritual adventure, 33

Presence: angel of, 85; coming face to face with, 190; fixing one's attention upon, 124; meditation upon the perfection of, 198; requesting protection from, 112. *See also* God; I AM; I AM THAT I AM

Present, as the seat of malleability, 125. *See also* Moments

Preservation: ritual of, 41; room of, 209

Pressing, toward the mark, 11-12

Principle: applying the, of internal Reality, 91; of correspondence, 190; of love, 190; of redemption, 119. *See also* Law; Laws; Precepts; Principles

Principles: absorbing the cardinal, 65; misapplication of cardinal, in school, church, and society, 59. *See also* Law; Laws; Precepts; Principle

Pristine state, despoiling of, 66

Problems: find the way out of the maze of, 66; prolonging of, 88; as a result of auric contact with humanity, 88; solving world, 71-72

Progress: discontent as the hallmark of, 165; evolutionary astral, 150;

For information on The Summit Lighthouse, Church Universal and Triumphant, Summit University, Montessori International, and conferences and seminars conducted by Elizabeth Clare Prophet, free literature, and current *Pearls of Wisdom* sent weekly to you, write to Box A, Malibu, CA 90265, or contact any of the following centers:

Church Universal and Triumphant
International Headquarters
Summit University
Montessori International
Box A
Malibu, CA 90265
(213) 880-5300

Church Universal and Triumphant
Los Angeles Community Teaching Center
1130 Arlington Avenue
Los Angeles, CA 90019
(213) 737-6739

Church Universal and Triumphant
Keepers of the Flame Motherhouse
2112 Santa Barbara Street
Santa Barbara, CA 93105
(805) 963-3371

Church Universal and Triumphant
San Francisco Community Teaching Center
2109 Fourteenth Avenue
San Francisco, CA 94116
(415) 564-6433

Church Universal and Triumphant
Retreat of the Resurrection Spiral
First and Broadmoor
Colorado Springs, CO 80906
(303) 475-2133

Church Universal and Triumphant
Minneapolis/St. Paul Community Teaching Center
1206 Fifth Street SE
Minneapolis, MN 55414
(612) 331-6960

Church Universal and Triumphant
Chicago Community Teaching Center
2001 West Bradley Place
Chicago, IL 60618
(312) 477-8980

Church Universal and Triumphant
Detroit Community Teaching Center
23647 Woodward Avenue
Pleasant Ridge, MI 48069
(313) 545-6769

Church Universal and Triumphant
Washington, D.C. Community Teaching Center
4715 Sixteenth Street NW
Washington, D.C. 20011
(202) 882-1900

Church Universal and Triumphant
New York City Community Teaching Center
P.O. Box 667
Lenox Hill Station
New York, NY 10021
(212) 362-3708

Summit University®
A COLLEGE OF RELIGION, CULTURE AND SCIENCE
OF CHURCH UNIVERSAL AND TRIUMPHANT

In every age there have been some, the few, who have pursued an understanding of God and of selfhood that transcends the current traditions of doctrine and dogma. Compelled by a faith that knows the freedom of love, they have sought to expand their awareness of God by probing and proving the infinite expressions of his law. Through the true science of religion, they have penetrated the 'mysteries' of both Spirit and Matter and come to experience God as the All-in-all.

Having discovered the key to reality, these sons and daughters of God have drawn about them disciples who would pursue the disciplines of the law of the universe and the inner teachings of the 'mystery schools'. Thus Jesus chose his apostles, Bodhidharma his monks, and Pythagoras his initiates at Crotona, Gautama Buddha called his disciples to form the *sangha* (community), and King Arthur summoned his knights to the quest for the Holy Grail at the Table Round.

Summit University is a mystery school for men and women of the twentieth century who would pursue the great synthesis of the teachings of the ascended masters—the few who have overcome in every age, the many who now stand as our elder brothers and sisters on the Path. Together Gautama Buddha and Lord Maitreya sponsor Summit University with the World Teachers Jesus and Kuthumi, El Morya, Lanello, and Saint Germain, Confucius, Mother Mary, Moses and Mohammed, the Archangels Michael and Gabriel, and "numberless numbers" of "saints robed in white"— the Great 'White' Brotherhood. To this university of the Spirit they lend their flame, their counsel, the momentum of their attainment, and the living teaching for us who would follow in their footsteps to the source of that reality they have become.

Founded in 1971 under the direction of the Messengers Mark L. Prophet and Elizabeth Clare Prophet, Summit University currently holds three twelve-week retreats each year—fall, winter, and spring quarters—as well as five two-week summer retreats and healing weekend retreats. All of the courses are based on the unfoldment of the inner potential of the Christ, the Buddha, and the Mother. Through the teachings of the ascended masters given through their messengers, students at Summit University pursue the disciplines on the path of the ascension for the soul's ultimate reunion with the Spirit of the living God.

This includes the study of the sacred scriptures of East and West taught by Jesus and Gautama; exercises in the self-mastery of the energies of the chakras and the aura under Kuthumi and Djwal Kul; beginning and intermediate studies in alchemy under the Ascended Master Saint Germain; the cosmic clock—a new-age astrology for charting the cycles of karma and dharma given by Mother Mary; the science of the spoken Word in conjunction with prayer, meditation, and visualization—the key to soul liberation in the Aquarian age; weekly healing services, "Be Thou Made Whole!" at the Ashram of the World Mother in which the messenger gives personal and planetary healing invocations; the psychology of the family, the marriage ritual and meditations for the conception of new-age children; counseling for community service through the sacred labor; the teachings and meditations of the Buddha taught by Gautama Buddha, Lord Maitreya, Lanello, and the five Dhyani Buddhas; and individual initiations transferred to each student from the ascended masters through the messengers.

Summit University is a twelve-week spiral that begins with you as self-awareness and ends with you as God Self-awareness. As you traverse the spiral, light intensifies, darkness is transmuted. You experience the rebirth day by day as the old man is put off and the new man is put on. Energies are aligned, chakras are cleared, and the soul is poised for the victorious fulfillment of the individual divine plan.

In addition to preparing the student to enter into the guru-chela relationship with the ascended masters and the path of initiation outlined in their retreats, the academic standards of Summit University, with emphasis on the basic skills of both oral and written communication, prepare students to enroll in top-level undergraduate and graduate programs and to become efficient members of the national and international community. A high school diploma (or its equivalent) is required and a willingness to become the disciplined one—the disciple of the Great God Self of all.

Summit University is a way of life that is an integral part of Camelot—an Aquarian-age community secluded on a beautiful 218-acre campus in the Santa Monica Mountains west of Los Angeles near the beaches of Malibu. Here ancient truths become the law of everyday living to hundreds of kindred souls brought together again for the fulfillment of the mission of the Christ through the oneness of the Holy Spirit.

For information write or call Summit University, Box A, Malibu, CA 90265   (213) 880-5300.